U P H I L L   B A T T L E

Uphill Battle

CYCLING'S GREAT CLIMBERS

OWEN MULHOLLAND

VELOPRESS® *Boulder, Colorado*

Distributed in the United States and Canada by Publishers Group West.

Library of Congress Cataloging-in-Publication Data
Mulholland, Owen.
    Uphill battle : cycling's great climbers / Owen Mulholland.
        p. cm.
    Including bibliographical references and index.
    ISBN 1-931382-12-3
        1. Cyclists—Biography. 2. Bicycle racing—History—20th century—Anecdotes.
    I. Title: Cycling's great climbers. II. Title.
    GV1051.A1M85 2003
    796.6'092'2—dc21
    [B]   2002044601

VeloPress®
1830 North 55th Street
Boulder, Colorado 80301-2700 USA
303/440-0601 • Fax 303/444-6788 • E-mail velopress@7dogs.com

To purchase additional copies of this book or other VeloPress® books, call 800/234-8356 or visit us on the Web at velopress.com.

Cover: Presse Sports (front), Graham Watson (back)
Cover and interior design by Kristina Kachele
Interior composition by Liz Jones

For René Poulain, who "rescued" me when I was racing in France and showed me the real depths of the bike life; my son, Emile, for whom, someday, I hope these stories will be as inspiring as his all conquering legs are now; and Kathy, my tandem partner and life partner, who has shown me vistas beyond competition, vistas of just how entangled the metaphors and actualities of tandem life and love life can be. May it ever be so.

CONTENTS

IN-THE-KNOW spectators at bike races congregate on the uphill sections. They know that it's on the climbs they will have the best views of the peloton and will see the riders either attacking or digging deep into their reserves to stay in contact. That's why when you see photos of climbs like L'Alpe d'Huez in the Tour de France or the Passo del Mortirolo at the Giro d'Italia, roads are lined with thousands of fans cheering on their heroes. They have come to see a show, a spectacle, and for the really big occasions these fans camp overnight on the mountainside to stake out the best places to watch.

Owen Mulholland knows about these things. He is one of those fanatic followers of cycling. He has stood by the roadside, raced in the mountains of France, ridden the great passes, and followed some of Europe's grand tours from a privileged seat in a press car. In addition to following the sport diligently, Mulholland loves reading about its history and retelling the best yarns for new generations of readers. That's what he has done in this book, which not only examines the careers of cycling's greatest climbers but also describes and elucidates the deeds that made them famous.

If you have picked up this book, it is likely that you have already looked at some of the photos or seen historic cycling pictures in other publications.

Old photos are great. They give you an insight into the types of bicycles and the condition of the roads in different eras. What they don't tell you is what the riders and spectators in the photos are saying or thinking or feeling. That's where a writer like Mulholland comes in. He brings to life the incidents those photos depict, takes you into the time and place, and gives the stories a context that you can understand and appreciate.

The opening chapters of this book chronicle the first confrontations between cyclists and mountains in the formative years of the Tour de France. It's almost impossible for today's cycling fans, accustomed to seeing men like Lance Armstrong pounding up smooth mountain roads on less-than-twenty-pound bikes fitted with twenty different gears, to identify with the sport's pioneers. But that is what Mulholland sets out to do. He writes about the dreadful state of "roads" that were no more than mule tracks; the inhuman length of some of the Tour's early stages that forced the racers to be in the saddle for up to twelve hours at a stretch; the heavy, single-gear bikes they had to ride; and the draconian rules that forced them to make their own repairs, even when a bike frame broke!

Besides discussing the careers of pre–World War II grand tour winners like Ottavio Bottecchia, Lucien Buysse, Alfredo Binda, André Leducq, and Antonin Magne, the author reveals stories of the men who were great climbers but didn't have the luck to win the Tour itself. The most famous of these was the French hero Eugène Christophe, whose hopes were dashed on more than one occasion by a broken bicycle. Another was Vicente Trueba, a tiny Spanish climber, who was the first man to win the Tour's King of the Mountains contest, introduced in 1933. Then there was the youthful René Vietto, a charismatic rider from the French Riviera. Vietto rode his first Tour at age twenty, won three mountain stages in the Alps, but lost his chance of greatness by giving up his bike to rescue his French national teammate Antonin Magne in the Pyrenees.

Similarly, Mulholland's postwar subjects include such riders as Wim Van Est, Tom Simpson, Raymond Poulidor, José Manuel Fuente, Roberto Laiseka, and Julio Perez—all of whom offer compelling stories about their exploits in the mountains of the Tour or Giro. Among the most enthralling tales is the one told in Chapter 27, which is mostly a first-person account of the dramatic alpine stage of the 1975 Tour de France that saw the superstar Eddy Merckx succumb to the upstart Bernard Thévenet. Merckx, of course, the five-time winner of the Tour and the Giro, is featured prominently in this book, as are the other multi-time winners of grand tours—Fausto Coppi, Louison Bobet, Jacques Anquetil, Bernard Hinault, Greg LeMond, Miguel Indurain, and Lance Armstrong.

The heartbeat of *Uphill Battle* ultimately lies with the group of "pure" climbers who not only distinguished themselves by their uphill skills, but also achieved victories in at least one of the three grand tours. This group includes Jean Robic of France, Charly Gaul of Luxembourg, Federico Bahamontes of Spain, Luis Herrera of Colombia, Andy Hampsten of the United States, and Marco Pantani of Italy. These riders personified the epic nature of man against mountain, a lone, lightweight figure sprinting away from the pack, and racing up a switchback road at a tempo that no one could follow. Robic and Gaul won Tour stages by ten minutes or more. Bahamontes once stopped at the top of a pass waiting for the other riders while eating an ice cream. Herrera rode the Tour when he was still an amateur, in 1984, and won the mythical stage to L'Alpe d'Huez. Hampsten confounded the best Europeans at the 1988 Giro by taking the pink jersey in a mountain blizzard and clinched the race by winning an uphill time trial at record speed. And Pantani, years before his more recent troubles, toyed with champions like Indurain and Gianni Bugno in the mountains of the Giro.

Wonderful stories, well told.

ANY RETROSPECTIVE OF the last century of road racing must focus on Europe, and even more so, France. It was here that all the original mountain challenges were met and overcome and it was here this most epic of the sport's dimensions were created. The stories I have selected from the traditional events are my personal favorites. Many of these stories occurred in the Tour de France and this book reflects that bias. My apologies to those who will search for stories not told. I can think of several, myself.

But there had to be limits. Just as I didn't include, say, Joachim Agostinho, the gifted Portuguese rider who won a stage to l'Alpe d'Huez and challenged Eddy Merckx on Mont Ventoux, so too have I chosen not to pick from the annals outside the classic repertoire. Rob Parsons, John Allis, Bob Cook, George Mount, and Mike Englemann, to name but a few, all put up memorable rides in American mountains. Starting up their road would have meant a second book. And so too, with the women. Who, who saw it, could forget the impact of Maria Canins on big-time women's tours, and how Jeannie Longo transformed her body and style of racing to meet that challenge?

I have meant for this book to be a source of inspiration to a primarily American audience. In my forty-two years of racing I have seen a heretofore unimaginable transformation of our sport. There was a time when there were no national cycling publications. One had to wait until the end of September to find out who won the Tour de France in July. And it was pure fantasy to imagine an American might do well in Europe, let alone win a major tour.

Yet for all the progress it seems to me many of the current generation inhale their cycling in a sort of vacuum. They enjoy the excitement of cycling, the fitness, the fraternity, and the adventures the cycling life inevitably bring. But the sense of being an individual ripple in a long river is often missing.

However much one likes one's own accomplishments, they can take on even more meaning, can be even more inspirational, when seen in the context of other generations. Or so it has seemed to me, and for those who are similarly inclined I offer this selection of stories that have given passion to my own cycling.

FIRST AND LAST I must thank John Wilcockson for giving me this opportunity to make systematically public what up to now I have either known privately or written about in small snippets. John gave me my first European assignments in 1972, and as he single-handedly transformed the landscape of American cycling journalism he was kind enough to find a place for my work. Thanks to him I was able to follow an entire Tour de France in 1985. He has waded through this manuscript and made several insightful corrections. He even changed the caption of a historic photo. Due to his vast experience he recognized the picture could not have been where the caption said it was. One look at the background and he knew where it should be. He is a mountain and I am honored to be a foothill.

In addition to his own genius, John has assembled a talented team, without whom this book would have been impossible. Editor Amy Sorrells conceived the initial project and came all the way to my home to discuss it. Later, Theresa van Zante and Renee Jardine, managing editors, were of infinite service in providing technical guidance and enduring the limitations of my modest computer skills. Copyeditor Chrisona Schmidt subjected the text to microscopic examination; it was humbling to see her corrections to the submitted text and realize how right they were.

My sense of historical importance is undoubtedly the legacy of my father. His inspiring bedtime stories of ancient heroes very much prepared me to recognize the significance of their modern counterparts on two wheels. My twin brother, John, who raced in Italy, has been a lifetime resonance chamber for this transition. How many times did he call me from Europe at 2 A.M. (my time) and lovingly torture me as to who I thought might have just won Paris–Roubaix or the Tour of Lombardy. "What? Vanderaerden? He hasn't had his old form for a couple years. Surely you can do better than that!" Amazing where inspiration can come from.

I saw my first magazine on the Tour de France in 1961. Before that I didn't realize the difference between Tour and tour. I was instantly fascinated, but it was so difficult to find information. And then, racing in France a decade later, I met René Poulain. Open a closet in his house and there was shelf after shelf of cycling magazines and books going back to 1800s. He fed my starving intuitions with facts, figures, and unlimited stories. René and his well–informed wife and daughter would engage me in quiz games: "Why was Eddy Merckx almost not selected for the 1964 amateur Belgian world championship team?" and that sort of thing. In the succeeding thirty years he has given me a steady stream of documentation, and even more, such insight. What parallels can a particular event impart? Which point of view will reveal the most satisfaction? And he practices what he preaches. Even though he's approaching his eightieth year, he recently rode from Lake Geneva to the Cote d'Azur via every pass he could include in a very serpentine itinerary. René is the perfect embodiment of a Bike Guy.

The list of knowledgeable people who have directly and indirectly contributed to this book is probably almost unlimited, but a short list has to include Bob and Barbara George, Les Woodland, Bill McGann, Peter Nye, Mike Turner, Otis Guy, Jiri Mainus, David Walsh, David Epperson,

Pierre Chany, Claude Sudres, Joe Harvin, Mike Neel, Bob Tetzlaff, Emile Waldteufel, Shelley Verses, Felix Magowan, Chris Koch, Victor Vincente, Peter Rich, Michael Aisner, Karl Napper, Dave Staub, Victor Linart, Jock Wadley, René de Latour, and Georges Pagnoud. It is not possible to quantify their individual contributions to my appreciation of this great life game that unifies, as Tour founder Henri Desgrange used to say, *"tête et jambs"* (head and legs), but without their (and so many others') collective input I would have remained unenlightened about our beautiful sport and this book would have been impossible to write.

WHEN THE FIRST two-wheeled vehicles were first added to our arsenal of transportation options roughly a century and a half ago (much more or somewhat less, depending on one's definition) no one could have dreamed of the myriad permutations this deceptively simple device would evolve into; the process is hardly concluded as the recent rise of the mountain bike attests. The essential attraction, however, remains the same. The bicycle remains the most efficient device ever invented for transforming the relatively paltry power of the heart into forward motion.

Boys being boys (with, yes, a few women), the search for a pecking order soon followed the invention of these machines. By the late nineteenth century track racing was huge in the United States (the first world championships were held in Chicago in 1893), and in Europe the track scene was complemented by a road scene as well.

On the road the creation of new races resulted in a competition to see who could sponsor the longest event. Some sort of outer limit was reached in 1891 with the first Paris-Brest-Paris. At just under 800 kilometers it took close to four days to complete! (The track version of this one-upmanship led to the Six-Day races—a non-stop event, originally for single riders, lasting six days. Without the Lord's mandated day of rest on Sunday one wonders where the limit of this formula might have ended!)

In 1903 the Tour de France represented a solution to the problem of how to attract public attention without creating an even longer race. The single day races, then as now, have a tremendous following both among the riders and the public, but if one were to poll the planet's population as to which race is the most famous, it would indisputably be the Tour de France. Not only is the bicycle mechanically efficient, it also takes a substantial load off the legs because the racers are in the saddle most of the time. The Tour de France was the first race to fully exploit this combination of efficiency with ease, which allowed competitors to prolong their efforts over enormous distances and sustain those efforts day after day.

From the beginning the race was one of superlatives. We have to take ourselves back to 1900 to appreciate just how superlative. In that year a seventeen-year-old Belgian farm boy named Cyrille Van Hauwaert caught the bike bug and began training hard. His rides carried him farther and farther from home until one day he returned after a 150-kilometer loop. This ride had been so exciting he could hardly contain himself, but to gain maximum effect, he managed to stifle the urge to burst out the story to anyone who would listen. Instead, he waited for dinner when the whole family was gathered. And family meant *family* in those days—siblings, parents, grandparents, a great-grandparent, aunts and uncles, a cousin or two—all seated at a large circular table. Cyrille said grace along with the rest, and bit his tongue waiting for his moment . . . which finally came when someone, fishing for a new line of conversation, asked Cyrille how his training ride had gone that day. "I went farther today, up toward Oostende (then pausing dramatically), where I saw the ocean." Forks dropped, mouths gasped, eyes stared, and stunned disbelief marked every countenance. Four generations sat at that table, all had heard of the ocean only 75 kilometers away, but none had ever seen it.

The Van Hauwaerts were, in their day, a typical family, not unlike others European families. So now, through those eyes, gaze upon a bike race 2,428 kilometers long (the distance in 1903, and this distance would double in the ensuing years) linking most of the major cities in France. However superhuman the men of the Tour appear today, imagine how they must have appeared then!

This book is primarily concerned with performances in the mountains, probably the dimension of greatest magnitude in any modern tour. Yet it's important to appreciate how much mountains had been avoided, even after thirty years of cycling competition. The avoidance is easy to understand. On heavy single-gear bikes with one modest brake and tires ill-suited to the few stony goat tracks that did traverse the mountains, it's no wonder that major climbs were considered off limits. I have a picture of a hill in the 1905 Tour of Lombardy in northern Italy. In those days it was very much a flat race around the Po Valley and this hill was just an 80-meter bump. Yet the picture, taken from the top looking down toward the bottom reveals the problem. Those in the distance on the flat are still riding, but no one on the upper portions of the climb is. Some are pushing their bikes, others carrying them, and one appears to be resting. Not much of a "race." More a neutral zone between race zones.

Yet in the same year, 1905, the Tour de France ventured into the forbidden zone, big climbs. It's just impossible to separate the Tour from so many innovations, which, accumulated, turned it into a colossal collective diorama where entire populations could see played out their wildest projections of the humanly possible.

The history of the first third of the Tour de France is inevitably intertwined with Henri Desgrange. He was quite a character; in fact, it would be nice to have read the comments of his Austrian contemporary, Sigmund Freud, had he ever had the chance to analyze him. Not that it really matters if Desgrange was abused as a child or suffered from oedipal conflicts, but finding a consistent line of explanation that unites the many facets of Desgrange's personality is no easy matter. He could be simultaneously creative and conservative, autocratic and solicitous, a braggart and fearful, racist and democratic, and so on. From the vantage point of nearly a century's hindsight, he is the obvious figure on which to hang our gratitude for this amazing cultural and sporting creation.

But when the magnification is turned up he shrinks a bit in one's estimation. Just as the Tour de France was actually the inspiration of Geo Lefevre, so too was the innovation of mountain climbing the brainchild of another associate, Alphonse Steinès. Desgrange was only too happy to be called the "father of the Tour," but his initial reaction to many of the suggestions that we recognize as the indelible soul of the Tour were often laced with ridicule and bombast.

The Tour was just two years old (1905) when Steinès' pestering finally wore down Desgrange's reservations. But there was a caveat. "Okay, Steinès," Desgrange allowed, "we'll include these mountains even though there is a huge risk here. Therefore, the responsibility for their successful execution is all yours." Of course when the riders successfully mounted the Ballon d'Alsace, Côte de Laffrey, and Col Bayard the "father of the Tour" was only too glad to take the credit.

Actually, Steinès had had a bigger vision all along, the Pyrenees and the Alps, but he didn't mind testing his ideas on these smaller climbs. Most riders had been able to ride up these hills (for the most part on special bikes with low gears allowed for the occasion) and the public now had another dimension to ponder with ever-growing admiration. To the distance, the hours, night and day, cobbles and mud, hot and cold, mechanical failures and famine was now added the ability to ascend in an attempt to yet again expand the public's appreciation, if not adulation, of these men. . . . Men who looked like men off the bike, but who must be something very different on the bike in order to manage such a feat of athleticism and will.

In his own way Steinès was as obstinate as Desgrange and by May of 1910 Desgrange just couldn't hold him off anymore. Desgrange was torn. If the participants could actually ride over these gigantic mountains their performances would obviously galvanize public adulation even more than the challenges that Desgrange and his team had introduced in previous years. But what if the racers couldn't? What if this challenge were truly inhuman? It would make the Tour a fiasco, a joke, a gesture of futility. This possibility had to be avoided at all costs. Desgrange considered the Tour to be "his baby." He may have been an unreasonable tyrant, but at least in his own mind everything he did was to improve the Tour.

The Tour was just two months away. Desgrange couldn't take it anymore. He ordered Steinès to go down to the Pyrenees, evaluate the conditions, and report back if this was something that could be seriously considered.

In the Pyreneen foothill town of Pau, Steinès hired a driver to take him up the Tourmalet. The first six kilometers were at least feasible, even if the rude track was barely wide enough for the car and the surface no more than an assemblage of rough rocks and potholes. But at six kilometers they encountered a snow bank. Steinès got out and began shoveling. The driver scratched his head. "Monsieur, it's one thing to be brave, another to be stupid. It's six o'clock and night will soon be upon us. The bears will be coming out. Normally they like sheep, but if you are up here . . . " He let the implication silently sink in, expecting Steinès to succumb to reason and get back in the car. But Steinès was obsessed. He just *had* to get to the top. The driver gave him an ever-expressive Gallic shrug, muttered uncomplimentary things under his breath, and told Steinès that he would drive around and meet him on the other side.

As the car putted off back down the mountain the foolishness of the city-slicker's bravado began to sink in. His smooth leather shoes were fine for the sidewalks of Paris, but little help in snowdrifts. His cane was too narrow to give support in the snow. And no matter how thick his coat he could already feel the chill seeping into his bones.

He pressed on as best he could until a shower of snow from above gave him a moment of panic. "A bear?!" he wondered as he searched the hillsides. No, but it was something alive—a shepherd, who in this context became a savior. Steinès gave the young man some money and begged him to lead him to the summit. By the time they struggled to the summit of the Col dark had engulfed them and the shepherd lost no time wishing the old eccentric good luck as he hurried back down to his sheep.

Steinès had never seen real dark. In Paris there was always at least a little light. Snow covered everything. The contour of the road was totally indiscernible. He heard a stream and thought he might be able to follow it, but about that time he stepped off an edge, the snow underneath broke away, and he slid in a mini-avalanche to the bottom of the ravine.

Meanwhile, the driver had rounded up a rescue squad of locals to save this madman from himself. They reached Steinès about 3:00 A.M., on his back, exhausted from his struggle in the snow. He was helped down the mountain and taken into a home where he was able to clean up and collapse into bed, sleeping for twelve hours.

Once aroused and fed he knew he had to contact Desgrange immediately. He was taken to a local telegraph office where he transmitted the following message: "No trouble crossing Tourmalet. Roads satisfactory. No problem for cyclists. Steinès"!

Desgrange, totally unaware of what Steinès had endured, began typing at once for the next day's edition of *L'Auto,* at the time the sponsoring paper for the Tour. "The route of the 1910 Tour de France will include the

Pyreneen cols of the Peyresourde, Aspin, Tourmalet, and Aubisque." The dice had been thrown. There could be no going back now.

That colossal stage was almost the end of the Tour, but by the barest of margins it wasn't. And in being a success, however slim, once again the public's comprehension of what these supermen on bikes could do was exponentially expanded. Once again the Tour de France had grabbed the imagination of the public and pushed it to levels never before conceived. What had heretofore been considered impossible had become, at least for a few, the norm, and ever since then the Pyrenees have been on the Tour menu.

Never content, Desgrange added the Alps the following year (1911). Desgrange was more than pleased with his discovery of the Col de Galibier. He wrote, "Oh Laffrey! Oh Col Bayard! Oh Tourmalet! You are no more than little hills compared to the Galibier, vulgar babies who must tie on your bonnets, bow down, and salute this giant from far below!" However racy and inaccurate the words (the Tourmalet is easily comparable to the Galibier), he once again stirred the ardor of the fans now intoxicated by the quest for ever higher obstacles to be surmounted. This new dimension was to blossom into something quasi-mythological and make the Tour de France (and its imitators) into a legendary race.

A monument to the Tour de France and Henri Desgrange sits near the summit of the Galibier, there to remind every passerby of its significance. There's a wonderful cartoon penned in 1953 depicting Louison Bobet struggling up the mountain slopes. Each peak above is in the shape of the head of a former Tour winner, each one looking down on Bobet to judge if he is a worthy successor. Where else across the modern landscape can one discover such mythological anthropomorphism uniting nature and man in such a terrible life-affirming dance?

1

WITHIN TWO YEARS of its inception, the Tour de France was ready to break new ground. That "new ground" tilted uphill. The limitations of single gears and heavy frames had, until 1905, eliminated major hills, not to mention true mountains, from the itinerary of any competitive event.

Henri Desgrange, titular father of the Tour, decided to risk riding in a following vehicle to watch this historic second stage in 1905 from Nancy to Besançon. I say "risk" because the stage included a major climb in the Vosges mountains, Le Ballon d'Alsace. It's a twelve-kilometer grind with some sections as steep as 10 percent grade. The idea had come from Desgrange's colleague Alphonse Steinès, and Desgrange was torn between the curiosity of seeing how the stars of the day would handle this new challenge and the fear that if it was a fiasco he'd be blamed for desecrating the reputation of his beloved Tour de France. Curiosity trumped fear, and the next day he filed this report on the front page of his newspaper, *L'Auto*.

At the foot of the hill six men were leading the race and all changed to bikes with lower gears. Lucien Petit-Breton was held back by a poor bike change and never able to catch up. That left five who immediately engaged in a struggle I will qualify, without exaggeration, as one the greatest epic struggles of all time.

The next forty minutes are ones we will never forget, because forty minutes is all it took for a winner to emerge on the summit from the combat on the slopes. This was an average of 18 to 20 kilometers per hour!

The first four or five kilometers passed without incident until Henri Cornet[*] suddenly attacked in an effort to drop the others. To our surprise Louis Trousselier was the first to concede.

Now there were only four, and still this was too much for Cornet, so again he arched his back and accentuated his rhythm, forcing the others to respond to the assault. But the strength of Emile Georget betrayed him forcing him to be the next to let up.

No more than three! And a little farther up the hill, Cornet, who gave frequent looks back over his shoulder revealing a ferocious appearance, had the satisfaction of seeing his great rival, Hippolyte Aucouturier, become detached. We couldn't believe our eyes.

But the biggest surprise of this amazing sporting drama was reserved for the end because we saw, all of a sudden, René Pottier, focusing all the energy of his being, past Cornet. This began a ferocious duel between the two survivors. Gasping for air, rivulets of sweat coursing down their faces, their bodies swung in time with their pedaling.

Cornet lost two lengths, then another, and another, and that was it. The victory must go to Pottier, who now launched himself alone, admirable in his desperate vigor, his body flattened over the handlebar,

---

[*] Henri Cornet was declared the winner of the previous (1904) Tour de France after the top four were disqualified. He remains, at age twenty, the youngest-ever Tour winner.

eye on the ground, in order not to relax in the slightest before the pines parted and the summit of the Ballon was attained.

We didn't have much time to congratulate the heroes of this formidable athletic effort. Pottier made a quick change back to his regular machine, followed by Aucouturier, Cornet, and Trousselier. Actually, Cornet was left standing for twenty minutes waiting for his normal bike because his mechanic's car had broken down on the climb. Even sadder was poor Dortignacq, who had two flats and had to take two hours for the climb riding on his rim!

Pottier tried to hold his hard-fought lead all the way to Besançon. At the sign-in control town of Montbéliard, eighty-four kilometers from the finish, he had only a three-minute advantage over Aucouturier. When the latter arrived in Montbéliard and discovered the modest gap he said, "I'll catch him." Aucouturier was as good as his word, passing and dropping Pottier and going on to win the stage by ten minutes, although a substantial portion of that ten minutes was attributable to an untimely flat suffered by Pottier.

While Pottier took the title of first uncrowned King of the Mountains, he also revealed that it would take more than pure climbing to win the Tour. Indeed, Pottier retired the next day, suffering from a painful Achilles tendon, and Trousselier emerged as the overall winner in Paris over Aucouturier after a ding-dong battle all around France, one of the best ones being on the stage from Grenoble to Toulon over the Côte de Laffrey and Col Bayard climbs.

There was no shortage of passion for the Tour in 1904, as spectators actively intervened to slow down rivals of their favorites. Obviously that passion had to be managed, especially after the enthralling additions of 1905 and its three big climbs. But if it could be managed, Desgrange knew he had a unique event on his hands, one that could galvanize his nation like none other, short of war.

Pottier learned his lessons from 1905 well and returned in 1906 to dominate the race and its climbs, winning five of the thirteen stages, which encompassed no less than a 1,652-kilometer increase over the previous year. One "gimmick" Pottier added was to mount foot rests on the front fork so he could "freewheel" down the mountain on his fixed gear. (It wasn't until the following year that Emile Georget rode one of the first true freewheels.)

Pottier was a complete rider. He had set numerous records on the track, from one to one hundred kilometers, and had done very well in several classics. Now, at age twenty-seven, having dominated the Tour throughout, he appeared set for a remarkable cycling career. But somehow his focus had been too extreme, to the neglect of other parts of his life, and he committed suicide by hanging himself in January 1907 after suffering a romantic rebuff.

Convinced that mountains were a good thing, Desgrange was eager to add more to the menu. For 1907 he added the Col de Porte in the Chartreuse region of the western Alps. It dwarfed the Ballon d'Alsace, and Georget used his new freewheel to win the stage over the Porte by outcoasting the others on the descent into Grenoble.

The trend was obvious. France is framed between very impressive mountain ranges, the Pyrenees and the Alps. The Tour would inevitably invade them; the only question was when. Desgrange was mightily impressed that these madmen on two wheels had surmounted with aplomb every new challenge he had thrown at them. The public couldn't get enough of it and the daily sales of *L'Auto* soared. Still he held off until 1910, when his colleague Steinès used a disingenuous telegram after a springtime reconnaissance to trick Desgrange into accepting that the

Pyrenees could be successfully added to the Tour itinerary.

The "appetizer stage" from Perpignan to Luchon over primarily the Col de Port and Col de Portet d'Aspet proceeded without undue drama. Octave Lapize proved his climbing credentials by arriving in Luchon with eighteen minutes over Emile Georget and twenty-two minutes ahead of the race leader, François Faber. (Faber remained the race leader. Since the race was decided on points in those days, these time gaps weren't as significant as they might appear.)

A fever of apprehension gripped the entire Tour entourage on the eve of July 21. At 3:30 in the morning the Tourmen would have to tackle the single greatest challenge ever thrown at them. The 326-kilometer stage from Luchon to Bayonne surmounted no fewer than four giant cols—the Peyresourde, Aspin, Tourmalet, and Aubisque. Desgrange had never really ventured into the big Pyrenees before, and now that he was there he lost his nerve. He cabled his lieutenant, Victor Breyer, to hurry down to Luchon to take his place. Breyer arrived and Desgrange, making his excuses, slipped out of town and back to Paris. Clearly he anticipated a disaster and couldn't bear to see a debacle with his own eyes. The extent of his concern is shown in another way as well. For 1910, he introduced the *voiture balai,* the broom wagon, to sweep up riders who couldn't finish; for this terrible stage only, they would be allowed to complete the stage in the broom wagon and start again the next day.

The signal to start came sharply at 3:30 A.M. and into the dark canyons the peloton crept. It wasn't until daylight and the first climb that things, as expected, started to break up. Lapize was out to show that his win the day before was no fluke. He quickly disappeared up the track (one could hardly call this potholed, rock-strewn path a bona fide "road") and reached the first two summits, Peyresourde and Aspin, in first. But Gustave Garrigou caught Lapize on the day's most difficult climb, the

Tourmalet, where they passed and repassed each other in a slow-motion dance. Lapize held on to a small 500-meter lead at the summit even though he, unlike Garrigou, had walked at times.

Breyer, with Steinès, picked a spot three-quarters of the way up the Aubisque to observe the riders. Breyer wrote:

> According to my calculations the first riders should come by me in about 15 minutes. The quarter-hour passed, then another, and another, and all this time I was alone in this wondrous mountain landscape under a cloudless blue sky and a burning sun. An absolute silence reigned in this intimidating region so alien to man. An hour passed and the fear of a disaster began to gnaw at my guts. It was as though the Tour de France had fallen into a void.
>
> And suddenly I saw him, a rider, but one I didn't know. His body heaved at the pedals, like some automaton on two wheels. He wasn't going fast, but he was at least moving. I trotted alongside him and asked, "Who are you? What's going on? Where are the others?" Bent over his handlebars, his eyes riveted on the road, the man never turned his head nor uttered one sole word. He continued and disappeared around a turn. Steinès had read his number and consulted the riders' list. Steinès was dumbfounded. "The man is François Lafourcade, a nobody. He has caught and passed all the 'cracks.' This is something prodigious, almost unbelievable!"
>
> Still the minutes passed. Another quarter-hour passed before the second rider appeared, whom we immediately recognized as Lapize. Unlike Lafourcade, Lapize was walking, half leaning on, half pushing his machine. His eyes revealed an intense distress. But unlike his predecessor, Lapize spoke, and in abundance. "You are assassins, yes, assassins!" To discuss matters with a man in this condition would have

In 1905, René Pottier was the first man to the top of the Ballon d'Alsace, the first mountain introduced to the Tour de France.

been cruel and stupid. I walked at his side, attentive to all he said. After more imprecations, he finished by saying, "Don't worry, at Eaux-Bonnes I'm going to quit."

It took me some time to recover my composure. Eaux-Bonnes was the control town at the foot of the last descent, from which there were still 150 kilometers yet to go to the stage finish at Bayonne. We got in the car and drove to Eaux-Bonnes. Lafourcade had arrived 17 minutes ahead of Lapize, but he was spent. He rested five minutes and left. The descent into Eaux-Bonnes had given Lapize new courage and he continued.

Now Breyer and Steinès drove to the finish, where they saw Lapize come across the line with his Alcyon teammate, Aldo Albini, an Italian. Ten minutes later Faber arrived after having suffered five punctures in the closing kilometers. He remained the race leader. After that the gaps grew. Garrigou, in eighth, was fifty-six minutes down. Henri Cornet, the 1904 winner and still only twenty-six years old, was 4.5 hours down. These were still the early finishers. Finally, search parties were organized to retrieve those poor wretches who had collapsed by the side of the road. Of course the broom wagon would have eventually found them, but stuck behind the last rider, it could have been very late at night and who knows what the condition of these desperate men might have been by then? One death from an inhuman experiment and all Desgrange's carefully nurtured goodwill for the Tour could have instantly evaporated.

Having survived this trial, the riders now headed back toward Paris. Lapize and Faber fought for every point, but the gods intervened by showering bad luck on Faber. On one stage he had to ride for a considerable distance with half a handlebar and one pedal! It was too much, and Lapize emerged a worthy, but lucky, winner.

The 1911 Tour was the first to have a modern look, going completely around the country and penetrating deep into the intimidating heights of both Alps and Pyrenees. The Tour organizers have been developing these themes ever since, but 1911 was the year in which those themes were fully introduced.

A rich group of possible winners was in the field at the start, and as usual, foreseen and unforeseen consequences reduced the group of contenders. An early crash eliminated Lucien Petit-Breton, winner in 1907 and 1908. Faber, still licking his wounds from the previous year, used the Ballon d'Alsace as a centerpiece for a fabulous solo breakaway in which he finished seventeen minutes ahead of the next rider (not his old rival, Lapize, who mysteriously lost his strength, finished in *tenth* place, and abandoned the race the following day). It would have been 2 minutes and 20 seconds longer than that, but Desgrange personally stopped Faber for that length of time because he had blasted through a *contrôle* without signing in.

Emile Georget was flying down the Ballon in first place when he encountered a motorcycle coming up the hill. Brakes in those days were not in the plural. One lever pressed a metal spoon directly on the front tire. Knowing his brake would never help in the instant of decision, Georget chose to fly off the road rather than hit the motorcycle. He cartwheeled off a cliff and was seriously bruised; the bike survived intact. Summoning all his willpower, he climbed back to the road and finished the stage in 43rd place.

Georget must have recovered quickly because two days later he tackled the new mountain, the Col du Galibier (2,556 meters or 8,385 feet), with, as they say in French, *panache.* The twelve-kilometer climb of the Col du Télégraphe is a killing little warm-up before a five-kilometer descent leads to the true start of the Galibier: a combined thirty-three kilometers of climbing with gradients averaging 7 percent but pitches as steep as 14 percent. Georget's technique was simple. He was the only man who was able to ride the entire distance without dismounting, even in the mud sections between walls of snow. He kept the pressure on over the top and all the way down the long descent to Grenoble, where he won the stage by more than fifteen minutes.

Nevertheless, the very regular Gustave Garrigou held the race lead by a few points over the young Normandy rider, Paul Duboc, who preceded Faber by one point. The race was far from over! Faber won the stage into Nice, but then Duboc won two consecutive, the second being the first Pyrenean stage. His form appeared to improve every day, and with the giant four-col Pyrenean monster next on the menu, everyone concerned with the race was hard-pressed to see how he could lose.

Duboc led by eight minutes at the summit of the Tourmalet and seemed likely to increase his lead over the final obstacle, the Aubisque. Everything appeared to be going well as he pounded up the Aubisque when he suddenly lost strength, his skin going deathly pale under the grime and sweat. He fell to the side of the road and vomited vile liquids repeatedly. He lay shaking from chills and was too weak to speak as rider after rider passed by. The consensus was that Duboc had been poisoned, although exactly how and by whom was never determined. If the intent was to eliminate him as a threat for the overall lead, the perpetrators were successful.

Duboc eventually recovered and finished the stage in 21st place, and he even won the next one. But it was Garrigou, like Lapize the year before, who won the race, on the strength of his own abilities, but also because of the bad luck of others.

To say the French public was enthusiastic about this colossal mélange of athleticism, displayed over an enormous disparity of terrain and sprinkled with incidents of high drama, would be a gross understatement. The deeds continue to search for words to properly exemplify them. As long as the Tour suffers from this problem, it will be in good shape!

2

OF ALL THE stories that grace these pages, probably none is more famous than the repeated tragedies of Eugène Christophe. Viewed through a simple lens, cycling appears to be an elementary game of triumphs and losses. It takes an extra twist to turn the losses into tragedies, and it's that twist that turns cycling into something other than a simple competition. Race promoters go to great lengths to make sure their events meet the fairness test. But humans can set the stage only so well, and after that bigger forces can come into play, especially in a race as long as the Tour de France. In such an event cycling becomes truly great, for it rises beyond the necessarily personal concerns of the cyclists and reflects life as a whole. What did blue-footed booby or spotted hyena babies do to get pecked or bitten to death by their older siblings? Weren't the residents of Pompeii and Herculaneum innocently minding their own business on that fateful day in A.D. 79 when Mount Vesuvius blew its top and buried them all? These and countless other painful realities have to be reckoned with by persons evaluating the worth of an enterprise purporting to somehow measure the fullness of life, and if the showcase story is that of Eugène Christophe, the enterprise has met the test.

In 1912, Christophe was hardly an unknown. He turned twenty-seven that year and had already won the single-day classic Milan–San Remo and the French cyclo-cross championship. Few specialized then as they do now; and every road rider dreamed of the Tour de France. Twenty-seven may seem a little late to make a Tour debut, but Christophe was a model "late bloomer." From the perspective of his eventual retirement, at twenty-seven he was in his infancy.

But a robust infancy to be sure. Christophe entered the Tour intent on big things. He even trimmed his mammoth mustache in order to facilitate drinking. In the Tour that year he led the race through the Alps, winning three stages in succession. It was only the second time the Galibier had been included in the Tour route, and Christophe rode it in a way to guarantee that the phrase *seul en tête* (alone in front) would be added to the lexicon of heroic cycling. Having won stages 3, 4, and 5, he could be forgiven for thinking he could relax a little, and in a normal year he could have. But in those days the Tour was judged on points awarded according to finishing position. Although Belgium's Odile Defraye lost half an hour in the Alps, his finishing position on the majority of stages was still good enough that he and Christophe were equal on points following stage 5. Then, later in the race, with the help of a very organized team, Defraye was able to win overall. And while the French hailed their young star, Eugène Christophe, for finishing second, they mourned his misfortune and were sure he would win in the future.

Henri Desgrange, founder and chief "tyrant" of the Tour de France, saw the injustice of the Tour's ways and determined to make amends. For 1913, he declared that the Tour classification would be decided on time. (There was more to this change, which has endured to present times. From the French point of view a Belgian victory was more a blight than a compliment to the already illustrious list of winners over the Tour's first decade. Joke of the time in France: What's the worst thing you can call a Belgian? Answer: A Belgian! Desgrange was hoping to not only help Christophe but also eliminate any more wins by Defraye. Desgrange got a Pyrrhic victory: Defraye never won again, but neither did Christophe. Instead, the winners of the next six Tours were Belgians.)

In 1913, a fateful year for Christophe, he started the Tour expecting to win. Everything seemed to be in his favor: age twenty-eight, second-place finish the year before, a classification system that favored his style of riding. And he rode like a champion-to-be, staying close to the front and not wasting energy. After a procession across northern France, Defraye was in the lead by five minutes over Christophe in second. Things got serious in the Pyrenees. Philippe Thys, a rising star from Belgium and a Peugeot teammate of Christophe, led over the Tourmalet, but Christophe was hanging tough in second and expected to go into the overall lead on the next mountain, the Aspin, as poor Defraye had crashed out.

Once over the top, after a quick stop to whip the rear wheel around for the small cog side and to put on a rain jacket—not only for the occasional rain shower that day but to cut the chill wind on the descent—Christophe was off in pursuit. But not for long. A car collided with Christophe's bike, throwing him to the ground. He restarted but his bike didn't handle right. It was sagging, and just as he brought it to a halt he realized his forks were almost broken off.

Now begins the great Christophe saga. He knew perfectly well the Tour rule that every rider must finish each stage with the bike he started on. (In this regard the Tour of that time is reminiscent of mountain bike racing today.) Desgrange saw the Tour as a test of man *and* machine. The evolution to a test for riders with the machines being a neutral factor took many years. As recently as the 1950s, a mechanic stopping for a rider with a flat had to emerge from the following car with the tire separate from the wheel. Resigned to his fate, Christophe shouldered his bike and began walking the fourteen kilometers down the mountain road to Ste.-Marie-de-Campan at the foot of the Tourmalet.

It was a bitter stroll. Rival after dropped rival went whizzing past. Even running as well as he could and cutting a few corners, he took over an hour to get to the village. The first townsperson he saw was a young girl who answered his request by taking him to the shop of the town blacksmith, one Monsieur Lecomte, who is remembered for verbally guiding Christophe through the repair process. "Verbal guidance?" you can be forgiven for asking. "Is that all?" The sad answer is *yes* because another rule decreed that all repairs had to be made by the rider. Lest anything sneaky be attempted, at first race director Desgrange, then other officials and representatives of rival teams, like so many hungry vultures, gathered around the forge to make sure that Christophe did all the repairs alone.

Christophe got the knack quickly, but it was a four-hand job: one to hold the forks, one to apply the brazing material, and two to pump the bellows to keep the fire hot. M. Lecomte tried to discreetly assist with the bellows but was admonished to desist. Finally, after a discussion, a boy was allowed to occasionally pump the bellows and Christophe received a time penalty for the infraction.

After four hours of tension-filled toil Christophe was ready to mount his rejuvenated steed and set off once again in the waning light to tackle the Aspin. On his way out the door an official put his hand on Christophe's shoulder and reminded him that he had a minute's penalty for the assistance from the boy with the bellows. Christophe made an ironic grin. What difference did another minute make now except as an unnecessary pinprick? The other irony was not lost on him either. With the old points system he might have been able to retrieve this Tour, but never with the new classification based on time. That funky old stone blacksmith's shop still stands in Ste.-Marie-de-Campan, a historic monument with a proper bronze plaque on the wall describing the immortal drama played out in these premises on July 9, 1913.

Christophe had an off year in 1914, finishing in an anonymous eleventh place, and no doubt some thought he might be a one-year wonder for 1912. A certain intrusion into the proper Tour de France sequence began in 1914 that delayed confirmation of the foregoing suppositions. Like the rest of his generation, Eugène Christophe had to put his cycling career on hold for World War I.

Christophe got off easy. Unlike millions of his contemporaries, he lived. In fact, he lived long enough to suffer two more devastating broken forks in the Tour!

3

ONE OF THE endless sources of satisfaction provided by the pantheon of men (and women) who fill the annals of cycling is the variety they present. Despite their shared ability to pedal a bike quickly, the differences among them never cease to amaze. Consider one factor—destiny. While he was a teenager, Greg LeMond made a list of his cycling goals: World Championship, Tour de France, goals that in hindsight appear to have been totally justified. Eddy Merckx was the same sort. His fixation with cycling drove his teachers and parents a little crazy. In looking back, we have to admit that their ages obscured an amazingly prescient maturity.

At the other extreme are riders who practically fell into the sport. Events proved they had talent, but they never would have realized it without some weird accidental twist of fate that put them on a bike at the right time and place, and, voilà, a champion was born.

Ottavio Bottecchia is one of the best examples of the latter category. He came from northern Italy, where scenes of bucolic splendor belied the grinding reality country folks endured. It was a hand-to-mouth existence and most of people's waking energy went into survival activities. His family had neither the means nor, to be honest, the interest to educate the kids. They didn't have to be literate to cut stones, make bricks, and build walls, which was the line of work Ottavio, the youngest of eight children, came to specialize in. So identified with this line of work did he become that even after he had gained great cycling fame he was still called the "mason of Friuli."

World War I interrupted his life. Living near the Austrian border, he was soon at the front lugging supplies and building trenches along the hotly disputed frontier. Here his extraordinary strength was first recognized. Even on a lead-pipe army issue single-speed bike he could carry amazing loads up to the contested alpine crests. He also used a bike three times to escape from an Austrian prisoner-of-war camp!

One of his army buddies, Alfredo Piccin, tried to steer Ottavio toward cycling competition after the war. Piccin was clairvoyant in recognizing that this rather taciturn introvert had real possibilities, but it took a bit of convincing. It was Piccin who helped him learn to read and write and showed him enough of the surrounding world and the pleasures of cycling to finally get Bottecchia to consider something other than the stone cutting he'd always thought he'd do.

In his first year as a professional cyclist, 1922, the twenty-seven-year-old Bottecchia had collected an eighth place in the Tour of Lombardy, and the next spring he finished sixth in Milan–San Remo. Even better, he finished the Tour of Italy in fifth.

At the same time, in France, the Automoto team was looking for some good men to add to its lineup for the Tour de France. Four Italians were contacted and invited to come north, but only Bottecchia made the trip. Between his total lack of French and his natural shyness, there was considerable discussion about including him on the team, but in the end he was given the benefit of the doubt.

Automoto soon discovered that once on a bike this boy could talk just fine with his legs. He won the Tour's second stage by making a solo attack a kilometer from the line and taking the yellow jersey. Later in the Pyrenees he recaptured the lead, much to the delight of his team leader, Frenchman Henri Pélissier. That delight turned to anxiety by the end of stage 9 to Nice, where Pélissier, lying third overall, was almost a half-hour behind Bottecchia.

Henri Desgrange, the founder and boss of the Tour de France, had maintained a love-hate relationship with the Pélissier brothers for more than a decade. Henri Pélissier hated all the petty, tyrannical rules that Henri Desgrange imposed on the Tour. Year after year the Pélissiers quit in disgust rather than be subjected to some demeaning and trivial imposition. Desgrange excoriated the Pélissiers, particularly the eldest brother, Henri, and said in print that while the Pélissiers had no shortage of talent they could never win the Tour de France because they lacked the courage.

When Henri Pélissier stuck it out in 1923 and made a bold attack through the Alps on stage 10 to take over the yellow jersey, Desgrange was man enough to congratulate him. He wrote:

> Henri Pélissier has given us today a spectacle that ranks as art. His victory has the classicism of a work by Racine, it has the beauty of a perfect statue, a flawless painting, of a piece of music destined to be remembered by all those who hear it. We saw him climb using the full range of his abilities, from the force of his legs to the acumen of his mind. It was the surety of his judgment that allowed him to win the stage by taking advantage of Bottecchia's poor timing to change gears. You might say Pélissier knows how to play his instrument. His sense of tempo was no less impressive. He had, in his pedaling style and position, an amazing facility. With one exception he made all his attacks in the saddle, maintaining the beautiful position of a born

climber. From time to time he slowed to drink, but always without haste, as you'd expect from someone who knows his affairs. The enormous mountains seemed humbled, diminished under the victorious push of his muscles.

Henri Pélissier was not at all impressed by these voluptuous lines. He replied with sarcasm and truth:

What form Desgrange has! He merits entry into the Académie française, and me, to read him, I should be buried in the Pantheon. Oh Racine, sculpture, painting, music—my head swims! But I wonder if Racine ever had to work on command, to start a work at two in the morning and have it delivered by six in the afternoon, or if one of the painters that he evokes ever set his easel in the middle of a storm on a mountain? I wonder if old Desgrange, who supposedly follows the Tour, actually saw me, for I spent a long time on foot, at the side of Bottecchia under a burning sky, pushing the bike with one hand and with the other swigging from my bottle and sharing it with my companion who was worse off than I. There was no question, at the moment, of the *maillot jaune* and victory, Monsieur Desgrange. We struggled in a daze, like two soldiers lost in the desert, merely to survive, and if you had passed in our proximity, I, like anyone in my place, would have treated you as a murderer!

Both men captured aspects of the Tour, Desgrange the poetry and Pélissier the savagery. Henri Pélissier finally won his Tour de France with his faithful henchman Ottavio Bottecchia right behind in second. For Bottecchia there would be no more thoughts of life as a mason. It had been a surprising journey, but at last he had found his destiny.

And that destiny was France, even if his French vocabulary barely encompassed ten words. As my brother, who raced his bike in Italy in the late 1960s and then lived in the Middle East for twenty years and ran 10Ks and marathons with every nationality on earth, said, "Sweat cuts through a lot of shit." In Italy Bottecchia knew he would confront a sort of closed shop. Costante Girardengo, Gaetano Belloni, and the emerging Alfredo Binda didn't leave many scraps on the table after they were finished. France had a more open situation. The real problem for the 1924 Tour was how to handle the in-team rivalry that would exist between Henri Pélissier and Ottavio Bottecchia. They seemed pretty cool about the situation. Both had to thank each other for a lot from the previous year, and they seemed to have an unspoken agreement that they'd let the race sort things out.

Bottecchia was a truly complete rider, more so than perhaps even he dreamed. He won the first stage, and, although it wasn't obvious then, he was on his way to becoming the first rider to lead the Tour de France from beginning to end. Pélissier "cooperated" by having yet another fight with Desgrange's insipid rules and quitting on stage 3. The door was now completely open for Bottecchia. He totally dominated both Pyrenean stages, gaining so much time that he was content to follow the action all the way back to Paris, where, to enforce the point, he won the last stage as well.

He repeated his Tour victory, if not with quite the same mastery, in 1925. It's stupid to be too critical. There was one ghastly day in the Pyrenees from Luchon to Perpignan—rain, hail, mud, the works. Bottecchia didn't win the stage (that honor went to the rising young star from Luxembourg, Nicholas Frantz, who was to win the Tour in 1927–1928), but the essential object was achieved. His main rival ever since the start in Paris, the Belgian, Adelin Benoit, was left so far behind that Bottecchia had no more worries for the rest of the race. Protected by the strongest team, Bottecchia had a relative cruise back to the finish in Paris where, to emphasize his dominance, he won the prestigious final stage (again!).

This represented the apotheosis of the cycling career of the "mason of Friuli." In the 1926 Tour, he was one of twenty-two riders who didn't survive the Pyrenees, and the following June, while training for the 1927 Tour, he was found dead by a roadside in northern Italy. Nothing was ever proved about the cause of his death and theories swirl to this day. Not the least of the ambiguities is that his brother was also found dead on the same roadside two years later.

4

LUCIEN BUYSSE, 1892–1980

LUCIEN BUYSSE CAME from one of those dynastic Belgian cycling families. Think of the modern Planckaerts—father, son, cousin, and so on. It's almost easier to ask who (at least among the males in the family) didn't race. Lucien Buysse had no fewer than three brothers who were good enough to make the grade and turn pro. It is fascinating to speculate about the factors that occasionally allow such talent to burst forth so uniformly, although there can never be a definitive explanation.

Among the Buysses, Marcel was the first to show his talent. In 1913, at age of twenty-four, Marcel Buysse won no fewer than six stages of the Tour de France. The second of those stage wins, in the Pyrenees, put Buysse into the race leadership by six minutes over his teammate Philippe Thys. Then, on stage 9, disaster struck. Buysse's frame cracked and despite help from another teammate, Eugène Christophe, to make the repair, the Belgian lost more than three hours that day.

Remarkably, Buysse won four of the remaining five stages to finish third overall, though still those three hours behind Thys. Marcel was joined by his younger brother Lucien in the 1914 Tour, but both dropped out in the South of France. As it did for the rest of their generation, World War I put the Buysse brothers' racing plans on hold for an interminable four years. Of course, in the context of the times, they were lucky. In 1918 they were still alive, unlike many of the racers, famous or not, who were mowed down in the incredible carnage of Verdun, Marne, Ypres, and all the rest of the ghastly slaughterhouses that passed for battles. Loony as the bike races of that heroic epoch can appear to be, with their stupefying distances, unpaved roads, single-gear bikes, wretched food, and generally inhuman demands, compared to the "Great War" (as World War I is still frequently called in Europe), these two-wheeled competitions were veritable islands of sanity.

Certainly Lucien Buysse thought so. As a good pro he rode the complete season and did the six-day circuit. He even won the Ghent Six-Day in 1923, the year after his brother Marcel won it in 1922. Lucien also ventured across the Atlantic to take in the lucrative six-days in the United States, most notably in New York and Chicago. He and his wife had four children, but given the nonstop nature of his racing, it is a wonder that they found enough time together to bring a family into the world.

Through it all, Lucien Buysse never lost sight of his first passion, the Tour de France. After he and his brother both abandoned the 1919 Tour on stage 2, both victims of the war-shattered roads, Lucien didn't return to the race until 1923. He showed his climbing strength by finishing second on the big alpine stage to Briançon just behind Frenchman Henri Pélissier, who went on to win that Tour. Buysse was a solid eighth, a couple of hours back. Buysse moved up the rankings in the following two Tours, coming in third in 1924 and second in 1925—when he won two stages and gave valuable support to teammate Ottavio Bottecchia, the overall winner. But the aging Belgian seemed to lack that little something extra that separates champions from also-rans.

By 1926 time was starting to run out. For an endurance event like the Tour he was probably at the peak of his form, but at age thirty-four he knew well enough that the years when he could seriously dream of victory were numbered.

For the first time, the Tour commenced from a city other than Paris. Old man Desgrange knew that the long stages back to Paris from the mountains were a tedious bore for all concerned, so he concocted a loop that began at Evian on the shore of Lake Geneva, went clear around France in a counterclockwise direction back to Evian, and from there went straight to Paris in two days. That loop with the tail to Paris added up to 5,745 kilometers. It was a record distance, almost twice as far as modern Tours.

Stages of 350 kilometers (roughly 220 miles) were the norm. Not infrequently, stages began at 4:00 A.M. in order to arrive at the finish line before nightfall. All this on heavy, single-gear bikes on unpaved roads. The accomplishments of the riders of that era are not to be underestimated.

But you wouldn't find Lucien Buysse complaining. He had ridden the Tour many times, studied the route map in great detail, knew where to get off to change gears (by hand lifting the chain from one sprocket to another), and always had secret ambitions. The year 1926 began nicely: His brother Jules won the first stage. Other Belgians dominated as the race crossed northern France and ground down to the Pyrenees. Perhaps Buysse's biggest worry was that he was in the same team as Bottecchia, the man who had won the two previous years, and of course Buysse was expected once more to work for the Italian. It was an awkward position to be in; all he could do was hope something would break his way.

That break came on stage 10, the first Pyrenean stage, from Bayonne to Luchon via four killer cols: Aubisque, Tourmalet, Aspin, and Peyresourde. The stage began at 2:00 A.M., and hard as that may have been to bear in normal circumstances, in 1926 there were no normal circumstances. Even in the coastal town of Bayonne a chill rain was falling, and anyone with mountain experience could pretty well guess what conditions would be like on the summits. The riders tried to stay in a bunch at first where the lights of the leading and following cars could help the hapless herd navigate through and around the rocks and potholes, but such luxuries soon disappeared as the grind up the first mountain inevitably stretched out the group.

Difficult as all this was, no one was more prepared than Lucien Buysse. He may not have been the fastest climber, but he could do it damn near forever. This 323-kilometer stage was almost interminable. It never quite snowed, but on the highest peaks freezing sleet lashed the riders. The dirt roads turned into a quagmire and even Buysse, who led all day, had to walk lengthy distances. But Buysse had the right clothes, the right training, and a lifetime of built-up resistance. He knew when and what to eat, and where to stop to change gears. Most of all, he was inspired because Bottecchia was nowhere in sight. There was no instant communication in those days. Only rarely could he get any idea of what was going on behind. When the clouds parted, he could look back and see he had a substantial lead. He knew the route because he'd raced it many times, so he had a very good idea of where he was on the day's itinerary. He may not have been exactly sure of his lead, but he knew that if ever there was a chance to win the Tour, this was it.

This nightmare stage finally ended for him in Luchon at 5:12 in the afternoon after 17 hours, 12 minutes, and 4 seconds in the saddle, and he was the winner! An Italian, Bartolomeo Aimo was second at twenty-five minutes, Belgian Léon Devos, third at thirty minutes, and so on. The *maillot jaune,* Gustaaf Van Slembrouck, stumbled in 1 hour, 50 minutes after Buysse, and he was still in the top twenty on the stage. Night fell and the vast majority of riders were still out on the mountain trails, feeling their way like so many blind men reading Braille. By midnight, rescue parties were finally sent out in cars to find the miserable survivors, many of whom were too weak from hunger and stiffened by cold to be able to utter a word or even lift themselves into the vehicles. Others, such as Bottecchia, were found in farmhouses, having abandoned the race.

Buysse's performance was obviously an epic, but just to make sure, he repeated the performance on the following mountain stage in, mercifully, more benevolent conditions. The distance and number of climbs were almost identical, but his time from Luchon to Perpignan was almost five hours quicker. Still, he was again first by a good margin, and between these two colossal stages he had guaranteed his lifelong dream, a victory in the Tour de France.

5

ALFREDO BINDA, 1902–1986

IT'S AN ALL-TOO-COMMON yet natural tragedy in sports (and not only in sports; cuisine is even more so) that attention is focused on the moment only, and what happened yesterday dims all too quickly. To the degree that international cycling is appreciated in the United States, the Tour de France is recognized to the almost complete exclusion of other races. For those who focus on one domain of cycling, it's hard to beat the Tour de France, but there have been some worthy performances outside this peak of the pedaling pyramid.

The career of Alfredo Binda is not so well-known to us as that of Eddy Merckx or Bernard Hinault, but it should be, since the statistics alone give some measure of the man: three times world road champion, five times winner of the Tour of Italy, two times winner of Milan–San Remo, four times winner of the Tour of Lombardy, four times Italian road champion, Italian hour record holder, two stage wins in the Tour de France; and these are, of course, just the headlines. Need another index of his place in the cycling landscape? His name appears no less than 1,150 times on the World Wide Web!

It's not his fault that the modern media emphasizes France over Italy. Maybe if Greg LeMond and Lance Armstrong had crossed the Alps more often, Binda would be better known. Growing up on the French Riviera, adjacent to Italy, Binda could choose which way to go.

In his hometown, Cittiglio near Varese, his father pushed him into playing the trumpet in the city band at the tender age of ten. Alfredo enjoyed it, and the family enjoyed his modest contributions to the communal funds as well. Everyone had to struggle to survive. And with their poverty accentuated by World War I, he and his brother, Primo, were sent across the border to live with an uncle in Nice. This was where Alfredo Binda discovered cycling. For a few years he struggled to balance attending art school, working, and his growing passion for bicycle racing.

He first raced as a professional at age 19 in 1922, winning two local hill climbs. Then, on March 4, 1923, he broke through internationally meeting and beating the biggest names in Italian cycling, including the *campionissimo* of the day, Costante Girardengo. Binda had left them so easily on the last part of the muddy to Mont Chauve hill climb above Nice that on the way home to Milan by train, Gaetano Belloni had confided his fears to Girardengo, "If this kid from Nice comes down here to race against us more often we may as well pack our bags."

Girardengo tried to shift the focus, "I hear he plays the trumpet."

"Yeah, and he'll be playing taps for us," Belloni replied laconically.

The following year, 1924, they all met again in the last prestigious race of the season, the Tour of Lombardy. Binda was attracted by the handsome cash prime at the top of the first climb, the famous Madonna de Ghisallo, now famous for its sacred shrine to cycling. He had no trouble pocketing the money and then impressed everyone by hanging on to take fourth at the finish.

It was a fateful ride because he was immediately offered a contract by Eberardo Pavesi, director of the prestigious Legnano team, and Alfredo, still a hungry young man juggling conflicting parts of his life, was only too happy to devote himself uniquely to the object of his primal passion. If the French team Alcyon had made a slightly better offer than it did, the name Alfredo Binda would have become as notorious to the pelotons north of the Alps as it was to become to the pelotons south of them.

All champions need opposition in order to display their talents, but Italy has a knack for producing them in pairs. After Cougnet and Colombo came Girardengo and Binda (and later Bartali–Coppi, Baldini–Nencini, Gimondi–Motta, and Saronni–Moser). By the time Binda appeared on the scene, Girardengo had already pocketed six Milan–San Remos, three Tours of Italy, and so on. Like every old lion (he was nine years older than Binda) he did not enjoy being pushed from his place of preeminence. It was beautiful and sad.

By the mid-1920s Binda was in full stride and truly untouchable. The world gasped in amazement when Binda won twelve of the fifteen stages in the 1927 Tour of Italy, including nine consecutively! After four years of such demonstrations the organizers of the Giro (Tour of Italy) quietly went to Binda and opened a suitcase full of money. "Here it is, Signore Binda," they offered, "the money for first place in the forthcoming (1930)

Giro. You may have it now if you *don't* ride the Giro. We will accept any excuse. Of course we can't prevent you from riding, but in the long-term interest of the sport and the future of the Giro we hope you will understand a year's absence will help revive interest in Italy's greatest race." Of course Binda took the money, made his excuses, and headed to the Tour de France for the only time in his career. After four second places in the first six stages, he was lying third overall, but then a crash caused him to lose more than an hour on the flat stage 7. Binda's response was to win the next two stages, including the main climbing stage through the Pyrenees. But another crash and more delays forced him to quit the Tour on stage 10.

Because of the difficulties of travel and the more self-sealed nature of national economies of the time, top riders around Europe didn't meet nearly so often in head-to-head competition then as in our more modern times. In 1927, the first world championship for road professionals was held to rectify this problem. It was a great idea that had long existed on the track. Bring the best from every nation to one venue to provide an annual pecking order. "Sure," a Frenchman might say, "Binda can win an easy tour like the Giro, but we all know those pasta eaters aren't really tough, not like our snail eaters!" Belgians sneered at both countries for not having to endure the rugged cobbles of the north, nor the nasty weather every rider near the North Sea knew so well.

The UCI (Union Cycliste Internationale) found a fitting venue for a confrontation of this order, the motor racing circuit at Germany's Nürburgring. The diabolical ingenuity that had gone into its design to force cars to become airborne over blind hillcrests would certainly suffice to put the hurt on any cyclist. Besides being fit, one had to figure which gear to mount because in a race of this magnitude there was going to be no time to hop off and put the chain on another cog, as then happened in mountain stages of major tours. The trick was to mount a gear combination that not only would allow the rider to keep up with the undoubtedly fast start but also be competitive on the nasty climbs as the strength-sapping distance took its toll.

There weren't many early heroics; the severity of the course was just too intimidating. None of the many severe ramps could be climbed sitting down. Naturally, the repeated efforts, efforts that would be ameliorated by a modern derailleur, took their toll.

On the sixth (of seven) laps Costante Girardengo made his grand attack. Eighteen men remained in the lead peloton. Seventeen of them appeared, relative to Girardengo, to go backward. One man, Alfredo Binda, floated across the widening gap. Girardengo was not pleased to find who he had for company, but both the Italians put their heads down to make sure they would remain unmolested out front.

If Girardengo had dreams that some angel of mercy might crown the fifteenth year of his illustrious career with this one last glorious achievement, the nightmare of reality intervened. On the same hill that Girardengo had used the previous lap to launch his do-or-die effort, Binda showed the depth of form that had won him every major race he'd entered that year (except Milan–San Remo). So brutal, so total was Binda's dramatic jump, that not only could Girardengo not follow, he couldn't even ride. He had to dismount and walk! He was not alone. When the other exhausted riders attempted this final hill, they too had to resort to the two-foot gear.

Thirty kilometers of triumph remained, a relative promenade for Binda in front of thousands of appreciative fans who had no doubt as to who was the best rider in the world. His final victory margin of seven minutes, gained in only thirty kilometers on a superb and desperate Girardengo, spoke louder than any words about who deserved to don that first rainbow jersey.

Alfredo Binda repeated the rainbow performance twice more, collecting innumerable other victories, until a broken leg ended his superb career in 1936. But he hardly got a breather, for he was quickly recruited as the national team manager, a role that tested his mind as much as the roads had tested his legs. He needed everything he'd learned in his rivalry with Girardengo to help him choreograph the next generation of Italian *campionissimi*, Gino Bartali and Fausto Coppi!

6

VICTOR FONTAN, 1892–1982

ANYONE FAMILIAR WITH the history of the Tour de France knows the tragic story of Eugène Christophe, who had the misfortune to break his forks and as a result lose the race. (See Chapter 2 for Christophe's story.) Less well-known is a similar story concerning Victor Fontan.

Fontan was born in 1892 and grew up in the rural atmosphere of the southern Pyrenees. It was a hard but rewarding life. Like many young men in their late teens, he became infatuated with bicycle racing, only to have his budding career nipped by World War I. Twice wounded in the left leg, he got off lucky. That war chewed up most of his generation, a fact attested to by all the monuments commemorating the dead in towns throughout France.

He returned to his country life and rekindled his love affair with the bicycle. Fontan was what today would be called a "late bloomer." He was content to play with cycling and enjoy a local reputation. It wasn't until 1928, at age thirty-six, that he decided to "leave his garden" and participate in the big tours. In that year he finished fourth in the Tour of Italy, the best French performance since Jean Alavoine finished third in 1920.

He then went on to a fine seventh in the Tour de France, winning two stages and staging a great performance in the mountains.

With greater knowledge and the momentum of a lifetime he came to the 1929 Tour prepared to be more than a marginal player. He bided his time until the race hit his home turf, the Pyrenees. Climbing superbly with his young Spanish friend, Salvador Cardona, the two broke away over the mountains en route to Luchon, where Cardona got the stage and Fontan the yellow jersey. Imagine, thirty-seven years old and leading the Tour de France! With another mountain stage on the next day there didn't seem to be any reason why Fontan couldn't stay in yellow for some time to come.

In those days the mountain stages were true ordeals, more than 300 kilometers long, which necessitated beginning before dawn in order to finish before dusk. After only seven kilometers on stage 10 to Perpignan, Fontan slipped into a culvert and broke his forks. The rule that you had to finish the stage on the bike you started with was still in force.

Fontan was forced to walk to the next village, where a local took pity on him and offered all there was, a much-too-small tourist bike. For the next 145 kilometers poor Victor crawled along on this machine up and down the most difficult mountains in the world, all the while carrying his original bike on his shoulder!

Finally, recognizing the inevitable, that there was absolutely no way he could get to the finish before the time limit expired, exhausted in mind and body, he collapsed by the side of the road and sobbed.

Even for late bloomers there is such a thing as *too* late. Poor Fontan would never wear the yellow jersey again. Indeed, in an extra twist of ironic cruelty, he was forced to abandon the Tour for the last time in his beloved Pyrenees the following year.

If Victor Fontan could gain any solace from his incredible misfortune, it would be that Henri Desgrange, the race director, subsequently changed the rules to allow riders with mechanical mishaps to secure a new bike from the team car, thereby making the race merely difficult rather than absurdly difficult.

7

ANDRÉ LEDUCQ, 1904–1980

FROM ITS VERY beginning in 1903, the Tour de France somehow achieved larger-than-life status. Looked at from the cold light of the roadside, it's difficult to understand how a handful of guys crawling around the country lanes of France at fifteen miles per hour could conjure such emotion. Given the immediate spectacle . . . well, let's face it, there wasn't much of a spectacle. Today, of course, it's like a thousand-ring circus. Even if you didn't know the Tour de France was a bike race, you'd have to be deaf and blind not to be impressed by the hours of rolling hoopla. But in the early years things were visually more tame.

The key to its appeal, of course, was the Tour's ability to galvanize the imagination. Imagination has always played a big role in the collective Gallic psyche. To cite one of almost innumerable possibilities, if you'd been a good *paysan* struggling with the soil in the neighborhood of Vézelay in 1146, you'd have noticed a large crowd streaming into town and climbing to the church on the top of the hill to hear some guy named St. Bernard make an impassioned speech about everyone dropping their farm implements and saying good-bye to their families in order to go on an enormous trek of unimaginable difficulty and duration to fight some total strangers who were supposedly doing not nice things to certain holy sites in a nebulous place called the Holy Land. At the very least one would think there might have been some inquiries about the technical implementation of such a project. But accounts of witnesses record no hesitation. The "grandeur" of the project galvanized those present, and off they went, most never to return.

Projects such as the Crusades and wars of colonization have given national dream states a bad name, but the genius of something like the Tour de France is that it can take these same elemental desires for a huge, noble mission, full of danger and grandiosity and heroism and "we're special," and harness these truly profound human sentiments in a way that satisfies them while not destroying the society that produces them. The society itself, by sponsoring such an enterprise, grows to a higher level of civilization as an appreciation of every aspect of existence is enhanced.

Certainly Henri Desgrange, the "father" of the Tour de France, saw his "baby" performing this type of function, and it was from this order of concern that he based his decisions regarding how best it should be run. Desgrange's role as benevolent dictator (or not so benevolent depend-ing on whom you talked to back then) was never questioned, even by those who violently disagreed with his policies. At bottom no one doubted his absolute devotion to the Tour. Never did the slightest hint of ulterior motive or personal gain besmirch Desgrange's pronouncements. He may have made mistakes, made decisions that produced results different from those intended, but his motivations were pure. He wanted the Tour de France to be the greatest sporting pageant on earth, an arena akin to the ancient Greek theater where one's most personal psychological and physical possibilities and pretensions could be projected onto a sort of national tableau permitting a collective catharsis.

So imagine his concern when he saw his "baby's" health failing dur-ing the 1920s. Trade teams (all bike companies) had become so pow-erful that they were able to ensure the eventual outcome in advance. The racing was predictable, the smell of "fix" gave off a nasty odor, and

France hadn't had a winner in seven years. Scandal! Humiliation! And time for radical surgery!

A revolution was needed, and when it came to boldness Desgrange had few peers. Trade teams in collusion? Okay, no more trade teams. Post-Tour bike sales a determining factor in race tactics? Okay, all bikes will be issued by the Tour organization and painted an anonymous yellow. Tired of foreign domination? Okay, the Tour will be open only to national teams, each representing the cream of sporting talent, and they will be inspired by national patriotism rather than filthy lucre!

Just imagine a proposal even vaguely approximating such a change in Tour structure today. Quite simply, impossible! Yet Desgrange issued his edicts on September 25, 1929, for the revamping of the 1930 Tour, and, with hardly a ripple of disagreement, the European cycling community saluted and said, "Yes sir."

Desgrange could barely hide his glee. The new formula electrified the public and restored flagging interest in the event overnight.

If this introduction to the 1930 Tour de France appears lengthy, it is because one needs to understand the background to fully appreciate the dramatic events that were to unfold in the Alps that year. In the first two and a half weeks, foreign threats diminished while French domination grew. Learco Guerra, the "Italian locomotive" (a great time trialist but no winged climber), remained the only man who had any chance of challenging André Leducq, the French race leader. The French team, saturated with talent, was full of potential race winners. But as Leducq emerged the best, the others forgot their personal ambitions and thought only of how to get Leducq safely to Paris in yellow. It was the kind of spirit Desgrange had dreamed of; the whole of France was on fire with love for these boys in blue who so epitomized the national ideal. The "Eight Tricolors" might as well have been the "Three Musketeers."

The final mountain stage from Grenoble to Evian via the Galibier didn't appear to offer any particular problem, its 331 kilometers being a normal stage distance in those days. After the Galibier there were still more than 100 kilometers of flat terrain before Evian, so whatever challenge the Galibier might pose, the remaining distance appeared to neutralize any hostilities that might be launched on it. Leducq went over the top in second position fifty seconds behind the leader and ten seconds ahead of Guerra and then commenced his customary rocket-like descent. Leducq was well-known for his downhill abilities; what appeared crazy for most others was well within his capabilities.

Nevertheless, in one of those little lapses that even the best can make, both of his wheels slid out on the gravel as he rounded a curve and he crashed at over forty miles per hour. He was pretty shook up, but he hadn't hit anything so the cost of the crash was extensive abrasions. Once the bike was retrieved and needed nothing more than handlebar straightening, the abrasions were forgotten and the pursuit was on.

A number of riders had seen the spectacular tumble, including Guerra, who was just sixteen minutes behind Leducq on overall time, and they had not hesitated a moment in attempting to take advantage of the situation. The descent of the north side of the Galibier ends in a short climb up to the next pass, the Télégraphe, before continuing down further into the valley of the Arc. But on that short sprint up the Télégraphe, Leducq found he had more problems than he'd supposed, for a pedal, damaged in the fall, broke off practically with the first out-of-the-saddle thrust. There had been no warning at all and Leducq was slammed to the ground.

With the previous crash he'd had some warning. Einstein's relativity can be empirical in myriad ways, and sliding out on a high-speed turn is one of the more elementary. Something that from an outside observer's perspective may appear to pass in an instant can also, to the subject involved, take plenty long enough for all parameters to be considered, not least of which might be something like, "Oh shit, this is gonna hurt!" But this time, all observers, inside and outside, were in agreement. One second Leducq was out over the bars adding his body weight to his already considerable power, and the next moment he was on the ground. No question about it, it was a hell of a slam. A doctor would have diagnosed shock.

But there was no doctor present, just a few teammates. Leducq may or may not have been in some sort of shock. His teammates only cared about whether he could ride a bike. How to tell? A moment later they were encouraged when they realized he was sufficiently lucid to say, "It's finished." That was a double message. On one level it meant he was coherent enough to understand that a mechanical breakdown of this order precluded finishing the stage without breaking the rules regarding the nonutilization of original parts. The other message was that if a solution could be found, he still had the strength to carry on.

It was the second part of the message that teammate Marcel Bidot tuned in on. Bidot's sense of improvisation, which he was to utilize many times in future years as the director of national teams, showed his natural prescience at this sort of thing. He stopped a journalists' car, borrowed a wrench from its tool kit, grabbed/begged/stole a bike from a spectator, unscrewed a pedal, put it on Leducq's bike, changed the toe clip and strap, and, ready-or-not, André Leducq was now in for the ride of his life. Bidot had no second thoughts. What Desgrange didn't know about the enforcement of his stupid part replacement rule bothered him not at all. That was the minor part. Catching Guerra was going to be the major part!

Leducq was now surrounded by five teammates prepared to kill themselves over the next ninety kilometers to make up the fifteen-minute gap on Guerra and the other profiteers. It was the kind of chase made for modern television. Between overhead projections from helicopters, motorcycles zipping back and forth, and radio communications, every second gained or lost would be documented. But 1930 was different. Neither the breakaway nor the chase got much information about the other. And spectators would have to wait a day before they could thrill to this Homeric chase described in lascivious detail by the handful of journalists present.

And it *was* a Homeric chase. Guerra was indeed a locomotive. While he was the driving force of this choo-choo, because, after all, he had the most to gain, he got just enough help to allow him to ride at this maximum. Behind, no one on the French team thought of anything but closing the gap and saving the mangled yellow jersey of their beloved "Dede" Leducq. No one deserved to win, no one deserved to lose. But "deserve" is a lost word in the cruel field of cycling combat. After more than two hours of absolutely intense, flat-out, unrelenting effort, the chasers won and Guerra and company were scooped up.

And then Leducq had the temerity (and strength and speed) to win the sprint for the stage victory! The Tour was now as good as won for Leducq, but there was still glory to be had. The French team won twelve of the twenty-one stages, including eight by Charles Pélissier (the last four in succession!), the youngest brother of Henri Pélissier, the last French winner of the Tour way back in 1923.

The crash on the Galibier had given all of France a scare, but in the end it affirmed the appropriateness and popularity of Desgrange's revolutionary new Tour format. It was a change that lasted for more than thirty years and sealed the love of the Tour de France in the heart of the French soul.

8

FROM THE PERSPECTIVE of the rest of Europe, until the last thirty years or so, Spain has been something of a land apart. Geographically, it is at one end of the Continent and separated from it by the very substantial Pyrenees mountains. The demise of Spain's great empire left it ill prepared to prosper on its own. Grinding poverty and despotic governments made for a volatile mix that exploded in the 1930s. The ensuing civil war was won by Generalissimo Francisco Franco, a dictator who as recently as 1972 enforced his rule by use of the garrote (a fiendish device that simultaneously drives a pointed screw through a victim's vertebra and strangles him).

It was not the most conducive environment for such a bourgeois activity as bicycle racing. Yet even here cycling competition gained its converts, testimony to the passion two wheels can engender. Most notably, the Vuelta a España debuted in 1935 as Europe's third grand tour after the Tour de France and Giro d'Italia. Spanish races were almost exclusively Spanish, and Spanish riders of any repute in the rest of the Continent had to leave Spain to achieve it.

Foremost among the early émigrés were the Trueba brothers, Vicente and José, along with Francisco Cepeda. (Cepeda was killed at the 1935 Tour when he crashed descending the Galibier. He was the first rider to die in the Tour de France and until Tom Simpson died in 1967, the only one.) Vicente Trueba established the stereotype for Spanish riders: short, lean, and born climbers. He barely topped 100 pounds, and his bike frame looked too big at eighteen inches.

What wasn't small was the kind of gear he could turn on the climbs. Like some other riders of his power-to-weight ratio, he could get away using gears that would have broken the legs of a normal racer. On any given race day he would at first be indistinguishable from the pedaling mass. Once on a hill he would remain content to follow the pace in a normal 44x24 gear. (Tour de France riders in those days didn't use derailleurs. They had a single chainwheel with a double-sided hub. Each side mounted two cogs. To change gears it was necessary to dismount, loosen the wing nuts, slide the rear wheel forward to get chain slack, move the chain over a cog, or take the wheel out and turn it around to get the desired ratio, pull the wheel back to get proper chain tension, and then tighten the wing nuts. Whew!)

Most riders on a long climb must adopt a steady tempo. If necessary, they will increase their speed gradually since big mountains give no chance to recover after violent efforts—unless you were the "Torrelavega Flea," as Vicente Trueba came to be known.

When he tired of the (for him) boring tempo, his legs would go into electric motor mode for up to a minute or two. If necessary, he could do this repeatedly. Most often, no one tried to follow. Once detached, he would jump off, move to a bigger gear, and proceed up the hill in a completely different manner.

With his body angled out over the front of the bike like a cherry picker, he would stomp away for up to half an hour. Not only could Trueba have done without a saddle in the mountains, but he might have done with only a half pair of handlebars as well. An accident early in his cycling career severed most of the nerves in his left forearm. He couldn't even carry a book in his left hand, but this didn't cramp his riding style.

Trueba wasn't a "complete" rider. Time trials, sprints, echelon riding—all were necessary evils for him. Still he managed to finish sixth overall in the 1933 Tour de France, and along the way collect first prize in the newly created Grand Prix de la Montagne (a.k.a. King of the Mountains).

Trueba had great resistance, the ability to keep driving all day back when "all day" was literally true. Stages of eight or more hours were common. Once away in a break with the right combination of riders, he could be a major force. While he would set the pace on the climbs, he could rely on his breakaway companions to help him on the flats.

There are numerous examples of Trueba's strengths and weaknesses. In the 1933 Tour he arrived at the summit of the mighty Col du Galibier with a lead of 12 minutes, 50 seconds over that year's Tour winner, Georges Speicher. One hundred kilometers later at the finish line in Grenoble the difference was reduced—5 minutes, 38 seconds. Such has always been the lot of the climbing specialist.

Nevertheless, Trueba acquired a reasonable fortune from his racing day. On retiring to his hometown of Torrelavega, he invested his hard-earned money in a china factory and a restaurant. The combination kept him wealthy and fat. His legend will live as long as cycling, an inspiration to the "fleas" of the sport.

9

ANTONIN MAGNE, 1904–1983
RENÉ VIETTO, 1914–1988

NOT ALL RIVALRIES end in acrimony. Cycling has witnessed some epic demonstrations of altruism, but can any top that of René Vietto in the 1934 Tour de France?

Just four years before, the Tour de France founder, Henri Desgrange, had changed the Tour from a competition between trade teams (as it is today) to one between national teams (like the world road championship). He was sick of the intrigue and suspicious results. He even provided all the riders with anonymous yellow bikes. Now *les coureurs* would be racing for higher rewards than mere money. In the overheated political climate of post–World War I Europe, no rider would dream of doing less than his utmost for the honor and glory of his country.

The experiment was a spectacular success. During the early 1930s the French national team riders more than confirmed Desgrange's wildest expectations. Not only did they win every Tour from 1930 through 1934, but they did it with a musketeer-like "all for one, one for all" attitude that drove the fans into paroxysms of ecstasy.

The fact that Antonin Magne was extraordinarily taciturn didn't bother the French at all. He'd won the Tour in 1931 and appeared ready to repeat that success in 1934. If he was a man of few words who rarely smiled, that was just fine with his countrymen. The poor *paysans* who made up the vast majority of bike racing supporters in those days knew from their own sacrifices working on farms and in factories that life was tough. They appreciated a man who took his job seriously, a man who had no time for useless frivolities.

The French team was on precisely the same page with the rest of the country. Magne was the obvious best on the team and until events proved otherwise, his countrymen were prepared to sacrifice everything to make sure he arrived in Paris in yellow. René Vietto, a new recruit to the team, was more than grateful for the opportunity to ride alongside his idols and never dreamed of anything other than being in total support of Magne.

Vietto was only twenty years old. He was an elevator operator in a big resort hotel in Cannes during the day and a fanatical young bike racer every other moment. Except along the seashore, every direction from Cannes is up, a direction that very much pleased the skinny kid who seemed to float over the brutal climbs. Not only did Vietto start winning any race that ended on an incline, he more than looked after himself on training rides with his neighbor, the famous five-time Tour of Italy

A breakaway with Apo Lazarides (right) on the Briançon–Digne stage gave René Vietto (left) the yellow jersey at the 1947 Tour de France, which he led until two days from the finish.

winner, Alfredo Binda. Binda was impressed and was magnanimous enough to say so. He claimed that Vietto could become the "greatest of all time. He is an incomparable stylist. He could start a race with a bowl of milk on his back and at the end it'd still be full!" With such credentials it's no wonder that Vietto came to the notice of the French team Tour selectors. Today, it would be unthinkable to throw a twenty-year-old headlong into the Tour, no matter what his supposed talents, but the decade of the 1930s was desperate. Certainly Vietto had no complaints.

The early part of the race unfolded more or less predictably. Vietto lost almost forty-five minutes on the first two stages due to a series of untimely flats, but the important thing, from the French point of view, was that Magne was comfortably in yellow over the Italian, Giuseppe Martano, by eight minutes at the foot of the Alps. Magne could afford to be generous. He was delighted to see his young countryman fly away over the Galibier to win by three minutes into Grenoble. Not at all dismayed, Vietto took the next mountain stage as well. A flat stage followed, but the decidedly difficult stage from Nice through the Maritime Alps to Vietto's hometown of Cannes was a must win for the *enfant terrible,* and he didn't disappoint. His three consecutive mountain stage wins vaulted Vietto up to third on general classification, and he had every intention of improving on that in the Pyrenees, although challenging Magne never crossed his mind, as events were to show.

The first day in the Pyrenees and all was going well until Magne crashed descending the Col de Puymorens. Immediately Vietto stopped, gave Magne his front wheel and waited for the spares van to show up. Magne still had bike problems and waited for another teammate, Georges Speicher, to show up before chasing after his rival Martano.

Poor Vietto was left to sit on the stone parapet for a long time before finally getting a new wheel and finishing the stage with Speicher four minutes back. Pictures of Vietto's disconsolate, teary image made every paper in France, and on that day was born "Le Roi René" (King René), not only because of his climbing prowess but also because he was a master of those sacrificial sentiments that the French so desperately needed and admired. Unknown to everyone, those ghastly minutes on the wall by the road were to remain the high points of Vietto's cycling career.

Nevertheless, Magne lost 45 seconds to Martano and was less than three minutes ahead of the Italian going into the next stage. As for Vietto, he dropped to fifth on G.C. Not at all the direction on G.C. the young "Cannois" wanted. He vowed to make amends on the following mountain day.

On the second climb, the Portet d'Aspet, Vietto held a small lead over Magne at the summit, but he slowed in order to make sure Magne was on his wheel for the descent to help his leader chase Martano. A little lower down Magne hit a stone with such force that it threw off his chain, which got tangled around the cranks.

Unable to continue, Magne could see the Tour slipping from his grasp. Vietto and teammate Roger Lapébie were long gone, the rest of the team way behind, and the spares van god knows where. And then an apparition. Could it be the heat, the altitude, the fatigue, or was that really his teammate, René Vietto, standing before him ready to change bikes?

Blithely unaware of Magne's fate on the downhill, Vietto had flown ahead, having heard and seen nothing. It was only when a course marshal on a motorcycle zoomed up to explain things to Vietto that he come to a halt, and then turned around and rode back up the hill! Vietto went in the reverse direction of the race in order to save his leader. The point can hardly be overemphasized.

When Vietto reappeared, Magne knew better than to question this gift from god, or whomever. He grabbed Vietto's bike and raced off down the mountain to hook up with Lapébie on an ultimately successful mission to save his precious jersey.

Vietto won two climbing stages in the Alps the following year finishing eighth on G.C. After that, injuries plagued him for three years, injuries a modern sports doctor would easily interpret as too much too soon. He came closest to winning the Tour in 1939 at age 25, when he wore the yellow jersey until stage 15, when he cracked on the Izoard climb to concede the overall victory to Sylvère Maes of Belgium. Vietto finished second. He returned to his beloved Tour when it revived after World War II in 1947. He again wore yellow for ten days and held off all challengers until the nineteenth of twenty-one stages, when he succumbed to the relentless pressure of a 139-kilometer individual time trial.

Knowing the hands of time had passed him by, Vietto retired to his pig farm in the Pyrenees after finishing two more Tours. He would return to the Tour at age 72 when he was brought to the finish of the Alpe d'Huez stage in 1986. There Vietto participated in a roundtable discussion with Bernard Hinault and Greg LeMond. Unknown to anyone at the time, Hinault had asked LeMond to cool it while climbing the grueling Alpe. They finished arm in arm. Shortly thereafter Le Roi René gave a paean to the concept of sacrifice, which LeMond appeared justified in interpreting as a pat on the back from the old master for his sacrificing to let Hinault win the stage. Moments later, when asked about the outcome of the race, Hinault pointed to the upcoming time trial and intimated that the race was far from over. LeMond was stunned, and René Vietto needed no further proof that his glorious era was indeed in the past.

10

JEAN ROBIC IS remembered as one of those "characters" who give the sport so much more interest than a list of statistics would imply. Born in Brittany, France, in 1921, he first came to national notice when he won the French cyclo-cross championship in 1945. In 1950 he won the world championship at that specialty. But he was truly devoted to road racing, even though his short stature meant that he rarely went beyond being a climbing specialist.

He never recognized any personal limitations, and if he didn't do well he always had an excuse. He got the nickname "Biquet," or "Little Goat," for his habit of braying a lot. His other nickname was "Tête de Cuir," or "Leatherhead," because he took to wearing a leather helmet after several crashes. Yet his irascible, feisty nature endeared him to his homeland in northwest France where such personality traits were not all that abnormal. (Bernard Hinault, the "Badger," also came from Brittany.)

After a six-year layoff due to World War II, the Tour de France returned in 1947, much to the relief and delight of the French public. Of course the riders were ecstatic too, and none more than Robic, who, to the amusement of everyone, fancied his chances in his debut Tour. "Ah, good ol' Jean," they'd chuckled knowingly, "he may be delusional, but you *'av to give eem credit for being poseeteeve. Sure he can climb a hill here und zer, mais zut alors, mes amis, Le Tour de France is not for zee chickens who can hop!"*

The race was controlled from the start by old stager René Vietto (whose story appears in Chapter 9), but he came apart in the last time trial, a little bagatelle of no fewer than 139 kilometers! Robic had already won three climbing stages in long solo breaks, but in between he had been erratic. He came back once again in this monumental four-hour ordeal under the blazing sun to secure third on general classification, far better than the café hounds of his hometown had ever dared hope.

But surely that was all he could hope for. The new leader, Pierre Brambilla, a French-based Italian, was strong and experienced and never once on the last day did he or his Italian teammate Aldo Ronconi, who was second on G.C., quit the wheel of their little nemesis, Robic. No one expected otherwise, of course.

About 120 kilometers from Paris the race traversed Rouen and climbed out of the Seine River valley. After the Alps and Pyrenees the Côte de Bon-Secours was a mere bump but, not totally unexpectedly, Robic put in a furious attack. Brambilla responded instantly, and after a few hundred meters of desperate effort Robic slowed, apparently resigned to the futility of the move. Just then a counterattack by Edouard Fachleitner blew by. Brambilla tried to go with this second attack, but he hadn't gotten his second wind, and when he faded Robic managed to rev up again and grab the wheel of Fachleitner.

Brambilla organized his forces and began the expected chase. But it didn't make a dent in the difference. "Fach" and Robic were riding like madmen. As the kilometers rolled by, Brambilla's Italian teammates started to melt and he was left to do most of the work alone.

Fachleitner, only four minutes down on Robic on G.C., could have sat on and then tried to make a break for Paris on his own, but he never did. There was talk of money changing hands. But whatever it was, Fachleitner worked with Robic all the way to Paris, where they arrived thirteen minutes ahead of Brambilla's small group.

So Jean Robic became the first and only rider to win the Tour on the last day when it's a road stage (in contrast to a time trial). His unique feat is called "le Miracle de Bon-Secours," or "the miracle of good-help hill."

The win made Robic—who raced that first year for the West France regional team—more intolerable than ever. As a Tour winner he had to be included on the national squad the following year. But when reminded of the great men such as Louison Bobet on the team, he sneered, "What's he done that I haven't?" Robic had a point. He'd won the Tour and Bobet's three Tour victories lay in the future. But Bobet had won lots of races outside the Tour that Robic hadn't. Robic was pint-sized sand-paper and everyone dreaded his presence.

In the event, Bobet finished the 1948 Tour in fourth (after leading the race until the last stage in the Alps), while Robic was a distant sixteenth overall. Robic returned to the regional team for the next three Tours, finishing fourth overall in 1949, when he won a mountain stage in the Pyrenees and was the only climber able to challenge the Italian super-champions Fausto Coppi and Gino Bartali in the Alps. Back on the national team in 1952, at age thirty-one, Robic again won a stage and took second to Coppi at L'Alpe d'Huez, to be the best French rider, finishing fourth overall.

In 1953 Leon Le Calvez took over the West regional team and invited Robic to come home and lead his local boys against the big guns. Robic jumped at the chance. It was the kind of challenge that appealed to him, and of course there was no opposition to the idea from anyone associ-ated with the national team.

Le Calvez really believed in his new charge and desperately wanted to see him in yellow. But how? He looked at every aspect of the race—and despaired. Unless the time trials were hilly, and few were, Robic would lose time there to the likes of Coppi, Hugo Koblet, and Bobet. If he could get the team to pull Robic up to attacks on the flat, it was all that could be hoped for. In the mountains it was pretty well every man for himself. If only Robic could go downhill as fast as he went up. How many times had Le Calvez seen Robic arrive on some mountaintop a minute or two ahead of the nearest rival, only to lose it all going down the other side. It wasn't as though Robic was a terrible descender, but he was so light bigger guys would just eat him up.

What to do? What to do? Even as the 1953 Tour began, Le Calvez could think of no solution. Nine stages passed, and the Pyrenees were imminent. Le Calvez was desperate. Finally, on the very eve of the mountains, it came to him. Too light on the downhills? Of course, add weight! "How could I be so dense?" he berated himself. "The answer is so obvious."

Secrecy would be required. That evening, in the stage town of Cauterets—where Robic took second on the uphill finish and moved to within five minutes of race leader Fritz Schaer of Switzerland—Le Calvez found an excuse to leave the team dinner table early and quietly slipped out the back. A few blocks away he knocked on a door. It opened and greetings were exchanged, but Le Calvez's attention went immediately to the forge where a pot of lead sat bubbling. From his pocket he produced an aluminum water bottle, standard for the day. In less than a minute it was full, and in less than an hour it was cool enough to heft back into his pocket and return to the hotel as clandestinely as he had departed.

He collected the team mechanic who followed along obediently, and the two went to Robic's room. Robic responded to the knock with curiosity, as well as a touch of annoyance. The team leader wasn't accustomed to being disturbed at this late hour, even by the team director.

"Jean, I'm sorry to disturb you," Le Calvez apologized. "I have your water bottle ready for tomorrow."

Robic was not amused. But before he could advise Le Calvez to seek psychiatric assistance, the director produced the bottle and handed it to Robic. Instinctively, Jean reached for it, involuntarily preparing to grasp a few grams.

Le Calvez couldn't help but smile when he saw Robic's shock at his arm almost falling off. Before Robic could become too agitated, Le Calvez explained, "Jean, here is your salvation for the mountains tomorrow. Not the uphills, just the down."

Robic did the impossible—he laughed. *"Merde! Quel coup!"*

"Yes," the director agreed, "at nine kilos [20 pounds] this bottle will almost double the weight of your bicycle!"

Turning to the mechanic, the crafty Le Calvez added, "And you, my dear Vaslin, must be careful how you give this to our esteemed team leader. There are three passes tomorrow and if Jean is in the lead on any of them he must stop as though in need of assistance. You will leap out of the car, a wheel in your hand, bend over the bike while appearing to change a wheel, and slip the bottle into the cage. Remember, the whole operation will not succeed if you're spotted by a commissaire. As you know, you can only hand up food and water in the designated feeding zones.

"Once at the bottom, Jean, gently drop the bottle off with some spectator. We'll pick it up and be prepared to have it back to you on the following summit."

With smiles all around the three retired for the evening.

The next day things went pretty well as planned. On the descent of the Tourmalet, when Robic was knocked off his bike by a motorcycle, spectators were reduced to ethnic slurs about the brightness of Brittany brains in order to explain the apparently inexplicable alacrity with which Robic scrambled after his water bottle as it rolled toward a ravine. At day's end Robic could afford to overlook such comments. He had won the stage and donned the *maillot jaune!*

The trick was such a well-kept secret that it might have been used in following years, but Robic being Robic, he was so tickled at having deceived everyone that he boasted about the gimmick to a reporter.

Dear Robic, you are much missed!

11

FAUSTO COPPI, 1919–1960

A TALL, RATHER frail-looking young amateur cyclist, accompanied by two friends, hesitantly knocked on the door. Moments seemed like hours before the sound of shuffling feet told them their knock had been heard. The door opened, revealing an imposing figure. Weighing at least 250 pounds and wearing black eyeglasses, the man had, at least, a reassuring voice.

"Hello, Domenico," he greeted them, "I've been waiting for you and your friends. Please come in." Handshakes were made, and the moment he grasped the tall one's hand, he exclaimed, "Ah yes, you must be the young Fausto Coppi about whom we've heard so much of late."

The young men were ushered down a hallway into a simple room whose main adornment was a massage table. Each undressed to allow the renowned "Wizard of Cycling," the "Muscle Magician," to work his magic on them. His name was Biagio Cavanna and by 1938 he was a legend in cycling circles. All the greats of Italian cycling for two generations, men such as Costante Girardengo, Alfredo Binda, and Learco Guerra, passed through his hands.

Now he was starting on a third generation. As the three hopeful amateurs prepared to leave, the blind masseur pulled Coppi aside. Fausto almost trembled in his presence. Cavanna spoke seriously now, all trace of warmth gone. The old man had just made a discovery and in his own way was as excited as the shy youth in front of him.

"Listen to me," he intoned. "My hands see more than my eyes. My ears hear what can't be heard. Your lung capacity, heart strength, and muscles indicate you can become a great champion. Believe me, I am not mistaken. Will you do as I say?"

Coppi could barely stammer, "Of course."

"Then do not race for the next three months."

"But I must race," Fausto replied. "It's how I make my living."

"I am sorry for you," Cavanna sighed. "There is nothing I can do for you. You see, you must build yourself up. Eat meat every day."

Even though he could not understand the master's reasoning, Coppi returned home, determined to follow the advice. He abandoned the rest of the season and prepared the following spring under the direct "gaze" of the blind man. The rest of the story is, of course, history. Fausto Coppi remains the greatest cyclist Italy has ever produced, and for exactly twenty years his superb physique received daily attention from the blind wizard.

That physique needed all the help it could get. When Coppi stepped into the arena of professional cycling, he soon found himself the natural antagonist of Italy's former greatest cyclist, Gino Bartali. Their relative merits fuel an ongoing argument in many of Italy's bars and cafés. The late 1940s and early 1950s were a golden age of sorts in cycling, for there was an abundant supply of truly superb professional bike racers. A third great Italian, Fiorenzo Magni, the Swiss pair Ferdi Kubler and Hugo Koblet, Belgians Alberic Schotte and Rik Van Steenbergen, Frenchmen Louison Bobet, Raphaël Geminiani, and Jean Robic, just to name the elite, all contributed to the Coppi legend, for it was against such giants that Coppi was measured and found superior.

But Coppi's impact on the sport went beyond an impressive list of victories. He may have been born in poverty, but he had the appearance of an aristocrat. In class-conscious Europe (more so then than now) cycling was commonly viewed as a lower-class sport, something farm boys and factory workers utilized to escape a life of drudgery. Bartali was adored because he fulfilled the ideal of a "champion of the people." He was a little bit short and thickset. His skin was a little dark. He loved to talk in that hyperexpressive manner so loved by Italians; he could be moody; he smoked and drank, was superstitious, and was so religious that he was called "Gino the pious." And he was as tough as nails. In contrast, Coppi looked and acted like someone from the upper class. His tall, slim, almost feline body was crowned by a face that would have made a Roman senator proud. And his distinguished appearance was just the beginning. He committed himself to cycling with a professional attention to detail formerly unknown. In large measure due to Cavanna, Coppi followed a strict regimen—select foods, mineral water, proper sleep, cleanliness in all matters, and so on. He transformed the public image of the sport. Now everyone admired Coppi.

Coppi created a revolution in every dimension of cycling. Before his time saddle boils plagued riders during stage races. The continuous attention of a doctor and fresh clothes for each rider every day almost eliminated this scourge. Coppi insisted on using gloves not just because they were comfortable but to protect his hands from abrasions during the inevitable crashes. He elevated his *gregarii* from bicycle slaves to real teammates. With them he took strategy and tactics to a new level. Having them infiltrate breakaways to control his adversaries was one of his innovations. Having backup bikes was another. He was the first to use an especially light bike for time trials. He consulted with many manufacturers to improve everything from toe straps to tires to clothing to derailleurs. Most of these changes were made with utilitarian benefits in mind, but sometimes his recommendations were based on a more stylish image he thought the sport should have.

Thanks to Coppi's proper comportment (before the *damma bianca* affair), his kindness, and his fabulous prestige, professional cycling entered into a new era, a mutually beneficial climate in which organizers, journalists, sponsors, the riders, and the public came to occupy a much more harmonious atmosphere.

In the not inconsequential opinion of Raphaël Geminiani, once a teammate of both Coppi and Bobet and later team director for both Anquetil and Merckx, Fausto Coppi was the greatest rider of all time. Geminiani is perfectly aware that Merckx amassed the best record of any rider, but he is adamant that Merckx rarely faced opposition of the caliber of Coppi's days. What would Merckx's record look like if his victories between the ages of twenty-three and twenty-six were excised, as Coppi's were by the war?

These suggestions put us on the slippery slope to cross-generational comparisons, a slope I don't wish to slide down. But some measure of comparison is necessary to determine the full value of the man. As Einstein showed at the beginning of the century, relativity enters into all matter(s). At the very least, Fausto Coppi was the pivotal person in the history of our magnificent obsession.

Of all the elements that constituted his influence, his supernatural performances were the foundation of everything else. Coppi fans love to list these performances and describe them in lascivious detail. For them, each one is a love affair. Here are two that show his prowess in the particular domain that is the subject of this book, the mountains.

After World War II the sporting war between Fausto Coppi and Gino Bartali resumed. They beat each other often enough to give their partisans plenty of ammo to argue the superiority of their respective idols. Coppi wanted 1949 to be different. He would turn thirty that year, and Bartali thirty-five. For the first time in his career he intended to ride the Tour de France. In those days the Tour was open to national teams, which meant Coppi would have to spend over three weeks in close proximity to Bartali. He hated the idea because Bartali grated on his every nerve. But if he could make a definitive statement in the earlier grand tour, the Tour of Italy, his job in the Tour de France might be made easier.

As though reading his mind, the Giro (Tour of Italy) organizers included a stage of such epic proportions that the winner was sure to become an instant legend. From the first pedal stroke in southern Italy, Coppi looked forward to this 254-kilometer monster through both Italian and French Alps. Between Cuneo and Pinerolo it would scale no less than five first-category mountains: the Maddalena, Vars, Izoard, Montgenèvre, and Sestriere.

The cycling gladiators arose at 4:30 that grim morning of June 10, 1949. A big breakfast and time to digest were needed before the start at 7:00. Outside, as the rain poured down, the riders became more morose as they contemplated how the precipitation would complicate their efforts to survive the muddy roads. Asphalt had yet to reach these remote mountain passages.

When Fausto attacked midway up the Maddalena, he did it with such authority that no one, not even Gino Bartali himself, could make an effort to react. There were 192 kilometers remaining, approximately eight hours in which Coppi proved there was no one to race against except himself. That day Bartali served as a sort of backlight. Already 2 minutes, 40 seconds down at the summit of the Maddalena, the gap grew inexorably to 6 minutes, 55 seconds on the Izoard and 11 minutes, 52 seconds at the finish line. Without Coppi, Bartali's second place would have looked fabulous. Others arrived well over an hour later. Coppi was on the podium when Bartali, covered in mud, rode by below. At last Bartali had to admit the new order of things, and he lowered his head. Coppi returned the nod in reciprocal homage.

His epic ride was described by an observer:

This singular combat, beautiful in its cruelty, was emotional in intensity. Victory accompanied him from the beginning. It could not be doubted. On these grim climbs he pedaled irresistibly. What force could have stopped him? Three flats went almost unnoticed. From time to time he arose out of the saddle, perhaps to give his derriere a break, but it seemed as he danced on the pedals that he needed to discharge excessive energy, like a giant awakening from a long sleep. One saw his muscles under the skin looking like young snakes attempting to break free of their confines. Throughout he rode with an absolute calm as though no one was chasing behind.

Twice since, this stage has been included on the Giro itinerary. In 1964 Franco Bitossi won it. In 1982 Giuseppe Saronni beat Bernard Hinault by half a length. The next day's headlines in the Italian sports paper *La Gazzetta Sportiva* screamed, "Saronni won, but the triumph is for Coppi!"

Coppi went on that summer to become the first man to win both Giro and Tour in the same year. He returned for another triumphal appearance in the Tour de France in 1952. He won where and when he pleased. Among the stages he dominated was one that concluded with an obscure serpentine path featuring twenty-one numbered hairpins. It has since become famous as the road to L'Alpe d'Huez. He had no need to win the stage except that desire and pride forced him to fly away up the dirt track.

One of the race directors, Jacques Goddet, rode alongside on a motorcycle. Reflecting on what he saw that day, he wrote, "This Coppi, this was not the Coppi of the average stage. This was a fighter unchained, a wild beast on the track of its prey, and from our vantage point we could scrutinize his visage, read his eyes, and in them we perceived the gleam of a cruel animal, a tiger bounding on its victim." It is no wonder that the cycling world still mourns his untimely death from malaria in the early hours of 1960.

12

B & C , BARTALI AND COPPI

THIS IS A BOOK ABOUT great climbers. Certainly Gino Bartali and Fausto Coppi were two of the greatest; many would argue that they were the greatest of all time. Any attempt to compare riders from different generations quickly descends into probability theory, possibility theory, could-have-been theory, and so on. A waste of time that could be better spent appreciating riders in their own context where evaluations are far easier to discern. Normally, that context is the rider confronting some task while considering his rivals' possible moves.

For these two Italians, considering each other's next move was a full-time occupation. It's necessary to recall Gino Bartali's place in the scheme of Italian cycling in 1939. He turned pro in 1935 before his twenty-first birthday and swept through the ranks like a firestorm. None of that slow apprenticeship stuff. In just four years he'd won numerous prestigious one-day races, the Tour of Italy twice, and the Tour de France once (which would have been twice if he hadn't slid off a bridge into a raging torrent).

Bartali was so good that he rose to the top immediately. There were never more than a few riders at the top and teams were formed with the exclusive purpose of keeping their leaders up there. Most riders had no personal ambitions. Certainly no young rider would join Bartali's team daring to dream of personal performances. A newcomer would be honored just to be hired and become a good slave to his leader.

It was into this atmosphere that the seemingly timid nineteen-year-old Fausto Coppi walked in 1939. He showed some promise as an amateur and was recruited to Bartali's Legnano team. Coming from poverty, he was more than grateful for the opportunity to be on one of Italy's best teams. And yet, looking back, which no doubt Bartali did in his night-mares, Coppi showed a quiet assertiveness that a normal *gregario* would never reveal. Questions over the dinner table, a certain sense of personal pride—these were the types of hints that Bartali completely overlooked. No ordinary team member would have dreamed of challenging the boss.

Coppi incubated in 1939 and got his chance in the 1940 Tour of Italy. War was already raging across northern Europe, but in the ominous twi-light Italy gave herself one last time to indulge in her preferred form of warfare: cycling titans in their annual Giro showdown.

After being severely injured in a crash early in the race, Gino lumbered on, driven by pure willpower. Recognizing his unexpected vulnerabil-ity, Bartali's rivals attacked repeatedly. The team director, Pavesi, was in a terrible bind. On the one hand he wanted to support Bartali. Gino wasn't dead yet, despite being in the center of a piranha-like feeding frenzy. Pedaling with only one leg, he valiantly attempted to respond to every acceleration. Even with all his superb talent and determination, however, he was weakening and clearly couldn't carry on like this.

On the other hand, Pavesi's mandate was to supply a Giro winner. Indisputably, that had been Bartali before he was wounded. Next to Gino there was one teammate left, that skinny Coppi kid. And he looked good, no sign of stress. Pavesi's anguish resolved itself in a pattern to make Freud proud. Pavesi made a face to Bartali that appeared to say, "You're still the leader." Then he turned to Coppi and made another facial ges-ture that screamed, "Attack!" And the whole time Pavesi could dissimu-late to himself that he hadn't actually "said" anything.

Fausto needed no further encouragement. He went on the offensive to win stage 11 by four minutes and take the coveted *maglia rosa* (race leader's jersey) with the full support of Bartali.

There could be no denying it. With Coppi's win, Italy now had two *cam-pionissimi*. An unspoken peace pact existed until the Tour of Emilia the following spring. These national one-day classics were all the Italians had, since international races elsewhere had fallen victim to the war. Understandably, they took on the stature formerly enjoyed by the select handful of international classics. Furthermore, these domestic classics composed a points series that counted toward the Italian national championship. Gino had won it in 1940 and very much wanted to repeat his success in 1941.

The night before the race the team gathered in Gino's room for the usual prerace discussion of tactics. Coppi opened with a request: "I would like to attack from the start. I don't have very good form and am a little sick. I hope to make an effort you [Bartali] can profit from. This way you can warm up easily and follow the chase. After a short escape, I plan to quit."

"I don't see any problem with that," Bartali replied.

But things went a little differently. Coppi escaped all right and stayed escaped all the way to the finish.

The moment Coppi got to his hotel room, Bartali was waiting. "So, you don't have any form?"

"But no one chased me."

"You could have quit."

"But I wasn't sick anymore. The race made me feel good."

"Thanks for the explanation," Gino responded sarcastically. On the way out of Fausto's room he discovered a map of the race route, outlined and detailed. At the time such documents were not routinely furnished to the racers.

"So what's this?" Gino demanded. No response. "Do you need a map to choose which road on which to take your sick leave?"

"But I got the map before I was sick," Coppi replied lamely.

"You should have warned me that racing was a remedy for illness!" Bartali retorted with growing sarcasm. Storming out of the room, he made a mental note. "This man is dangerous. I lost seven minutes today."

Their meetings became increasingly rare. By 1943 Bartali was hiding out trying to avoid the war and Coppi was soon to become a POW in North Africa.

Racing didn't begin again until 1946. Bartali turned thirty-two that year, Coppi twenty-seven. Nothing had changed except Coppi's team. He was now in the Bianchi *squadra* (team) and free to race as he wished.

Bartali recognized Coppi's natural gifts. He wrote:

On a bike Fausto was like a god. When he got off he was a mortal, but when he pedaled he was supernatural. His suppleness, his form, this plasticity in motion constituted a complete spectacle. It's easy to understand the enthusiasm of so many to see him in action.

But all the same, fatigue could mark his organism. Certain traces did not escape the critical eye I had. I studied every centimeter of his hide. I knew it almost as well as my own. As team captain in 1940 I had explained my weak points to the team. At that time I was far from supposing that I was exposing myself to a rival. It was necessary to discover his fallibilities. At last, one day, my endless scrutiny was rewarded. In the hollow of his right knee a vein inflated along five or six centimeters. This happened between kilometers 160 and 180 of a race. At this moment I knew Fausto was vulnerable.

I needed to be sure, so I assigned my faithful Giovannino Corrieri to look for the vein during the 1948 Tour of Italy. The moment Corrieri saw the sign he came dashing through the peloton, shouting to me, "The vein! The vein!" Of course, no one knew what he meant, but when I heard those words I attacked. At the finish line Fausto was four minutes back.

Bartali was convinced that Coppi was more than blessed by the gods. He was sure that Fausto had discovered a secret, some magic that made him, on certain days, beyond reach.

One day in the 1946 Giro, Bartali saw Coppi drink a small bottle of some liquid and throw it in the grass by the roadside. "What the hell is it he drinks?" Bartali asked himself.

The first thing I did was note precisely where he threw his bottle. After the Giro, which I won by forty-seven seconds over Fausto, I drove to the spot where the bottle was, and after a little searching, found it. The next day, first thing, I went to my personal doctor and asked him to identify it.

The result was a big letdown. No drug. No magic. Just a French mineral water that could be bought anywhere. I immediately bought a case.

Still, I was not satisfied. It was necessary to establish a plan of investigation. I demanded that my team manager make every effort to book into the same hotel as Coppi and to get a room as close to his as possible. You understand, this wasn't always so easy. Even during the Tour de France when we were on the same national team when I would like to have shared a room, Fausto kept his distance.

The active phase of my inquest began just ten minutes before the start of every stage. This was work, ultracondensed! The moment I saw Coppi and his companions leave the hotel I would tiptoe into his room and search everything. Glasses, bottle, tubes, cartons, suppositories, wrappers—nothing escaped my eye. Poor Fausto. He never understood how he aroused all my *Toscanerie,* all my bitterness and aggressiveness.

The biggest problem with my "operation wastebasket" was to get to the start on time. Coppi always left at nearly the last moment, so I hadn't much time to do my "work." How many times did I rush up to the commissaires at the last second, hand trembling, to sign in just before I would have been disqualified!

Bartali seized every opportunity to derail his "young rival." For example, on the eve of the 1947 Milan–San Remo classic, Gino had a miserable cold and felt he had no hopes of doing well the following day. Walking down the street that evening, he was intercepted by Serse Coppi (Fausto's brother) and Serse's teammate, Luigi Casola.

Serse, in all innocence, asked, "Hey, Gino, want to go to the movies with us?"

Bartali didn't much care for films, but the thought of depriving Fausto of two fully rested *gregarii* was all the motivation he needed. After three hours of Rita Hayworth, they adjourned to a restaurant for a nightcap of white wine and tortellini. It was 2:00 A.M. when they returned to the hotel.

No one seems to remember how Fausto's "boys" felt the next day. All eyes were on Gino Bartali. He won!

For the most part Coppi suffered the surveillance in silence. There were times, however, when he was content just to follow Bartali. The worst of such moments came in the 1948 world road championships. While others escaped, Coppi and Bartali played a game of "after you." Finally, eons in arrears, they both quit.

The Italian Cycling Federation exercised its muscle in a communiqué: "In the World Championships they have forgotten to honor the Italian prestige that they represent. Thinking only of their personal rivalry, they abandoned the race, to the approbation of all sportsmen." A three-month suspension began immediately.

Until 1949 Fausto had avoided the Tour de France. This race, disputed by national teams, threatened to recreate the 1948 world road championship fiasco every day. To make matters worse, Gino had won the Tour in 1948, ten years after his first win. Never mind his thirty-four years, Gino must be treated as an equal.

A peace pact was signed, but it was a cold war all the way. Coppi's statement just prior to the Tour revealed his underlying bitterness. "A team of twelve modest, united riders is stronger than a team divided among different leaders. It's obvious that neither of us will be the mercenary for the other. Consequently, each of us tries to pass the other, to create as big a difference as possible. This is why I have always reproached Bartali for his poor team spirit and why I don't like to race with him."

Things came literally to a boil on the stifling hot fifth stage, the 293 kilometers from Rouen to St. Malo. Coppi got away at the forty-second kilometer with seven others. By the seventy-fifth kilometer the gap was six minutes and the Tour was on its way to big changes. Suddenly, Jacques Marinelli, the *maillot jaune,* collided with a spectator and crashed. Fausto couldn't avoid him and joined Marinelli on the ground. Marinelli was able to remount immediately, but Coppi was stuck. His bike was a wreck. The Italian following car, driven by Tragella, stopped and offered a bike that wasn't Coppi's. Fausto growled, "I want my bike or I quit." Bartali came by, saw the mess, and cried, "I'll wait for you." Finally the second car arrived with the team director, Alfredo Binda, at the wheel. On the roof was Fausto's bike.

The group was barely under way when Fausto began to complain of various problems—hunger, fatigue, fever, and so on. His speed dropped to a walking pace and finally Bartali took off. Gino lost 5 minutes, 30 seconds that day, Fausto 18 minutes, 43 seconds.

That night the full story came out. In short, when Coppi discovered that Binda wasn't following him, he thought the directeur sportif preferred Bartali. Under those conditions, Fausto didn't want to continue. The arguments raged through the evening, first around the dinner table and then in the hotel lobby.

Into this bedlam walked a bold, old man. With him walked his dog. He went right to Coppi. "Listen," he said, "I have no one except this dog. And because I am an admirer of yours I baptized him 'Fausto.' I trust he will never betray me as I will never betray him." Tipping his hat, the man and his dog departed. From that moment, Coppi's glacial indifference began to thaw. Finally he could hear that Binda had been legitimately delayed and that the delay had nothing to do with preferring Bartali.

With the fratricidal warfare laid to rest, the Italian team went to work to rectify the gaping time losses. The mountains, of course, gave Bartali and Coppi the chance to get back to the top of the general classification list where they belonged. So superior were they to everyone else that on successive days in the Alps Bartali won on his birthday, and Coppi flew away the following to take the yellow jersey. It was one of the greatest comebacks of all time.

The glow didn't last long, however. The following year, for example, Bartali won the Italian national road title, and with it the right to wear the champion's red, white, and green jersey. Not long after was the Tour of Italy, and Bartali took great delight riding at the front where the fans could recognize him from afar. All day long the peloton cruised through a shouting chorus of "Bartali! Bartali!" Just as intended, the sustained adulation got on Coppi's nerves.

But Coppi was not without his own weapons in this psy-war. On his team was Antonio Bevilacqua, the Italian national pursuit champion. He too had the right to wear a red, white, and green jersey, but only on the track. Coppi commanded him to wear it and ride in front of Bartali. The *tifosi*, on seeing the jersey from afar, went into raptures as usual, yelling "Viva Gino!" and only at the last moment recognized their error. Bartali was not amused, but Coppi was and happily paid the daily fine for Bevilacqua's violation of the rules.

The rivalry gradually diminished because even Bartali's fierce desire to win couldn't overcome the tick of the inner clock. Their last chapter was a touching one. At the end of the 1959 season, Gino, retired since 1954 and now director of his own team, signed Fausto Coppi (age 40) to be his team captain for the following season. Teammates again, twenty years later! It was not to be. That winter Coppi contracted a fatal illness while on a hunting trip to Africa. The rivalry and, yes, camaraderie (they even sang together on occasion) finally ended and the cycling world mourned.

13

GINO BARTALI, 1914–2000

THE TOUR DE FRANCE is always looking toward the future. It strives to be one of the great sporting events of the world by being open to more riders, providing a formula that will produce a worthy winner, visiting nearby countries, and allowing media from just about everywhere to have access to the three-week drama. And yet the Tour never forgets its past. Little and large motifs pervade the annual itinerary, giving added pleasure to those who care to dig under the surface. The year 2000 was a natural opportunity for the Tour to look both ahead and behind. In marking out the stage from Cannes to Briançon, the organizers intended not only to give the riders a proper test in the mountains but also to remind the current generation of an earlier generation who set out to race in 1948. The sporting comparison would be stimulating enough, but in 1948 there was an extra dimension that no one would have wanted to see repeated fifty-two years later.

In 1948 Gino Bartali returned to the Tour for the first time since 1938, a Tour he had won. No rider in history had been able to win a decade after a previous victory. But the swarthy thirty-four-year-old Tuscan showed no signs of his age. He won the opening stage and then two in the Pyrenees, but the Italian still allowed young French star Louison Bobet to take the lead by an enormous 21 minutes, 28 seconds.

Yes, there were three mountain stages on the menu between Cannes on the sunny Riviera and Lausanne, Switzerland, but Bobet appeared to be a man who could not be dismissed casually. A few minutes gained here and a few minutes gained there were not going to eradicate over twenty-one minutes!

However, an off-stage drama on the eve of the great Cannes-to-Briançon challenge temporarily overshadowed the race. The leader of the Italian communist party (at the time the party was a major player in Italian politics), Palmiro Togliatti, was shot and gravely wounded by the extremist Antonio Pallante.

As the Italian team began to leave the dinner table, an Italian journalist approached Bartali, "Gino, we have to go."

"Where, to the sea?"

"No, back to Italy."

Gino could feel the blood boiling in his forehead. "I know what you're thinking; I'm old. That you've come here for nothing. It's useless to follow a race in which all you can write is 'poor Bartali.' But let me tell you this. Tomorrow I'll be so far ahead of the others a watch won't do you any good. And above all, don't bother asking for an interview when I'm wearing the *maillot jaune!*"

"No, no, Gino," the poor reporter protested, "it's not that at all. Italy is on the edge of a revolution." And then the reporter told Bartali about the assassination attempt.

Bartali was stupefied. He immediately phoned home to Florence and was reassured that everything appeared normal. He promptly forgot about the affair until later in the evening when he received a direct call from Prime Minister Alcide de Gasperi.

Gasperi didn't bother with formalities. His voice was filled with tension. "Things are going badly here, really badly. Listen, Gino, I want to know one thing. Do you think you can win the Tour?"

Bartali was puzzled. "I'm not a magician. The Tour isn't over until Paris and there's still a week to go."

The tension in Gasperi's voice rose almost to the level of desperation. "This is important, Gino, no longer just for you but for Italy, for everyone. If you win the Tour, it will take everyone's mind away from our troubles here. It could save the country!"

Bartali muttered a lame affirmation and said *arrivederci.* He wasn't prepared to speak to the prime minister with the bold pronouncement he'd given the reporter. But that pronouncement was a lot closer to Bartali's intentions.

The following morning the riders were up for a 4:00 A.M. breakfast and a 6:00 A.M. start in anticipation of a ten-hour day. (Oh yes, things have changed a bit!) A fine rain added a dreary, ominous air to the morning.

At 11:00 they began the first climb, the Col d'Allos. A few escaped, the most important being Jean Robic, the surprise winner of the previous Tour. Bartali wasn't bothered by his 1-minute, 5-second deficit at the summit. Even the miserable weather couldn't disturb the Tuscan's serene confidence. He felt on top of his considerable form and couldn't imagine anyone being able to stay with him whenever he chose to attack. All that mattered was to wait for the right time. Bartali had a motto, "never too hot, never too cold," and a day like this revealed it was no idle bravado. Sure, half the peloton might be still on his wheel, but he knew they were together in appearance only. To one degree or another they were already tired, frozen, and riding on willpower alone, praying for no increase in tempo. All that mattered was to wait for the right time.

That time came nine kilometers from the summit of the Col de Vars. In that era (and almost to the end of his racing days) Bartali preferred the old Campagnolo shifting system, a complicated arrangement that necessitated loosening the rear wheel with a remote lever, pedaling backward while moving the shifting fork (which in turn moved the chain onto the desired cog), allowing the rear wheel to move in the dropouts to take up the chain slack, and then securing the wheel with a reverse twist of the original lever. Most riders found this quite a challenge on the flat, but Bartali claimed there was less friction in the system (no tensioned idler wheels). He had so mastered the intricacies he made it appear easy. More importantly, when the others saw Bartali go through all the motions in order the drop the chain on the sixteen-tooth sprocket, they knew what was coming. They also knew there was nothing they could do about it!

Bartali loved the feeling of the big gear in his legs and had no doubts that he could stay in it for the remaining nine kilometers of the climb. Immediately he stood on the pedals and an ever widening gap appeared behind him. At the summit Robic remained ahead with a slim lead of thirty seconds. More interesting to Bartali was the presence of the national soccer team giving him the full *tifosi* treatment, and he waved his appreciation.

On the descent Bartali rocketed by the frozen little Robic, who was en route to losing twenty-five minutes over the final climb! Although no riders were close enough to appreciate Bartali's solo recital, one who did get a good view was a privileged guest for a day, French entertainer Maurice Chevalier.

Over the last climb, the Izoard, Bartali pounded like a well-oiled metronome. In this sort of mood and form it didn't appear Bartali needed to let up before Paris. Mercifully for the others, the stage ended in Briançon. Bobet managed to hang on to his yellow jersey by a meager 1 minute, 6 seconds.

In Italy, as hoped, Bartali's victory helped ease the concerns of the country's leaders. At the hospital the son of Togliatti gently opened the door, tiptoed across the room, and whispered in his father's ear, "Papa, Bartali has won the first alpine stage. He's almost the *maillot jaune."* A contented smile illuminated the old man's face. The revolution could wait.

The following alpine stage gave Bartali every reason for confidence. It was even longer and more mountainous than the one just completed. En route to Aix-les-Bains it would go over the Lautaret, Galibier, Télégraphe, Croix de Fer, Porte, Cucheron, and Granier. It's a route the Tour has followed many times since—in two stages!

Lance Armstrong's mastery in 2000 proved his ability to dominate such stages. But proceeding down the list of general classification, one could be forgiven for having doubts. David Millar, the precocious Scot, between coughing fits in Briançon, termed this eight-hour ride "sadistic." One wonders what adjectives he would have conjured if the 2000 Tour had followed the 1948 route more closely!

In any event, Bartali did the expected, winning by six minutes into Aix and two minutes into Lausanne, thereby assuring his triumph in Paris. Anyone across the Alps who had thoughts of revolution, of rushing to a neighbor with a gun and crying that now was the time to throw off the yoke of this miserable government and these thieving capitalists, met louder cries from those crowded around the radio. "Shut up, fool, Bartali's winning the Tour de France!" And Italy was saved.

14

HUGO KOBLET, 1925–1964

THE SWISS RIDER Hugo Koblet was perhaps the best example of a cycling supernova. Arguably, he lit up the cycling sky more brilliantly than anyone before or since, but only for two years. Until 1950 he was known, to the degree that he was, as a track racer, his only significant road wins in four years as a professional being two stages of the Tour of Switzerland.

No one, least of all Koblet, could explain his instant transformation that year into an all-conquering road rider. His name on the list of entrants for the thirty-third Tour of Italy caused no comment. Italy had seen lots of foreign riders better known than Hugo Koblet enter their sacred national event and go home far from first place. However much the Italians warred against one another, they always closed ranks to gang up on an outsider. Besides, this was still the era of Coppi-Bartali-Magni dominance. Challenging them was inconceivable.

Coppi was the defending champion, having dominated Bartali in their legendary 1949 Giro duel. Koblet, finding a form neither he nor anyone had dreamed possible, was only too happy to take advantage of the Italians' rivalry. Coppi crashed on the first mountain stage and broke his leg, clearing the way for Koblet to roll across the snowy passes in the style of a pursuiter. He appeared to flow rather than pedal, and for a little while Fausto Coppi was forgotten as the public flocked to the roadside to watch the birth of this new superstar.

In the end Koblet won the 1950 Giro d'Italia by more than five minutes over the homeland favorite, Gino Bartali. Everyone, including Bartali, had the impression that the divide between first and second could have been substantially greater if Koblet had so desired. Thus the order established in Italy since 1909 had finally been upset—a non-Italian had won.

France got to see this new wonder the following year in its own tour. If Koblet could win, it would be an impressive victory, for also on the start line were Bartali, Coppi, Magni, Robic, Bobet, Geminiani, Ockers, Bauvin, and Ruiz. It was one of the most superlative lineups in history.

Koblet played with them from the beginning. He won the first time trial and then created his own on the stage from Brive to Agen. With 140 rolling kilometers left in the stage the tall Swiss rolled off the front and defied the whole peloton. There was a lot of pride in that peloton, pride that was indignant at being so obviously insulted. After a while all the teammates had been burned up and it was left to the stars to save the day. They buried themselves in pursuit, but still the gap grew!

Meanwhile, Koblet cruised along, hands on the tops of his bars, the picture of unforced elegance. Approaching the finish line, he sat up to comb his hair, and as he crossed under the *arrivée* banner he started his Swiss chronometer to see how much damage he'd done.

He had to wait 3 minutes, 35 seconds before the chasers arrived, with Koblet climbing to third on G.C.

The popular French singer Jacques Grello, who was following the Tour for the newspaper *Parisen Libéré*, characterized Hugo Koblet as "the pedaler of charm," a sobriquet that aptly graced the gentle Swiss for the rest of his days. All of Hugo's rivals now knew that anyone who could pedal that fast and remain charming would leave them to race for second place.

In the Pyrenees, Koblet disappeared with Coppi on the stage to Luchon, to take the overall lead. To be fair, the redoubtable Coppi was not at his best. His brother, Serse, had been killed in a bike race shortly before the Tour, leaving Coppi a shadow of his normal self.

Both the public and the other riders showed great sympathy for the stricken champion. The day after leaving the Pyrenees he finished in a back group more than a half-hour behind stage-winner Koblet. So when he revived in the Alps, attacking over the Vars and Izoard climbs, he was given some leeway. Only the French regional rider Roger Buchonnet chased. For a time they were together, but at the summit of Vars, Coppi was forty seconds ahead.

When the gap to the peloton had yawned to nine minutes, Koblet decided to take things in hand. His acceleration, as smooth as an electric car winding up, soon left him chasing alone after his idol. Only six years younger than Coppi, Koblet had grown up marveling at the Italian's mastery. Unknown to observers, Koblet had not embarked on this chase to limit Coppi's advantage. Koblet already had the better part of an hour's lead on the Italian ace, although Frenchman Raphaël Geminiani was still only ninety seconds back on G.C. Koblet's overall lead became nine minutes by the end of the stage but that was almost incidental. Now that Coppi had gone off to attempt this ride of prestige, the gracious Koblet wanted to be close enough to show that Fausto really deserved this stage win and that it wasn't just a gift.

On the Izoard, Koblet regained enough time that he could see Coppi on the hairpins above, about two minutes ahead. The speed with which the gap had been closed indicated that Fausto was paying for his earlier efforts. Koblet sensed this and discreetly slowed. In between rode an inspired Buchonnet.

At the finish in Briançon, Coppi did indeed win the stage, with Buchonnet second and Koblet third. When a reporter asked Koblet how he felt about losing the stage, he replied, "Yes, I am disappointed to finish third. My dream was to finish second—behind Coppi."

Hugo Koblet won the 1951 Tour de France by twenty-two minutes. The second place finisher, Geminiani, told anyone who would listen, "I won! I won!" When reminded of a certain Hugo Koblet, Geminiani replied seriously, "He doesn't count. I'm the first human! If I thought there were two Koblets in this sport I'd search for a different line of work."

The magical form that had come so easily then disappeared. The beautiful Hugo came closest to it at the Giro in 1953 (losing to Coppi by just 1 minute, 29 seconds) and 1954 (second to Swiss teammate Carlo Clerici). On retiring from cycling in 1958, he wandered into journalism for a while, but in some way he was deeply lost. Maybe the capriciousness of life was just too much for him. On or off the bike his charm continued to enchant everyone who met him. In 1964 he died in a road accident in an apparent suicide.

15

AN EXCEPTIONALLY INFORMED reader might wonder at finding Wim Van Est in a book about great climbers. He was a rather thickly built Dutchman who was definitely not on any list of uphill specialists. However, as I stated earlier in this book, I attempt to explore the full spectrum of mountain achievements, and the adventures of Wim Van Est in the 1951 Tour de France certainly merit his inclusion.

Between the Depression and World War II Van Est had a pretty grim childhood. In the rare event that a little meat or fish was available for the family dinner, his father would often pretend he wasn't hungry so the kids could have more. Even before he was a teenager, Van Est was contributing to the family income. Although he was attracted to bike racing, it was several years before he could afford even a simple bike. Facing so many obstacles, he did not reach the upper levels of cycling until a rather advanced age. He was twenty-six when he turned pro in 1949. He won his first classic, the derny-paced Bordeaux-Paris (550 kilometers), in 1950 and was only too pleased to find out what the Tour de France was all about when he was invited to join the Dutch national team in 1951.

Van Est reveled in the early flat stages across northern France. He loved to attack when he was hurting. Why? "If I'm hurting," he reasoned, "the others must be dying!" And he was right! After twelve days of battling, Van Est rode into yellow on the doorstep of the Pyrenees after leading a ten-man group into Dax eighteen minutes ahead of the pack.

He had never seen a real mountain before in his life. The Netherlands isn't the best place in the world to familiarize oneself with topographical extremes. Of course he'd heard about the quasi-mythological snowy peaks that determined the outcome of the Tour and had been told a rider of his type was supposed to be handicapped on the big climbs. He had no idea of his true potential in a mountainous domain but was determined to defend his precious *maillot jaune* as best he could.

That first day in yellow the first real challenge came with the climb of the Aubisque. He fought to hang in and was successful. At the summit he looked around and was pleased to see many famous faces close by. He knew, of course, there was still a long way to go that day, but he had survived his first test with honor. He was still "there."

He was not a bad bike handler. He hung right in on any criterium, no matter how complex the course. But mountain descents were something new. He was holding his place in line when . . . well, he never could quite explain it. One moment he was flying down the road and the next he was flying through the air.

Poor Wim had carried too much speed into a turn, misread its decreasing radius, and eventually was forced into the low outside retaining wall. The wall might have restrained a car, but for Van Est it served as a catapult. He came to rest some seventy-five meters (about 250 feet) below. Riders who stopped to look for him had a hard time seeing him at first. His yellow jersey was just a dot below.

Could the tough Dutchman be alive? wondered the onlookers on the parapet above. Then those with better eyes spied movement, a wave of the hand, and a yell that might mean he was all right. He was too far away to hear anything distinctly.

With conscious existence confirmed, rescue became the next order of business. This was before the advent of helicopters and sophisticated forms of retrieval. Van Est was a long way below and down a steep cliff. The outside of the road was a sheer ten-meter wall above the precipitous slope of the mountain itself. But human ingenuity is never more fertile than in a crisis. The *directeurs sportifs* and mechanics and riders conferred for a few seconds and quickly agreed that the rope they so obviously needed and didn't have could be provided if they got together all the extra tubular tires available and wound them together.

They lowered a man down the wall, paying out the tubular "rope" slowly, and then continued to belay as the rescuer slipped down through the cliffside shrubbery to the inert figure. Van Est was certainly happy to have someone show up. He would have attempted to move earlier, but the cliff was so steep he was afraid the slightest move would send him rocketing further down.

With the tubulars in hand he was quickly on his feet and dragging himself, hand over hand, back to the road. On gaining the top of the wall, his first question was, "How's my bike?" But by now the Tour doctor was on the scene. He gently explained there was no way Wim could be allowed to ride on. The ambulance was waiting. With tears in his eyes, Van Est climbed in. To quit the race at all was something he'd never contemplated, but to quit it while in yellow put him in a very small group of riders indeed—one he wished he could avoid.

It wasn't as bad as he feared. Being rescued by a rope of tubulars caused a public sensation. He was an overnight hero and received far more publicity than he would have otherwise. Nor did it hurt his chances in future Tours. He went on to win more stages and even wear (twice) the yellow jersey again.

Nor was his late start in cycling much of a handicap. At age thirty-nine he won Bordeaux–Paris again!

16

NO ONE EVER worked harder to make himself a great cyclist than Louison Bobet. He attempted to copy Fausto Coppi's "scientific" approach to achieving maximum fitness, taking great care to balance diet, rest, and training regimens. Many nights he went to bed "hungry as a wolf." Yet for all his application, big-time success came only after years and years of struggle, years that included disappointments so great and physical suffering so severe that any lesser rider would have been tempted to choose another occupation.

The southern side of the Col d'Izoard in the eastern French Alps is famous among geologists for its unusual distribution of different types of rock strata. However, one needn't be a geologist to appreciate the bizarre formations, created by disproportionate erosion over the millennia, that look like enormous stalagmites. About a quarter-mile below the summit on this southern side next to the road and set into one of these rock towers are two life-size facial profiles set in bas-relief, those of Fausto Coppi and Louison Bobet.

Both monuments are intended to remind the passerby of heroics that were performed on this mountain. Coppi's career was so prolific that a monument on almost any mountain pass in Europe would be justified, and recently a large sculpture dedicated to the Italian *campionissimo* was placed on the Pordoi pass in the Italian Dolomites. But for Bobet the Izoard was almost unique. His first great defeats and triumphs took place on its rugged slopes, giving him a measuring device to gauge his progress, or lack thereof. At the peak of his career, he "owned" the Izoard, always demolishing the peloton and soaring alone up its never-ending gravel-strewn track.

Bobet's first encounter with the Izoard came in his second Tour de France, that of 1948. Just a week remained and the young rider from Brittany found himself in the yellow jersey with a massive 21 minute, 28 second lead over the Italian challenger, Gino Bartali. Who could blame Bobet for daring to dream dreams? Bartali had won the Tour in 1938, but old Gino was now thirty-four years old. It wouldn't be unreasonable to suppose that Bartali was on the decline. Meanwhile, Bobet had gotten through the Pyrenees quite well and didn't see why the Alps, which were to be crossed in three gigantic stages that year, should be that much more difficult.

The first of these three stages went from Cannes to Briançon by way of the Allos, Vars, and Izoard passes. To make matters more challenging, freezing rain fell all day. Bobet shadowed Bartali until nine kilometers from the summit of Vars. At that point Bartali shifted gears and simply disappeared into the gusting mists. So much for the decline theory!

Still, Bobet was far from dead, and he, along with the few others who could, gave chase with everything they had. But the grind up the Izoard was just too much. It was an eternity of agony. Finally, in Briançon, Bobet was relieved to find he had saved his yellow jersey by 1 minute, 6 seconds. But he had lost over twenty minutes on this one stage (which had taken more than ten hours to complete) and, assuming Bartali could put up a similar performance the next day, there didn't appear to be much hope for Bobet. The scenario played itself out just as Bartali wished and Bobet feared, leaving Bartali comfortably in yellow and Bobet down in fourth by the time they got to Paris.

Two years later, in 1950, Bobet's fortunes in the Tour had vacillated tremendously, but during the final week in the Alps he found new inspiration when his teammate, Raphaël Geminiani, won the stage to Gap. The next day followed the classic route over Vars and Izoard, and Bobet determined that now was the time to see what he could do. He succeeded in getting away on Vars and, even with a puncture, stayed away over the Izoard to take 2 minutes, 52 seconds from the yellow jersey, the Swiss rider Ferdi Kubler.

The intoxication of being alone on the Izoard with a substantial lead had both short- and long-term implications for Bobet. Long-term it was a reminder of what he could do and would do, and short-term it made him hatch a scheme to win the Tour on the next and last day in the Alps.

At the first feed, with 180 kilometers to go, he and Geminiani decided to skip their musettes (shoulder bags of food handed up at the feed zones) and attack at the base of the climb to St. Nizier. The breakaway went perfectly and Bobet's lead grew at one point to 4 minutes, 30 seconds. The Tour was in the balance as the mad gamble seemed to be paying off. But then Geminiani started to fade, a head wind kicked up, and Kubler, enraged by what he considered an underhanded trick, refused to give up. Once across the Rhône River and on the slopes of the Col de la République, Kubler finally managed to catch, and then drop, Bobet. His supporters were devastated, but it was just the type of epic effort that makes the Tour de France so revered.

Bobet's incubation period wasn't over. He had to wait until 1953 and his sixth participation in the Tour de France before it all came together. Even then it wasn't easy. His erratic performances didn't inspire the total confidence of his teammates on the French national team. Matters came to a head at dinner in Béziers, where two teammates in a ten-man breakaway group had beaten him to the finish line, thereby depriving him of the stage time bonuses. Over soup, Bobet, with a considerable edge in his voice, asked Geminiani why "Gem" hadn't let him by as had been agreed. With more than a little sarcasm, Geminiani replied, "Excuse me, little one, but I don't think you can expect me to dismount before the public in order to cede my place to you." Relations at the table deteriorated from there, with forks in the en garde position, before the men retired to their rooms.

In the morning, the directeur sportif, Marcel Bidot, guided a reconciliation conference that resulted in a legal document being drawn up and signed by all. It stated that the signatories (i.e., every member of the team), would selflessly support Louison Bobet in his role as team leader, and Bobet, in turn, agreed that if he won the Tour he would give all his earnings to the team. After that, harmony reigned.

Entering the Alps, Bobet was in third on G.C. and, remembering his experiences of 1948 and 1950, knew that the duo of Vars and Izoard gave him the opportunity he desired to take the race lead. Teammate Adolphe Deledda joined an early break on Vars, while Bobet stayed at the head of the rapidly dwindling peloton. When the Spanish climbing specialist Jésus Lorono attacked, Bobet comfortably accompanied him. Deledda was first over the summit, but on being informed of Bobet's attack cut his own effort. Meanwhile, Bobet dropped Lorono on the descent, caught the waiting Deledda at the bottom, and soon after caught and dropped the two men who had broken away with Deledda.

Before the real Izoard begins there is a long (twenty-kilometer), gentle climb up the valley of the Guil, and here Deledda showed that his signature on the Béziers document was for real. Deledda held nothing in reserve; he gave every last bit of his not inconsiderable energy to place Bobet in the freshest possible condition at the foot of the Izoard. The plan worked perfectly. All those years of trying finally came together. Bobet was untouchable, and he knew it. Only once was he distracted, and that was near the summit about where the Coppi and Bobet plaques are today. There, at the side of the road, was none other than Fausto Coppi himself and his famous "companion," the "Lady in White" (or "Damma Bianca" as she was known in Italy). (Coppi had won the Tour the year before but now he was recovering from yet another terrible bone-breaking crash.) As Bobet cruised by, he yelled to Coppi, "Thanks for coming!"

Even a flat on the descent couldn't disturb Bobet's calm, and in Briançon, he learned that he had taken no less than eleven minutes out of the now former wearer of the *maillot jaune,* Jean Malléjac, who dropped to second, 8 minutes, 35 seconds behind the new leader. Nothing could keep Bobet from wearing yellow into Paris this time.

In 1954 there was no discussion of Bobet's leadership possibilities. From the start of the Tour, Louison rode with dominating aggression. When the 1951 Tour winner, Hugo Koblet, got away with a very good group on a flat stage, Bobet and one other rider bridged up. Later Koblet asked Bobet, "Was it just you two who came across to us?" When he got an affirmative response, he half muttered, "I would never have believed such a thing possible."

Full confirmation came once again on the Izoard, only this time forty riders were together at the bottom. Bobet didn't hesitate. He immediately went to the front and set a killing tempo. One by one riders dropped off until Bobet was once again gloriously alone at the summit. At Briançon, he was just under two minutes up on second place, Kubler, but Bobet was better on every terrain, including the time trials, so once again there was no real challenge to his final victory.

Such was Bobet's form in 1954 that he went on to take an epic world road championship at Solingen, Germany, on a day of wild storms that only added to the luster of his victory.

The year 1955 brought the Tour de France once again into Bobet's crystal ball. Of course he wanted to win it for all the usual reasons, but a victory in 1955 would be unique because up until that time no one had ever won three successive Tours. By now Bobet was definitely the man to beat. Winner of the two previous Tours, wearer of the distinctive world champion's rainbow jersey, and at age thirty supposedly at the very peak of his physical possibilities, how could Bobet lose?

Actually, a number of men had very clear ideas on how Bobet could lose. Although each one had individual aspirations, they all knew they must share the job of attacking this apparently invincible monolith. In short, it was going to be all against one. Then there was the case of Charly Gaul. Bobet had hardly heard of him yet, but the little Luxembourger was about to make his debut in the Tour and reveal climbing capabilities that would terrify even Bobet. Finally, there was a secret problem. Bobet had developed a boil on his bottom, and as the race progressed it proved ever more distracting, not only because it was painful but because he had to disguise his discomfort.

From the beginning the French team knew it was in for a no-quarter war. For the most part they were inspired and rode exceedingly well, keeping Louison in touch with the front day after day. However, on entering the Alps, Charly Gaul appeared out of anonymity and flew away to a nearly seventeen-minute victory on the Galibier stage. Bobet and the French team were in shock.

Shock, yes, but capitulation, no. There remained the Ventoux to replace Bobet's beloved Izoard. At the time Bobet was third on G.C., 11 minutes, 33 seconds behind teammate Antonin Rolland. Thirty kilometers from the foot of the Ventoux the French plan went into operation. Geminiani attacked alone and after a few kilometers was joined by Kubler and Gilbert Scodeller. It was a burning hot day, a fact that worked in Bobet's favor. Gaul was still so new that very little was known about him, but this day was to reveal a vulnerability: He hated the heat.

Ten kilometers from the summit and Bobet went on the attack. This attack wasn't decisive, but the large number who had just been hanging on disappeared. A little later he went again, and then again, and this time he was on his own. He soon caught the three breakaways, but any hope he had for help from Geminiani was eliminated when Gem gasped, "I'm cooked. But go, you can win!"

The problem was that from the top of the Ventoux sixty kilometers remained to the stage finish in Avignon. Behind him at the summit came the Belgian, Jean Brankaert, at 1 minute, Giancarlo Astrua, Pasquale Fornara, and Geminiani, at 3 minutes, 40 seconds, and Gaul at 5 minutes, 28 seconds. What could Bobet do but go for it, but he warned Bidot that if the chasers got to within forty-five seconds, Bidot should let him know and he would wait for them. Bidot had enough confidence to think Bobet could pull off this exploit—until Bobet had a flat. He lost nearly a minute. The gap dropped to forty-five seconds with five kilometers to go, and Bidot decided Bobet could still win. Bidot was right. Bobet took the stage by forty-nine seconds over the first chase group and moved into second place on G.C., now 4 minutes, 53 seconds down on Rolland.

In the Pyrenees, Gaul attacked on the 249-kilometer stage from Tolosa, Spain, to St. Gaudens, as expected, but when the gap was two minutes, Bobet set off in pursuit and almost caught him by the finish! Bobet was the new *maillot jaune.*

The greatest potential threat now was his ever worsening derriere, which caused unending agony. It made him slump to third in the final time trial, but he still had almost five minutes in hand on Brankaert when they rode into Paris. A third successive Tour victory ensured Bobet a measure of immortality in the annals of the Tour, but when the condition of his bottom became public knowledge, and with it the realization of what he had endured, his fans' respect and adoration knew no bounds.

Bobet loved cycling, and many adventures still awaited him, not least the adventure of the "Cheri-pipi" told in Chapter 18. His last Tour was in 1959. It was one Tour too many and he didn't have the strength to finish. But even here he showed his grit. He retired at the *top* of the Col de l'Iseran.

17

ON JUNE 9, 1999, the American Jonathan Vaughters won the Mont Ventoux time trial stage of the Dauphiné Libéré stage race. On the podium to congratulate Vaughters was an older gentleman, a head shorter than the American and carrying a noticeable paunch. He was introduced to Vaughters as Charly Gaul, the man who had held, until just minutes before, the record for the Ventoux climb.

It can be an alarming sight, what age can do to a man, for who could have guessed from his appearance that forty years earlier this same gentleman was one of the great climbing specialists of all time. Charly Gaul was born in Luxembourg in 1932 and burst on the professional scene in 1954, when he won the Dauphiné's predecessor, the Circuit des Six Provinces. Then as now, the race route always included considerable alpine excursions. That Gaul, then only twenty-one, could keep up with top pros in their final preparation for the Tour de France would have been amazing enough. But he did even more. On a stage that featured the Galibier, on a day when winter appeared in June in the form of a massive snowstorm, the *petit* Luxembourger annihilated everyone. Never bothering with so much as warmer gloves, Gaul flew up the climbs even as he endeavored to stay in the wheel tracks of the race vehicles through the snow.

To say that the race entourage was stunned hardly credits the atmosphere Gaul created. Top pros develop their reputations through years of preparation and suffering. They don't appreciate being reduced to the ranks of also-rans by cheeky kids from nowhere. They quickly assem-

A brilliant climber, Luxembourg's Charly Gaul (left) fought a hectic battle with Raphaël Geminiani (in yellow) to win the 1958 Tour de France.

bled dismissive arguments: No one wanted to risk too much in the atrocious conditions; Gaul was lucky because, being new, he wasn't taken seriously; this was a preparation race and not the time to go all-out, and so on. And while they dissimulated, fear stalked their hearts, for they knew they had just witnessed a phenom who would return to haunt their cycling futures.

They didn't have long to wait. The following year, 1955, Gaul entered the Tour de France and right away demonstrated all the strengths and weaknesses that were to characterize his performances for the next seven years. Coming from Luxembourg at a time when the Tour was contested by national teams, Gaul was burdened with poor support. The composite teams he ostensibly led could rarely help him when he really needed help. For example, only occasionally did they have the legs to cross big gaps. Under the circumstances, Gaul felt justified in refusing to share his winnings with the team. In turn, this led to bad morale and even less help. He quickly learned he needed to be surreptitious and wait for the most opportune moment to strike. Give Gaul a cold, wet, snowy day in the mountains and he was untouchable, but turn on the heat and he frequently wilted. And then there were times when he seemed to fall asleep at the back of the field, only to wake up later and find he'd missed the train.

But when everything came together he left everyone stupefied, seeing but not believing. Many tried to imitate his low gear technique but no one mastered it as he did. When Gaul decided to attack, he'd spool up the gear at a prodigious rate and then, and this is the unique part (at least until the "new" Lance Armstrong revealed himself in 1999), maintain that tempo as long as necessary. Twenty kilometers, no problem. Multiple climbs, no problem. As the French cycling journalist Pierre Chany remarked, "For the others Gaul wasn't a rival; he was a fatality." Gaul won two mountain stages in that 1955 Tour by such margins, given how much he'd lost elsewhere, that he was able to arrive in Paris in third place overall. There could be no more dissimulations. This guy was for real.

Being the kind of rider he was, it's no surprise that Gaul focused almost exclusively on events that featured big climbs, which, aside from some specialty hill climbs, meant the Tours of Italy and France. In 1956 he mounted his first invasion of Italy. Over two-thirds of that Giro d'Italia (Tour of Italy) passed with nothing particular being produced by the enigmatic *enfant*. Stage 19, with the three monster climbs (Passo Rolle, Brocon, and a summit finish on Monte Bondone), stood out as offering opportunities to some, desolation for others. The race leader, Pasquale Fornara, had used every bit of brain and muscle in his possession to work his way into the *maglia rosa* (pink jersey the Giro leader wears). He had no intention of relinquishing that precious jersey to any of several Italian rivals who were all within ten minutes. To Gaul he hardly gave a thought. Gaul seemed content with two earlier stage wins and his twenty-fourth place at 16 minutes, 5 seconds certainly reflected that.

Fornara rode as a leader is expected to, at the front. His tempo discouraged any attacks over the first two climbs, and at the bottom of the Bondone, with fourteen kilometers remaining, his confidence revealed itself in even greater exertions. At first he hardly noticed the dramatic drop in air temperature accompanied by snow flurries. He had a race to win. Into the howling tempest he stomped—never to reappear. In less than a kilometer all his ambition left him and he was only too glad to rush into a farmhouse.

Bruno Monti replaced Fornara at the point of attack. He too began to dream dreams. Not much longer now and a lifetime's dedication would be repaid. Just one more kilometer, just one more kilometer, just . . . He was discovered in a roadside ditch, frozen, unable to speak, and in no condition to get back on the bike.

Nino Defilippis assumed the mantle of pedaling desperation until the sight of a basin of hot water held at the roadside by a farm family melted his resolved. "Not for 10 million lire would I start again," he declared, mostly to himself.

As each leader abandoned the race, he was replaced by another pedaling automaton, a cycling stoic endeavoring to ignore or transcend the frightening pain and ever decreasing capability to get one more rotation out of the legs. Each kilometer covered decreased the distance to the summit by that much and therefore gave rise to hope, but each kilometer also brought colder temperatures, down to zero degrees Fahrenheit, making the job intolerable for most.

Through this Siberian landscape pedaled one lucid rider, Charly Gaul. Apparently unaffected, his fluid style as poetic as ever. He spun his low gear to such effect that in the final four kilometers there appeared to be two races, one for him and one for the survivors far below down the mountain. In that short distance he inverted the race classification and emerged the race leader.

He wasn't as untouched as he appeared. He had to be lifted off his bike and carried into a hiker's refuge. Back at the hotel an hour later his jersey had to be cut off and he readily confessed that he had no memory of the final three kilometers. He had the appearance of having aged ten years in ten kilometers. All this from the man who supported the rigors of the day better than anyone! Thanks to the collective capitulation of sixty riders and his amazing talents, Charly Gaul became an instant legend.

For reasons explained in Chapter 18, 1957 is a year Gaul would prefer to forget. But in 1958 he returned to his amazing ways. Luxembourg was never able to furnish a complete national team for the Tour, so it was amalgamated with other minor countries such as Switzerland and/or Germany, and so on, depending on the year. Gaul was always the leader but never well supported.

At the opposite end of the spectrum was the French team, which had no end of talent. The problem for them was persuading professional rivals to kiss and make up for the month of July. The year 1957 had been an easy one for the national team director, Marcel Bidot, because the old guard had opted out for various reasons. Jacques Anquetil and the younger generation had dominated that 1957 Tour. But now the old guard wished to reassert its prior rights. Anquetil knew he had to accept Bobet, a triple Tour winner, as a teammate, but he drew the line at accepting Bobet's best friend, Raphaël Geminiani.

Geminiani was deeply hurt at being sacrificed and swore he would lead his regional Centre-Midi team into an all-out war with the French national team. He was as good as his word and attacked at every opportunity. By the end of the sixth stage to St. Brieuc out in Brittany, Geminiani had managed to gain ten minutes on Gaul, as well as all the big names in the French team, particularly Anquetil. At one point, when the Italian nemesis, Gastone Nencini, was a good distance up the road, the French team had implored Geminiani to help them in the chase. "Gem" took the greatest delight in teasing his old friends (but new enemies), "There must be something wrong with your eyesight. Can't you see the color of my jersey? Not the same as yours, is it? So, sorry, but you'll have to do your own chasing."

In the first time trial, more shocks occurred as Gaul beat Anquetil, the first time Anquetil had lost a Tour time trial. Anquetil, recently married, may have had his excuses, but he made it difficult for his comrades to put their full faith in him. In the Pyrenees Geminiani took the yellow jersey, only to lose it the next day to the Italian Vito Favero. All Europe was riveted by this splendid topsy-turvy combat. Should they support old (age thirty-three) Geminiani, obviously doing the ride of his life, and perhaps his last? Shunned by the national team, always cast in the role of first mate, wasn't his a brilliant performance in the role of underdog? Or what about these prima donnas on the national team? Louison Bobet, the former three-time winner riding well again, was he good for a last hurrah?

Nor could they forget that handsome young Norman, Jacques Anquetil. He had won the previous year and was within striking distance now. Maybe he was the man to get excited about.

Frenchmen couldn't be happy about an outsider taking their precious Tour, but in their sporting hearts they couldn't blame the Italians, Gastone Nencini and Favero, for stepping in and taking advantage of the French if the home boys were stupid enough to carve each other up. And then there was crazy Charly Gaul. No one knew what to think of him. He must be in pretty good form, having won the time trial. But he wasn't even in the top twenty on G.C. Surely the Tour in July wasn't going to see a miracle stage as the Giro had the previous month.

The next obstacle was the Ventoux time trial, and here Gaul stepped out from the shadows again to definitively win and set the course record alluded to at the beginning of this chapter. But interesting as that was, the real change for most people was that old Geminiani was once again back in yellow. This time he meant to stay in it. The next day, over baking hot roads to Gap, he took advantage of Gaul's need to stop to fix his derailleur. Charly never felt more isolated than during this all-day chase in the heat he hated, and it showed. At Gap he'd lost ten minutes, slipping to 15 minutes, 12 seconds down on G.C. The next day to Briançon he lost almost another minute to Geminiani.

"Imagine my feelings at this point in the race," Geminiani later wrote. "I began to believe that no one could take my *maillot jaune* away." Just four days to Paris, including the alpine stage the next day and the final time trial two days after that. Who could beat him now? He had enough cushion that he could lose a little here and a little there and still be in the lead. But that was only the safety net plan if things got desperate. He'd been riding the Tour de France since 1947. He knew the race. He knew himself. No, he wasn't going to be timid. Gem wanted to live up to his nickname, "Le Grand Fusil," or "The Big Gun." The term was originally coined to describe his excited style of speaking and shouting, but on the 219 kilometers from Briançon to Aix-les-Bains over five passes he had every intention of showing that he could shoot with his legs as well as his mouth.

The long drag up the Col du Lautaret out of Briançon was taken gently enough and served mostly to warm everyone up. Once over the top and onto the even longer descent the weather changed dramatically, with dark clouds scudding overhead followed by ever chillier gusts. As they rolled down the valley of the Romanche the weather became ever more menacing, and a violent storm broke over the defenseless riders.

But these guys were tough and used to a little rain. Their minds were focused on getting up the vicious Col de Luitel. Ten kilometers averaging 9 percent on a narrow switchback road quickly blew the compact group apart, and out front was Charly Gaul. His attack had been so explosive that no one had even attempted to go with him right away. Gem led the chase but was soon forced to recognize that trying to catch this "Angel of the Mountains" was the quickest way to lose the Tour.

Down into Grenoble and Gaul had two minutes on Federico Bahamontes, Anquetil, Bobet, and Geminiani. Now the Chartreuse trio of the Cols de Porte, Cucheron, and Granier commenced and Gaul danced across them like a kid happily playing in mud puddles. No matter how cold, no matter how violent the winds, no matter how wild the rain, Gaul spun along like some runaway electric fan.

Behind, chaos reigned. One moment Anquetil was leading the chase up the Porte, thinking all the while that this day could yet put him in a position to win the race, and the next moment he could barely pedal. He couldn't believe the transformation. All of a sudden he was cold to the bone. He had no power. "I became another person," he said. Bobet said he'd wait to help him, an extraordinary sacrifice for the old warrior who still had his own chance, but Anquetil waved him on. There was nothing anyone could do.

Gem became obsessed, and stupid. His toe clip broke and he insisted on changing the pedal. Back in the groove again, he passed up a chance to take on food at the feed station. To break his concentration for a second would be to lose his raging rhythm forever, or so, in his mania, he thought. But in time the raging elements and his raging hunger overcame the raging rhythm.

They were strung out now, each man on his own, slogging through the interminable rain: bicycle racing at its purest and most pitiless. Only Charly Gaul remained composed all the way to Aix, where, after finishing, he had plenty of time to change into dry clothes before watching his tattered foes totter in. Geminiani took more than fifteen minutes to arrive, Anquetil, over twenty-two! And these men, no matter how sorry their condition, represented the leaders of the chase. The majority took more than an hour longer to complete their calvaries.

Gaul was not yet in yellow. That honor went to Vito Favero, but by only a handful of seconds that Gaul easily erased in the final time trial. Meanwhile, Geminiani collapsed into the arms of his team manager, all the while sobbing, "Les Judas! Les Judas!" meaning the French team members who, he suddenly thought, owed him support.

Pick out your favorite opera, Greek tragedy, movie, and compare them to this. Between the weather, the formidable terrain, the dramatic Tour script, the cast of characters, and the star role of Charly Gaul, this Tour was hard to beat.

In the 1956 Giro and the 1958 Tour Gaul had provided dumbfounding performances. Yet through much of the year he hid in the peloton. But even here he was hardly anonymous. Everyone knew he was a bomb with a slow-burning fuse but no one knew how long the fuse was. Wherever he went, the Angel of the Mountains created tension, excitement.

His last great assassination was of Anquetil on the Petit St. Bernard pass on a giant 296-kilometer stage 21 in the 1959 Giro d'Italia. The weather wasn't such a factor that day, but Gaul's speed was. In one climb the little Luxembourger leaped over Anquetil and the other race leaders to vault into the *maglia rosa* with just one day left in the race.

Gaul continued to race well for several more years, but after 1959 his superpowers gradually began to fade. After retiring from racing in the mid-1960s he almost retired from life, scraping out a hermit's existence in a forest. Gradually, in recent years, he has been pulled back into the stream of cycling life. He spoke with kindness and generosity to Jonathon Vaughters that day on the Ventoux in 1999. I'd love to know if Vaughters had any idea who this man was who was congratulating him for his time trial win. Certainly the old Gaul appeared to see a bit of himself in the talented American, a transition of generations he could hardly have foreseen, but then the Angel of the Mountains always specialized in the unexpected.

18

BOBET AND GAUL, 1957 GIRO D'ITALIA

AMERICANS ON AN INAUGURAL TRIP to Europe are frequently amazed at the casualness with which Continentals "heed the call of nature." Public johns provide minimal cover and toilets are often unisex. If that isn't peculiar enough to Anglo sensibilities, one's visit to the urinal may be interrupted by a lady caretaker mopping around one's feet. Plays hell with one's concentration. Our sense of restroom etiquette takes a further beating when there are no restrooms. Families pull to the roadside for a communal pee with as much self-awareness as if they were having a picnic.

But it remains for competitive cyclists to bring these matters up to the level of a fine art. Just about anywhere and everywhere will do, even while riding. In Eddy Merckx's alphabet book ("A" is for Attacks, etc.) "E" is for ennui, accompanied by a picture of the great Belgian during a moment of human liquidity. Somehow one can't imagine American publications, obsessed as they are with digging out stories about drug abuse, infidelity, illegitimate children, financial mismanagement, and the like, portraying the mundane call of nature. The foregoing is not meant to be an exercise in cultural relativism, but a tour of the background necessary to understand how such minor matters could transform a great race.

The year was 1957. The event, the Tour of Italy. The principal actors:

LOUISON BOBET, thirty-two years old, three-time winner of the Tour de France, now attempting to be the first Frenchman to win the Giro d'Italia

RAPHAËL GEMINIANI, Bobet's right-hand man

CHARLY GAUL, twenty-four, from Luxembourg, a great climber and winner of the 1956 Giro

GASTONE NENCINI, twenty-seven, Italian, just coming into his own as a fine stage racer

With four days to go Gaul led the race, followed by Nencini at 56 seconds and Bobet at 1 minute, 17 seconds. The final two stages were flat. Barring accidents, all the action was expected to come during the two mountainous ones.

Most of the 242-kilometer fourth-to-last stage from Como to Trento was virtually flat. The sting in the tail came on the Monte Bondone. During the calm before the storm about a third of the way into the stage, Bobet signaled his team that he intended to enjoy the luxury of a dismounted pee. Bobet was no fool. He assumed that the normal professional etiquette reserved for such occasions would allow him an easy ride back to the peloton. Nevertheless, he went about his business quickly.

Nencini, seeing the entire French team stopped, decided to avail himself of a similar luxury. A little farther along, Gaul looked around, discovered he was practically alone, and so he too jumped off his bike.

A few seconds later Bobet, Nencini, and their respective troops came rolling past the race leader. Gaul, who had a passionate hatred of Bobet, "made an indecent gesture with his organ of virility," according to Geminiani, Bobet's teammate.

That moment's foolishness was to cost Gaul the race and give him the nickname "Cheri-Pipi" (literally "dearest pee-pee," as in "costly piss"). Bobet yelled to Geminiani, "We can't let this affront go unanswered. Hit it!"

The Italians immediately understood the situation and joined forces. The combined Franco-Italian teams covered the ninety flat kilometers to the foot of the mountain in less than two hours. Gaul, who never had a strong team, steadily lost time. On the climb of the Bondone, Bobet set the pace and finished two seconds ahead of Nencini, who took over the race leadership, and was no less than 8 minutes, 36 seconds in front of the Luxembourger. Yes, a very "cheri-pipi"!

Nencini had been on the ropes for much of the Bondone ascent. Bobet wasn't a flashy climber, just a very effective one. His pace was usually just a bit too demanding for everyone else. With this latest experience in his repertoire, along with the memories of his three Tour victories, Bobet felt justified that he had made an accurate assessment of the situation and would be in a position to administer the "coup de grace" on the following multi-mountain stage and win the Giro.

The next morning, leaving nothing to chance, Bobet's entire team went for an hour's warm-up ride before the start. The moment the flag dropped in Trento, Bobet's team attacked. By the summit of the first climb only six were in the lead, including the three leaders on general classification, Nencini, Bobet, and Gaul. It wasn't until the descent of the second pass that things broke apart.

Nencini punctured. The alliance of yesterday forgotten, Bobet and Geminiani went full bore. But a new alliance was born. Gaul waited for Nencini. Charly had lost all hope of winning the race for himself, but if he could keep the Frenchman from winning that would be a victory of sorts.

Up front, Bobet and Geminiani did all the work. The Italian with them, Ercole Baldini, refused to help relay them even though he was on a differ-ent team from Nencini. "I am an Italian," he explained. "If I help you they'll kill me."

On the last climb Gem dropped back and Bobet was all alone. From time to time Bobet could look down the switchbacks to see Nencini in his dis-tinctive pink leader's jersey. (Pink because the pages of the newspaper sponsoring the race, *La Gazzetta dello Sport,* are of the same color.) He was neatly tucked behind his pacemaker, Gaul. "I could see them gaining on me. I accelerated again and again with all my force," Bobet later recounted, "but I just couldn't go faster. Before the top they were on me. My last chance to win the Giro had disappeared." After three weeks of racing Bobet had lost the Giro by a mere nineteen seconds. And all for a "pipi"!

19

FEDERICO BAHAMONTES, 1928 –

IN 1954 THE SPANISH TEAM (from 1930 to 1961 the Tour was disputed by national teams, and again in 1967–1968) arrived at the Tour de France with a not-so-young climbing specialist, Federico Bahamontes. At age twenty-six, "Fede" or "Baha" (later the "Eagle of Toledo"), had acquired a reputation back home in Spain, but in those days Spain was another planet and reputations gathered there didn't necessarily impress elsewhere. The stereotypical Iberian rider was swarthy, short, useless on the flats and in time trials, and a pretty good climber, but was so out of it on general classification that no one cared what these riders could do once the race got to their terrain of predilection.

Jésus Lorono, Bernardo Ruiz, and Miguel Poblet were three Spanish exceptions to the foregoing description. But to be able to name only three riders in the immediate post–World War II period emphasizes the legitimacy of the general observation.

Initially, Bahamontes did little to distinguish himself from the stereotype, except for being a bit taller than the norm. He could usually be found at the back of the queue barely hanging on, a quarter-mile from the action up front, obviously intimidated by the tight intimacy of the heart of the peloton. Even modest descents revealed deeper levels of timorousness, leaving him dangerous gaps that, once on the flats again, had to be closed at considerable physical cost. Who could be blamed for assessing this supposed Spanish wonder as a wonder all right—a wonder he was in the race at all.

Such assessments were made before the big mountains where the one bullet in Baha's gun was fired. Yet even here he failed to fully impress. When he attacked, the sight was certainly dramatic, but it was so far from the finish no one was much concerned. His fixation on the Grand Prix de la Montagne (which in Spain meant more than the yellow jersey) removed him as a concern for those seeking a life in yellow. Still, even if he didn't win a stage, he couldn't help but bound up the G.C. list among the snowy summits, so dramatically that when the Tour entered the Alps by way of the Col de Romeyere and Baha took off, the leaders felt obliged to keep him in check by setting a hot tempo in pursuit.

They needn't have worried. At the summit they found the Spaniard standing by the roadside eating an ice cream cone! He thought it a great joke to "see who came after me." Needless to say, no one else was amused.

His erratic behavior continued, his fourth on G.C. in 1956 notwith-standing. The following year, midway through the Tour he quit—just pulled to the side of the road and quit. He spoke in the third person about himself. "Fede, he's not breathing well." His team stood around and pleaded. Not that they loved this Don Quixote of cycling, but he repre-sented a lot of lost money if he quit, money they expected to share.

Baha went silent when his protestations weren't heeded. Suddenly he reached down, took off his bike shoes, and threw them over a cliff. That got the message across!

He won two stages in 1958, but like everyone else was dominated by that other supreme climber of the era, the "Angel of the Mountains," Charly Gaul.

In 1959 no one would have expected more. That's one of the intrigu-ing aspects of great sport: The outcomes aren't predictable. The unfore-seen occurs. One difference for Bahamontes was that in that season (prior to racing for Spain at the Tour) he was on the Tricofilina-Coppi team with the aging Fausto Coppi. Somehow Coppi got to the eccentric Fede to take the Tour more seriously. All of a sudden the man was up front, infiltrating breakaways (on the flat!) and passing up mountain points in order to be in on the kill at the end of big mountain stages. Furthermore, the powerful French national team was paralyzed by the rivalry between Roger Rivière and Anquetil. The French regional rider Henry Anglade showed pretensions of winning the race. This had to be stopped at all costs, so Rivière and Anquetil collaborated to hinder Anglade so that the non-Frenchman, Bahamontes, could win. French fans were scandalized, but there was no denying that Bahamontes won the Puy-de-Dôme uphill time trial of twelve and a half kilometers in a commanding manner, leaving Gaul at no less than 1 minute, 26 seconds, but more importantly, Anglade, Rivière, and Anquetil at more than three minutes. It was the kind of performance worthy of a Tour winner.

Bahamontes was both pleased and disappointed. Such gaps over such great riders had been rarely seen. But when told he'd missed the yellow jersey by only four seconds, he replied in his curious style, "Me, if he had known that for only four seconds he could have taken the *maillot jaune*, me, he would have gone a little faster over the last kilometer." Hard to believe, but from this guy on that day he probably could have.

Bahamontes had no trouble picking up those four seconds and many more en route to Paris, where his triumph as the first Spaniard to win the Tour de France was celebrated not only in France but also in his home-land, even more enthusiastically. God knows, that poor country had lit-tle else to celebrate in those days.

Without the steadying hand of Coppi (d. January 1960) Bahamontes reverted to his former self, at least until 1963–1964. At the tender age of thirty-five and then thirty-six he once again focused on winning the race overall, and if he didn't win, it was because the course design put most of the mountain finishes far from the tops of the last mountains, and also because Jacques Anquetil was at the height of his powers, powers so great that when he had to he reinvented himself as a climber worthy of Bahamontes. And for this gift all Frenchmen were thankful. (Those years are covered in Chapter 21.)

Now in his seventies, Bahamontes has a famous bike store in Toledo, looks as fit and lean as ever, and is delighted to engage anyone in a con-versation about most anything. The man once considered a fool is now sought as a sage.

20

THE READER MAY reasonably ask, "What? Rik Van Looy featured in a book on mountain climbers?" The explosive Belgian with thighs massive enough to pull spoke nipples out of rims, the "Emperor of Herentals," or more often the "Emperor," the only man to ever win all the single-day classics, a sprinter so loaded with leg mass than he could barely survive the true mountains—how could such a man achieve sufficient notoriety in a book devoted to climbers? The apparent anomaly is explained by one word, "attitude."

Rik II (Rik Van Steenbergen was Rik I) recognized that the very gifts which made him the wonder of one-day races were to a considerable degree handicaps in other domains. But, as has often been pointed out, we do not ride with our bodies alone. "Heart," "will," "desire," call it what you wish, can go a long way to making the apparently impossible a reality. Known as a classic's specialist, Van Looy hated being stuck in one slot, however illustrious. Riding for an Italian team, he was regularly obligated to ride the Tour of Italy. For a man of his capabilities it was not especially remarkable to win several stages every year. Mario Cipollini is a more recent incarnation of the same role. Yet as much as Van Looy was admired for his electrifying sprints, his daredevil ability to navigate through a heaving mass of other sprinters to emerge once again victorious, he remained unsatisfied. The Emperor really wanted to be an emperor, a dominator, a master of all domains, and in the big tours that necessarily included the big mountains.

In 1960 he captured the climbing prize in the Giro (Tour of Italy), and he was much applauded for his enterprise. But it was obvious that he'd won it by grabbing points on every little bump for the three weeks of the race;

he had been relatively nowhere on the really big stuff. Yet he still dreamed of being a major player. Like all true winners he hated being anything less than first. (One of the great beauties of sport is that a field of play is provided for unlimited ego, and when the game is over everyone goes back to being human again. No doubt flaws in this structure can develop, but they sure beat warfare!) Once again wearing the rainbow jersey of world champion on his back, Van Looy wanted more than ever to show he was worthy of the jersey and not just in the relatively easy (for him) single-day races, but in a grand tour with the ultimate challenge of major mountains.

As the 1961 Giro unfolded, Rik's dreams of what he might do grew bigger and bigger. It had been a relatively quiet race full of tactical maneuvering, but there had been no big shake-up among the top men. One huge mountain stage loomed the day before the flat finish into Milan, and the main pretenders, each for his own reasons, decided that the Giovo and Stelvio passes would work to their own designs. The Giovo was a normally difficult climb, but the Stelvio is to Italy what L'Alpe d'Huez is to France. The Stelvio isn't as steep, but, from bottom to top, it's one of the longest and highest passes in Europe and features no fewer than forty-eight numbered hairpins. Also on the original menu for the day was the even more fearsome Gavia, which had been scheduled to follow the Stelvio. In those days it was mostly dirt and featured several pitches around 17 percent. Since climbing, particularly climbing for many kilometers, is in large measure an exercise in power-to-weight ratio, Van Looy knew there was no way he could lead on the Gavia. So imagine his joy when the announcement was made that the Gavia was excluded from the itinerary because the snow at the summit was too deep to be removed.

As the field set off that momentous morning, now just thirty-six hours from the finish in Milan, Van Looy was in fifth place on general classification, 4 minutes, 7 seconds behind the *maglia rosa* (pink jersey) of Arnaldo Pambianco. Jacques Anquetil, Antonio Suarez, Hans Junkermann, and Charly Gaul all expected to challenge Pambianco on the Stelvio, but no one expected Van Looy to be able to play that game too. While the leaders kept track of one another, Van Looy had no trouble rolling away up the Giovo. Everyone recognized his move for what it was, a defensive attack, an effort to gain some time so the later losses wouldn't be so great. However demeaning, Van Looy had counted on this gift.

He tried to find the proper tempo, fast enough to pull clear, but nevertheless at an economical rate that would leave reserves for the bigger challenge later. Over the Giovo summit he was 1 minute, 10 seconds ahead of the Italian climbing specialist, Vito Taccone, who, along with several others, caught him in the ensuing valley of the Adige. That was just fine with Rik. More than 100 kilometers remained, and he was only too happy to have some help around to share the work. So far, so good. His plans were working out perfectly. Everything that could be angled in his favor was cooperating.

Their time gap over Pambianco and company grew to 7 minutes, 20 seconds, making the German, Junkermann, the race leader on the road. Van Looy was a little surprised to see that Junkermann, a man who regularly made the top ten in the big tours, had been allowed to escape and fearful that his presence in the break would create a reaction from behind earlier than might have been otherwise expected. So imagine Van Looy's surprise when his little group began the long grind up the Stelvio, and Junkermann was one of the first dropped! However much Van Looy was bluffing, Junkermann had been even more so.

One by one, the others on Van Looy's wheel struggled and died. Fourteen kilometers from the summit and Rik II, Rik Van Looy, the supposed flatland one-day specialist, was alone in the lead of one of the world's two greatest stage races on its most famous mountain. Who could have ever dreamed, ever imagined? Even Rik would have pinched himself if he'd dared break his concentration for that long, for at this moment he was the race leader. He knew the odds of holding this exalted position were unlikely, but by god it wasn't going to be for lack of trying.

Now he gambled. There was no next mountain to hold back for. Just fourteen little (well, not so little on a big climb) kilometers stood between himself and the transformative dream he'd nourished for a whole year. It was an unnatural effort for this born "puncher" who specialized in dynamiting a peloton with explosive bursts. Anything like that now would only backfire, as he well knew. Already the steady, relentless effort, grinding up around one hairpin after another and then pounding between walls of snow, was starting to make inroads on his not inconsiderable reserves. He fought, and fought again, not just the gradient but his ebbing strength. The numbered hairpins appeared less quickly. The wet gravel underneath his tires became stickier. At times he checked for a lower gear and there was none. Then he had to dance out of the saddle, except it wasn't dancing anymore, it was slugging and heaving.

Five kilometers later a cavalcade of klaxoning cacophony from behind announced the inevitable, that Van Looy's glorious effort alone in front had come to an end. Charly Gaul, the famous "Angel of the Mountains" and former two-time Giro winner, came dancing by. And he would not be the last. Nine, now long, kilometers remained to the summit. Soon enough, others passed. But the Emperor did not fold, did not lose his style, his rhythm; he merely carried on as best his fading powers allowed, full of dignity and determination.

Gaul arrived at the summit 7 minutes, 40 seconds ahead of Van Looy, which, given Rik's lead at one time lower down, meant that the "Angel" had climbed the Stelvio no less than fifteen minutes faster! Rik Van Looy had lost his beautiful gamble, but he had gained something more precious: the admiration of everyone who appreciated great cycling. He finished a not dishonorable thirteenth on the stage and seventh overall. What other road sprint specialist could have done so well? The ultimate assessment was made by Gino Bartali, who had followed that day in a car and profoundly appreciated what Van Looy had attempted. It was like a benediction, coming from one of Bartali's stature: "For me, today Rik Van Looy has joined Fausto Coppi in legend."

21

JACQUES ANQUETIL, 1934–1987

JACQUES ANQUETIL WAS the first rider to win the Tour de France five times, a feat since repeated by three others. But in the years when he achieved this feat (1957, 1961–1964), along with two victories in the Tour of Italy, one in the Tour of Spain, the world hour record, and countless other wins, he appeared to be a new definition of the humanly possible. In public he retreated into an aloof shell, his riding more the result of an inexorable machine than something with a heart; the result was a chasm between his need for popular recognition and the public's search for a hero more like itself.

The key to many of his successes was his amazing ability racing against the watch. He had turned professional at the tender age of nineteen in the fall of 1953 and then won the most prestigious time trial event in cycledom, the Grand Prix des Nations. That ride catapulted him into the first rank of pros without the long climb through the ranks that normally produce social graces. While a rider can hardly be blamed for employing the unique talents his physique supplies, excessive reliance on time trials deprived the public of that *mano a mano* intensity they held to be at the core of their enthusiasm for the sport.

Jacques Anquetil, the first five-time winner of the Tour de France, had a labored, yet effective climbing style.

But fate, for lack of a better word, has a peculiar way of shaping destiny. Early in his career, Anquetil, in terms of his mountain riding, was somewhat dismissively described as "the man who can't be dropped but who can drop no one." This characterization combined a certain grudging respect with a yawn. If Anquetil could have gone on winning in the same old way, he would have. But each year some new twist arose that demanded he prove he was more versatile than anyone (perhaps even himself) had supposed. The twists that involve mountains require that Anquetil be included in this book.

In the 1963 season he turned twenty-nine and opened his yearly account of victories with one in the Tour of Spain (which at the time was held in April and May). That was the good news; the bad news was that he picked up a tapeworm, which forced him to take some time off the bike. Indeed, as the Tour approached, rumors abounded that he might not ride or might put in just a token appearance. Conveniently, the race went through his hometown of Rouen, and it was said he'd be checked by his own doctor and be ordered to retire from the event. Such talk also gave rise to vitriolic articles in the press saying he was scared of the opposition that year and looking for a way to avoid it.

Jacques kept his thoughts to himself, but from the first pedal stroke he appeared plenty healthy and intent on making it all the way to Paris. His two principal opponents were the great Spanish climber, Federico Bahamontes, and the second-year French pro, Raymond Poulidor. Both had superior climbing credentials and would take some watching in the mountains, but initially Anquetil thought he could rely on the old formula of limiting the damage in the mountains and more than compensating in the time trials.

The first alarm for the rider from Normandy came on the opening stage, when Bahamontes slipped into the winning break and gained one and a half minutes. While "Baha" was a former Tour winner, even beating Anquetil into third place in 1959, the "Eagle of Toledo" was primarily renowned for focusing on the King of the Mountains competition. That he was in an early break on a flat stage implied an atypical interest in the general classification results.

Jacques retrieved that deficit in the first time trial five days later, but the cushion Anquetil was accustomed to wasn't there. This is one of those "twists" alluded to earlier. No time cushion meant more attentive tactics in the mountains meant a level of climbing expertise not formerly displayed. Could Anquetil do it?

The answer was a resounding yes. On the first day in the Pyrenees, stage 10, Anquetil set the pace up the final climb, the Tourmalet, and easily won the sprint in Bagnères de Bigorre from Spain's Jose Perez Frances, Poulidor, and Bahamontes to take a mountain stage for the first time in a decade of competition.

But the thirty-five-year-old Bahamontes was just warming up. In the Alps he won the stage into Grenoble on his own and the next day went into yellow. But his lead over Anquetil was slim, only three seconds. One mountain stage, from Val d'Isère to Chamonix, remained. Its 228 kilometers, containing four major cols, appeared to offer every chance for Bahamontes to gain time on Anquetil. Finally the fans were going to get what they had so long hungered for. The pedaling metronome with a calculator for a brain was going to have to show some proper traditional heroic capabilities or the "Eagle" would fly away with the race. And there was the promising Poulidor (who could tell what he would do?). People had been waiting for this level of Tour excitement for years.

Just to make the stage extra epic, the weather switched to storm mode. The dark clouds, lightning, thunder, and lashing rain certainly added to the visual drama, but on this day the giants of the road really showed just how big they really were.

Things didn't get serious until the second climb, the Grand St. Bernard, where Bahamontes went away, but he knew his sub-two minute lead at the summit wasn't enough, so he didn't persist on the long descent. The third climb, the Col de la Forclaz (on the east side of Mont Blanc, not to be confused with a col of the same name near Lake Annecy), was only eleven kilometers long, but its upper stretches were unpaved and as steep as 25 percent.

It was here that Bahamontes, who was on his way to winning his fifth Grand Prix de la Montagne prize, gave his utmost. When the Eagle seriously soared, the ten-man lead group was immediately shattered. Only one man could give pursuit, Jacques Anquetil. Anquetil made no effort to match Bahamontes's sudden acceleration, but the most the Spaniard could gain was a few bike lengths. Pedal stroke by pedal stroke Anquetil pulled the desperate Spaniard back. Again Baha tried; again Anquetil slowly reeled him in. At the summit they were together.

There were twenty-six kilometers remaining, and now Bahamontes delayed as much as possible. Far better that they be caught and someone else win the stage winner's time bonus. Bahamontes made one more desperate effort on the last, short climb, but Anquetil was too strong for anything. At the finish Anquetil won the second mountain stage of his career, and although the victory was obtained in cold, rainy conditions, the reception he received was the warmest of his professional life.

The following year, 1964, marked the apotheosis of Anquetil's racing. He was forced to make a stupendous ride to win the Tour of Italy by nonstop attacks from all quarters. As the tapeworm incident the previous year had left him a bit handicapped for the Tour de France, so now the residual fatigue from the Giro handicapped him in the 1964 Tour.

Once again the great protagonists were Anquetil, Bahamontes, and Poulidor. The race started in Brittany and swept clockwise around the country, and for two-thirds of the distance, things were close to a draw among the top three. The Tour drew its breath on the rest day in the Pyrenean city-state of Andorra. Jacques appeared oblivious to the trials yet to come. He went off to a barbecue in the mountains with his wife and team director Raphaël Geminiani and didn't bother with the typical rest day ride. No one else was so casual. Everyone knows a rest day ride is necessary to maintain the body's habituation to the daily effort.

The stage following began with twenty-six kilometers straight up the Col de l'Envalira. Anquetil's casual preparation for the stage was almost suicidal. Not only had he not ridden on the rest day, he didn't even go for a warm-up ride before the start. Bahamontes, Poulidor, and others assuredly did, and from the first turn of the pedals it showed.

The hammer was down and there was no place to hide. There was no chance to warm up gradually and forcing too soon backfired. The mighty Anquetil was in serious trouble as he went slower and slower. He even felt so bad as to reach down to loosen his toe straps, preparatory to quitting the race. Then the teammate who had been shepherding him, the normally docile, even servile, Louis Rostollan, rose to unimagined heights when he addressed his boss imperiously, "Have you forgotten your name is Anquetil? You have no right to quit without a fight!"

These stinging words galvanized Jacques to struggle on to the summit, where he arrived no less than four minutes in arrears. It was a desperate situation, one that called for the kind of resources Anquetil possessed but perhaps took an emergency to produce. More than 150 kilometers lay in front of him, all downhill and flat, in which to retrieve the situation. Anquetil set about rectifying matters by making one of those ride-or-die efforts the "greats" seem to be able to produce in dire circumstances. That is, of course, one reason why they are "greats." Normal riders are overwhelmed.

Certainly Rostollan was overwhelmed when he attempted to hold Anquetil's wheel as the Norman descended into a cloudbank. If there were to be any hope, Jacques must use this descent as a low-energy opportunity to catch a chasing group in front of him. His engine, now very much warmed up, combined fabulous descending skills with his justifiably famous time trailing prowess, caught an important chase group, and used it to get back to the front, where poor Poulidor then had the misfortune to puncture and lose time on the run-in to the finish.

So Anquetil had saved the day, but was this near-fiasco a quirk or a sign of a deeper weakness? Poulidor and Bahamontes lost no time finding out by winning the next two mountain stages respectively. But then there was another time trial and Jacques once again relied on this staple to put himself in the race lead, by fifty seconds over Poulidor and three and a half minutes on Bahamontes. (What Bahamontes wouldn't have done for five mountaintop finishes, as seen in the Tours of 2000 and 2001!)

One mountain remained, and a rather special one at that. In the center of France there is a group of extinct volcanoes, or, as they're called locally, *puys*. The biggest, the Puy-de-Dôme, has a road to the summit. It rears up from the 900-meter plateau to 1,415 meters (4,642 feet). Nothing, one would think, that would intimidate men who had survived the Alps and Pyrenees. But the 515 meters of elevation gain come in only six kilometers for an average of almost 9 percent. The reality is even worse. The road gradually steepens all the way, making the last kilometers the most severe. On such percentages there is no momentum. One must work very close to one's maximum, and the slightest slip is immediately revealed.

Shortly after the climb began, Bahamontes took off. But Anquetil wasn't much worried about losing a minute or so to him. What worried him was Raymond Poulidor, whose progress in all departments over the previous couple years had been remarkable.

Normally, Anquetil would sit on a challenger and follow whatever pace was set. But Anquetil could sense his own frailty and so went to the psy-war department for help. As he later said, "All I cared was that I was directly next to Raymond. I needed to make him think I was as strong as he, to bluff him into not trying harder."

The tactic appeared to work. Several times Poulidor attacked, and each time Anquetil found the will to respond. The kilometers counted down. The *flamme rouge,* marking one kilometer to go, appeared in the distance. Anquetil recounted again, "I looked up at the *flamme rouge* flapping in the breeze, and thought, 'I'll make it now.' In that moment my attention lapsed. Poulidor had a length on me, a length I couldn't make up. I nearly collapsed."

Inspired by the gap, Poulidor gave it everything. The gulf yawned as Anquetil began to look like an overgeared tourist, heaving his body to turn his lowest gear. The mountainside rang with joy. Poulidor's home territory, Limousin, wasn't far away.

Poulidor pounded across the finish line and then could only wait, one of the few situations in which the more he waited the happier he became. At last Anquetil arrived and sagged into his helpers' hands, barely able to mutter, "How much?"

"You still have fourteen seconds," was the reply.

"That's enough. My god, a dog wouldn't have done it." Yes, it was only fourteen seconds, but it was enough to pull off his fifth and final win in the Tour.

Some two decades later, Anquetil lay in a hospital dying of stomach cancer. He was visited by his old rival, Poulidor. As they shook hands one last time, Jacques was still master enough of the situation to joke, "Well, Raymond, it looks like you finally dropped me this time."

22

TOM SIMPSON, 1937–1967

EVERY MAGAZINE SCRIBE resigns him- or herself to the necessity of editorial changes without consultation. There are usually good reasons for such changes, which have no implied critique of the work itself. But occasionally a change is made that alters the writer's original intent in a way that makes or him or her embarrassed to be associated with the published product.

Such a change happened to me once when an editor finished a piece I'd written about Tom Simpson by adding something to the effect that if he hadn't died on a mountain in the Tour de France he wouldn't be remembered well today. I was aghast to have my article so concluded when I had attempted for several hundred words to show otherwise.

I continue to assert, and I believe that even a passing familiarity with Simpson's career readily affirms, that he was one of the elite riders of his generation. He was not only the finest English road rider of all time, he was one of the finest in the world, period. In the course of nine years in the professional ranks he won four classics, the world road championship, and innumerable other races that aren't well remembered today but impressed spectators and fellow competitors of the time. Ask any pro if the aforementioned list of successes would constitute a successful professional lifetime, and the answer would be strongly in the affirmative.

Simpson was good and he knew it. He had been a pursuit champion as an amateur and carried that turn of speed into his professional riding. He could even sprint remarkably well, especially with a small group at the end of a long and tiring race. He comfortably beat Nino Defilippis in the 1961 Tour of Flanders and Rudi Altig in the 1965 World Road Championships—both clear examples of how he became more potent as the difficulties increased.

In shorter races he could climb with the best. He won the Mont Faron time trial, to cite but one instance, and in shorter stage races he was extremely dangerous. In the 1967 weeklong Paris–Nice stage race Simpson was in tremendous form, at one point breaking away with his teammate, Eddy Merckx, and then dropping Merckx on a climb without realizing it. (Simpson waited when he saw the gap he'd created.) Two days later in the final time trial he not only beat Merckx, but also such famous time trialists as Anquetil, Poulidor, and Felice Gimondi.

Cycling has a built-in escalator whose top floor is the Tour de France. Simpson seemed to have all the natural equipment to win it. His one complaint was that he couldn't go three weeks without an off-day, and Anquetil, for instance, never had an off-day. In 1962 Simpson even managed to get into the yellow jersey, only to lose it the very next day in the Superbagnères mountain time trial. Seeking to force him into a greater effort that day, his directeur sportif secretly ordered his mechanic to install a very high low gear on the bike for the time trial. Simpson counted on his fluidity, rather than brute force, to get up major mountains, and the unexpectedly high gearing turned out to be a ghastly, counterproductive mistake.

A single day in yellow, however, convinced Tom that the Tour was within his reach. More experience, greater physical maturity, a better team, and a year when Anquetil wasn't competing, and who knows what could happen? He had encouraging results and discouraging results, and certainly each year he put in a full season from February through October that always included sparkling performances in many events. But at night he couldn't stop dreaming of the ultimate, the Tour de France.

In the 1966 Tour he attempted an audacious break over the Galibier. Although he was caught by Anquetil and Poulidor, it was the kind of effort that convinced him he wasn't far from where he needed to be. Certainly his great start to the 1967 season did nothing to dampen those smoldering desires.

What didn't enthrall him was a reversion to the national team formula, which had been discontinued in 1962. All through the season riders competed for their trade team sponsors, and in Simpson's case that was Peugeot, the French manufacturer of bikes and cars. The riders were supposed to forget about those commitments and race for their respective countries. A small group of homegrown English pros with almost no continental experience were all Simpson could look to for teammates. More than ever he knew, he'd be on his own.

His game plan, therefore, was to ride cautiously on the flat and save himself for the mountains where the big time gaps would make all the difference. The 1967 Tour followed a clockwise direction across northern France before dropping south through the Vosges and Alps.

Simpson survived these tests fairly well. He had led almost the whole way in the team time trial, which was a mercifully short fifteen kilometers. The team was last, but the loss wasn't catastrophic. He punctured at the foot of the Ballon d'Alsace, the last of ten climbs that day, and got back to the front by the top, a superb piece of climbing. (Gimondi, the 1965 Tour winner, punctured at about the same time and didn't make it back to the front group, which highlights Simpson's capabilities.) Tom dropped back a short distance before the summit of the Galibier and regained the lead group on the descent. He even took part in the field sprint for fifth place on the Marseille velodrome and got second ahead of many reputed specialists.

And so to July 13, a summer scorcher that was already registering 80 degrees as the riders rolled out of the stage start in Marseille for the intimidating slopes of Mont Ventoux, the Giant of Provence. The long gradual climb to the true foot of the Ventoux shed most of the peloton, and Simpson, as expected, was the only member of his team to remain in front.

The summit area is lifeless, just a giant heap of white rock that on days like this acts as a giant reflector for the sun's rays. After seven miles in heat exceeding 100 degrees, Simpson started to drift back, eventually to be caught by a group of chasers about a minute down. The most famous man in this group was Lucien Aimar, winner of the Tour the previous year. Simpson refused to be content with his place in the scheme of things. He knew the Ventoux was the kind of mountain that could make or break a lot of dreams, and no matter how hot it was, he was still dreaming. Time after time he attempted to leave this little group and bridge back up to the men in front, but each time the elevated tempo proved to be too much and he was sucked up again by Aimar and company.

Suddenly Tom dropped from his little cluster of riders. Barely able to turn the pedals, he began to weave across the road. In a hundred yards he collapsed. The British mechanic jumped from the team car to help, and he and his rider were quickly surrounded by well-meaning spectators, to whom Simpson is reported to have appealed in whispered gasps, "Put me back on my bike." However apocryphal, this story has stuck because these, his last words, so epitomize his dedication to cycling. The mechanic and fans lifted him onto the saddle and got him going with a good shove. When the momentum dwindled in a few feet, Simpson began his former zigzag course. Another hundred yards and Tom again tottered from the bike, this time utterly spent. He immediately lapsed into a coma and nothing the Tour doctor or a local hospital (where he was taken by helicopter) could do brought relief. Within three hours Tom Simpson was dead, victim of his own indomitable will and the sorcery of his supposedly magical pills.

A monument marks the spot where he fell and is a mecca for cycling fans from around the world who wish to remember Tom Simpson as a complete professional.

23

RAYMOND POULIDOR, 1936–

IT'S A STRUGGLE to include Raymond Poulidor in this book. From his debut in the Tour de France in 1962 at age twenty-six, he showed great promise. Even with one hand in a cast he made a heroic breakaway in the mountains, and two years later he dropped his great nemesis, Jacques Anquetil, on the fearsome slopes of the Puy-de-Dôme to come within fourteen seconds of winning the *maillot jaune*. Surely a man of such talents must come into his own as a "grand," a "patron," a "vedette." Yet it never quite happened. Who can remember how many times he rode the Tour de France (okay, fourteen, a near record), yet one of his biographies is entitled *Glory without the Yellow Jersey.* Poor "Poupou" is remembered as the "eternal second" with three second-place and five third-place finishes in the Tour, but Joop Zoetemelk was the runner-up six times. The difference is that Zoetemelk won the Tour once.

In 1965 a first-year Italian pro, Felice Gimondi, surprised Poulidor. The next year, Anquetil retired from the race, but not before rigging things so that a teammate, Lucien Aimar, could win the Tour. In 1967 Poulidor sacrificed himself for teammate Roger Pingeon. In 1968 he had a terrible crash, directly hitting a kilometer stone with his face. Then came the Merckx era and no one could dream of beating him. But Poulidor endured. Twice in 1974 he managed to drop Merckx on the climbs, but never by enough to make up for losses elsewhere. He rode his last Tour in 1977 at the ripe old age of forty-one. He had always been a good trooper, often a brilliant one. The love that had gone to Eugène Christophe was poured on this similar modern figure who was often in that "if-only" position. Poulidor was a country boy. He faithfully tended his farm. He was faithful to his wife. His daughter married a famous cyclist, Adri Van der Poel. But all these attributes, however strongly they pull at the heartstrings, don't add up to inclusion in a book dedicated to the annals of cycling in the mountains.

But there were exceptions to Poulidor's also-ran status, and they really stand out. The first came in the 1966 Dauphiné Libéré race through the Alps, a standard warm-up for the Tour de France. The last climb of the last day had begun and two Spaniards appeared to be in charge, with Poulidor following on their wheels but not confident enough to do more. That is, until he heard Carlos Echeverria say to Francisco Gabica, "Menos rapido." Raymond would have been the first to admit that he was no worldly sort. His idea of heaven was to be at home on his farm, and he only traveled because of the demands his line of work imposed. However, he had made a couple of interesting trips to Spain to participate in the two previous Tours of Spain. From these he had returned with first- and second-place finishes respectively, not because of any particular one-day brilliance but because his deep strength kept him to the front day after day, and eventually the local boys had just had to give in. More importantly for the Dauphiné story, Poulidor had picked up some basic Spanish, enough to understand the full implications of "menos rapido" (slow down). He immediately attacked with the enormous force he could bring to bear, and presto, he was gone, winning not only the stage but the race as well. His fans went crazy, but as the full story unfolded, poor Poulidor again found his reputation a bit tarnished. A true "grand" would have created weakness rather than wait for it to be revealed.

Years came and years went and good ol' Poupou (Isn't that a sobriquet rich in cultural relativity? Its only rival, to my knowledge, was the Spanish Ferrys team that dressed their men in pink jerseys!) was always there, often the best Frenchman in Paris-Roubaix, well placed but rarely winning prestigious races, and often the victor of minor criteriums where his crowd support was overwhelming.

And 1972 promised to be another year of this sort. Eddy Merckx was still a colossus astride the era. The "Cannibal" was at the height of his devouring glory. The Paris-Nice stage race served as the early-spring setting to get the riders ready for the succeeding prestigious classics. Eddy had won Paris-Nice the preceding three years in succession, and this year appeared to follow exactly the same pattern. The traditional last day was a time trial up the Col d'Eze in the Grande Corniche behind Nice. On the morning of that hill climb the apparently unbeatable Belgian had what appeared to be a secure seventeen-second General Classification lead over Poulidor. At age thirty-six Poulidor could take considerable satisfaction in being second best to the greatest rider of all time—who was eleven years younger! If Poulidor could hang onto his second place, who could possibly ask for more?

One man harbored other opinions. That man was Louis Caput, Poulidor's directeur sportif. He had noticed that Merckx's margins of victory had diminished over the years and that Poulidor had trained through the winter like an enthusiastic amateur. If Poupou would believe in himself and give it everything he had, he just might pull off a surprise.

From the first pedal stroke it was obvious that Merckx was not at his best. That smooth overwhelming power observers were so used to enjoying wasn't quite there. He was out of the saddle in places he'd normally have stayed seated and just surged through. As the last man off, he got regular reports about riders ahead of him. All the reports were satisfactory, except one. Raymond Poulidor was actually gaining time! Merckx fought back. He used a bigger gear. He stayed out of the saddle longer in an effort to use his enormous supply of raw power. But he could not stave off this rebirth of an old dog. At midcourse Merckx had lost ten seconds, which still left him seven seconds of G.C. lead, but obviously the situation was getting desperate.

But Eddy Merckx could give no more, and dear "Poupou" could. At first Eddy was aghast. He hadn't sensed that he had gone so terribly slow and the gaps over other contenders were more or less what he expected them to be, so what was the difference this time? When Eddy looked at Poulidor's time, the situation became obvious. Eddy hadn't had an off day. He'd ridden close to his course record-setting pace of 20 minutes, 14 seconds of 1970. The problem was Poulidor had dug up a turbo somewhere. His time was 20 minutes, 4 seconds, a ten-second smashing of the old record for an average speed of twenty miles per hour!

Upon crossing the line Poulidor asked, "Did I win the stage?"

"Oh yes," came the happy response, "and the race too."

Poulidor could hardly believe his ears. "Are you sure? Make sure you confirm your calculations." Upon official verification, Poulidor smiled, self-amused, "I must be like good wine. I'm getting better with age. At this rate I'll be able to escape my own legend [of eternal second] and beat Merckx next year."

Everyone laughed. This was really too much to hope for. But guess what? Poulidor came back to Paris-Nice and won it again the next year!

24

EDDY MERCKX, 1945 –

THE NAME EDDY MERCKX is historic. "Isn't he the guy who makes nice bikes?" a young rider queries as he attempts to place the name. In a land where anything that happened the day before yesterday is written off with "that was then, this is now," it's difficult to demonstrate why "that was then" might have pertinence to now. But it's less abstract for one who rides a bike sportingly. Did you sprint to the bottom of the hill? Did you sprint up the hill? Did you sprint down the other side? No? Were you afraid you'd get tired? Now you know the relevance of Eddy Merckx. He did that all the time and, in his best years, never got tired. Quite simply, he redefined what was humanly possible on a bike.

All previous champions recognized their limitations, chose their targets, and then poured their talents into those events. The more frequently they could do this the greater their record, but no one, not even Fausto Coppi or Rik van Looy, attempted to win everything.

I have a prized possession, the *Eddy Merckx Alphabet Book.* The first entry under "A" is "Attack: a religion." Merckx is quoted as saying, "I acquired the habit of attacking when I was very young and have conserved it intact. I don't like to vegetate in the peloton, abandoning to others the position of command. Nothing good can come of this."

Others had thought of this too, but if they were more prudent it was because they were afraid they'd blow up. Merckx, for reasons that may someday be known to geneticists, functioned on another level. One French cycling magazine expressed it this way: "Victory was not sufficient for him. It was necessary for him to perform exploits and create legends. More than against his adversaries, whom he beat again and again, Eddy Merckx raced against himself, searching for an absolute that he frequently obtained."

The Belgian had won the world amateur road championship in 1964 at the tender age of nineteen, and he progressed through the professional ranks with steady improvement. By the time he encountered his first real mountains at the 1967 Tour of Italy, he was already the winner of four single-day classics, a short stage race, and a couple of six-day races on the winter tracks. At the 1967 Giro, he won the first mountain stage up the Block Haus climb, leaving little doubt that he would add masterful climbing to his already well-developed cycling capabilities. He returned to dominate the 1968 Tour of Italy in every department, but the lasting memory was up the fearsome Tre Cime de Lavaredo mountain in the Dolomites. While many were forced to walk in a howling snowstorm, Merckx, to quote an Italian newspaper, "climbed like a pursuiter."

Merckxists have no trouble reciting endless examples of these exploits. Here is one of my favorites from 1969.

Eddy turned twenty-four that year and at last felt he was mature enough to tackle the Tour de France. But all Belgium held its breath. The cycling-mad country hadn't provided a Tour winner for thirty years. It seemed to be jinxed. Just the year before, in 1968, Belgium's Hermann Van Springel had managed to lose the yellow jersey on the last day.

Still, the 1969 Tour began as well as any diehard Belgian fan could have wished. Although Merckx lost the prologue time trial by seven seconds to German specialist Rudi Altig, he took over the yellow jersey the next day after his Faema team won the team time trial, which just happened to pass by his parents' grocery store in the suburbs of Brussels! Two weeks later Merckx was solidly in command of the race with a lead of more than eight minutes on second place, Roger Pingeon. Normal tactics dictated a defensive strategy. "Let the others take the risk of attacking" was the standard advice.

The final week began with a classic Pyrenean stage of 214 kilometers over four passes. Huge headlines in a Belgian sports paper, *Le Sportif,* echoed the feelings of the nation: "The Prayer of All Belgium for Her Superchampion: Eddy—Be Careful!"

On that stage Merckx appeared to heed the advice over the first two passes. Always in the front five, where he could watch his opponents and avoid crashes, King Eddy, flanked by his loyal troops, appeared on his way to a stately coronation.

It sounds easy, and for Merckx it was, but many others felt the vise of fatigue squeezing them. All it took was a slight acceleration on a steep bit of the third climb, the Tourmalet, and gaps quickly yawned between groups struggling to limit the damage.

At the summit Merckx cruised serenely by with only his teammate, Martin Van den Bossche, able to hold his wheel. Within a few seconds Poulidor and Pingeon ground over the top, determination and anguish discernible through the sweat. But where was Gimondi, the Italian challenger? The 1965 Tour winner was having a frightful day and would ultimately lose even his third position overall.

Merckx extended the few seconds' lead into a minute on the long downhill. He seemed to be a man without a weakness. Uphill or down he was the best. By the end of the descent there were still 105 kilometers to go, so no one expected Eddy's lead to last. There were seven chasing seriously; the eighth member of the group, Van den Bossche, was, of course, being as much a drag as possible.

Before tackling the last monster climb, the Aubisque, Eddy grabbed a musette at the second feed zone of the day and rolled along hands-off, so he could stuff his pockets with fruit tarts, cream cheese sandwiches, bananas, and other in-flight refueling items.

Then he took out the route map from his jersey pocket for a clearer idea of what lay ahead. Later he described his thoughts at this moment. "I had just done a normal descent and was still gaining time, so I was pretty sure I could at least hold my lead on the final climb. The problem was that after that there were still seventy-four kilometers to the finish, mostly downhill and flat, where a chasing group would have a big advantage. I decided to make my decision at the summit."

The fans were ecstatic. Nationalism evaporated as the roadside rang with news of Merckx's audacity. They couldn't figure out why he should be attacking, when common sense said he shouldn't, but they were joyously grateful. The day would come when they would criticize him as the "Cannibal" for devouring his opponents at every opportunity, but at this moment Eddy's riding style was fresh air in a world grown stuffy after a generation of pedaling calculators who never did more than necessary. It may be crazy, a grand gesture signifying little more than exuberance, but they loved seeing the yellow jersey *seul en tête* (alone in front). "Yes," they said, reminding themselves of the supermen of the past, "this is how a truly great rider shows himself to the public!"

Eddy rolled up the Aubisque at a steady pace, working hard but not excessively, and still wondering what to do. Only at the summit, when he learned that the nearest chasers were now seven minutes adrift, did he resolve on a battle plan. "This is too good to waste. Go for it!"

The last swooping descent dribbled out onto the gently tilted plateau at the foot of the mountains. The profile map indicated a continued mild downhill, but the road was actually full of testy little bumps and exposed to adverse breezes blowing up from the hot plains toward the snowy peaks.

At last Eddy began to show signs he wasn't a prototype of the Terminator. Hints of weakness crossed his face and betrayed themselves in a slightly more heaving style as he lunged up those pesky bumps. A report that his lead had slipped to 6 minutes, 30 seconds confirmed this.

But wait, Eddy is through his momentary lapse, he's back on top of the thirteen-tooth cog and burning up those last twenty-five kilometers. Seven hours of labor have passed. Now, in the *arrivée* town of Mourenx-Ville-Nouvelle, Eddy is elatedly received. And then—silence. Underneath the nonstop blather of the announcer and the honking of Tour vehicles, people look at their watches and hold their collective breath. Every second adds to their estimation of this man and they mean to savor it.

It is obvious the chasers have had their hard times as well when 6 minutes, 30 seconds comes and goes. Another minute elapses before a distant commotion announces the arrival of the Pingeon-Poulidor group. Their deficit is just under eight minutes. In one day Merckx has doubled his lead!

In Paris, Merckx's final margin of victory will be 17 minutes, 54 seconds—more than the combined winning margins of the previous seven Tour winners! A new religion had been founded.

Late in the 1969 season Merckx was involved in a spectacular crash at a derny-paced track race in Blois, France. His pacer, Ferdinand Wambst, was killed, and Eddy suffered a cracked vertebra. The mending took much of the winter and ever after Merckx claimed he was never quite as good as before, continually suffering from back pains that forced him to stop during races and make frequent changes to his saddle height. On the surface this might appear a little difficult to believe. The majority of his great wins were yet in front of him—four more Tours of Italy, four more Tours de France, two of three world road championships, count-less classics, the world hour record, and on and on—but a close observer of his 1968 and 1969 years would have to admit that after his crash there was a growing loss, particularly in the mountains, of the sublime facility he had heretofore repeatedly demonstrated.

In some ways that made Merckx even more interesting. It's always a plea-sure to witness a genius at work, but humans love variety, and a repeated pattern, no matter how superior, can eventually become tedious. After 1970 he had to use his head as much as his legs, thereby confirming the favorite dictum of Tour de France founder, Henri Desgrange: Cycling is a sport for *la tête et les jambes* (the head and the legs).

The 1972 Tour of Italy provides a great example. That year a young climbing prodigy from Spain achieved full maturity. His name was José Manuel Fuente. He won his native tour, the Vuelta a España, in May, and in June was fully prepared to tackle the Tour of Italy. Merckx had also marked the Italian race as a must on his calendar, and their clash was greatly anticipated by race fans.

Course design for the big tours is not a casual affair. The organizers are always looking ahead to a host of parameters that will make the next tour memorable. History is one factor. No Giro can exclude the Dolomites, no Tour the Alps or Pyrenees. But these testing sections can be traversed in myriad ways and interspersed with all sorts of subordinate difficulties that might have huge implications for the overall outcome.

The Block Haus climb on the shores of the Adriatic stands alone. As such it is an isolated challenge, but properly utilized it is a great device for measuring who's who. Fuente understood the implications per-fectly. So did Merckx. As a new version of the Spanish flea, Fuente had to gain time wherever possible (i.e., on climbs), and the organizers certainly created this uphill fourth stage with him in mind. Only forty-eight kilometers long, with nearly two thousand meters (6,500 feet) of elevation gain, the stage appeared crafted for a pure climber. As already noted, Merckx had flown up this climb in 1967. He still had the build of a skinny junior then. Now, though his fat percentage was no greater, he was a robust adult. And he could no longer expect to run away from everyone else during a short stage of steep percentages. With most of the Block Haus climbed in the last twenty kilometers, it easily qualified as a challenge to measure who's who.

The short story is that Fuente rocketed up to the summit, leaving Merckx at no less than 2 minutes, 36 seconds. All sorts of big names, such as Felice Gimondi, were way behind Merckx, and no fewer than seven men, some of them famous sprinters (Marino Basso, Patrick Sercu), lost more than fifteen minutes and were summarily ejected from the race for exceeding the time limit. All this in less than fifty kilometers! The implications were alarming. Given the climbs to come, just where was Merckx, or anyone else, supposed to make up for the lost time?

Eddy had an answer up his sleeve, but he had to wait three days to show it. Meanwhile, the young Fuente, wearing the famed pink jersey, couldn't contain himself. He felt he was invincible. He had the strongest team, there were several climbing stages he felt were made to order for him, and overall he couldn't help but gain so much time that he could afford to lose a few minutes in the time trials and still be way ahead. While Fuente spouted off to pretty girls (of whom there was no shortage) and the press, Merckx plotted and fumed. The most Merckx would say was, "They talk decidedly too much, these Spaniards!"

The stage leading into the toe of Italy had no climbs comparable to the Alps, but it had one substantial incline after another. While Fuente's Kas team lolled around in the limelight at the stage start in Cosenza, Merckx took his Molteni men out for an hour's serious warm-up.

The first twenty-seven kilometers were progressively uphill, and Merckx attacked from the start. So violent was the Belgian's effort that only four men could hold his wheel after just the first kilometer. One was Fuente. Others came and went, mostly went. Fuente managed to hang on to the top of the first climb, the ominously named Valico di Monte Scuro ("Obscure," or better yet, "Dark" Mountain), but lost contact on the descent and from there on had to fruitlessly chase as the inspired Belgian, riding with the defending champion Gösta Pettersson of Sweden, increased the gap all the way to the finish. From being more than three minutes ahead of Merckx, Fuente was now 1 minute, 37 seconds behind; contrary to his expectations, the gap continued to widen (eventually to five and a half minutes) all the way to the finish in Milan.

Eddy had been the first to admit that Fuente was a better pure climber than he, not only because of Fuente's size but also because Fuente had just come off the Tour of Spain. With several mountaintop finishes in the 1972 Giro, it appeared on paper that Fuente should have the upper hand. Merckx never seriously considered losing. He analyzed the course in terms of his own strengths and went about setting up a victory on his own terms. On the Valico di Monte Scuro he attacked when Fuente least expected. Later in the race he didn't respond when Fuente broke away on the first of two mountains. He knew there was a lengthy exposed section into the wind between the two mountains. Eddy judged the situation perfectly. On the second climb he soared by a spent Fuente. The examples, from this race and many others, go on and on, and in the end they add up to a testimony about what a complete racer this man was. He was not only the strongest, overall, but the wisest as well.

It's difficult to imagine a *palmarès* (record) greater than the one Eddy Merckx assembled. He won every single-day classic but one. At one time or other he won just about every lesser one-day race on the calendar. He won all the short and long stage races. He was a splendid track rider. He raced the road intensely from the end of February to mid-October. He attempted to be fit, focused, and ready to win every race he entered. He came to be criticized for his maniacal attention to detail and desire to win everything. "But as a professional, isn't that what I'm supposed to do?" he more or less replied. As with any endeavor, people came to feel that too much of a good thing isn't a good thing.

That was then, this is now, a quarter century later. We live in an era of ever greater specialization. Tour riders don't bother with the classics, and vice versa. Top-level competition is so intense we bystanders can hardly urge the pros to do more than they do. If someone wins Paris-Roubaix in April, who can blame him for wanting to skip the Tour of Spain in September? And yet there is a certain romantic nostalgia for an era gone by when a professional racer felt duty bound by the very term "professional" to contest the entire season, particularly when that ethos was personified by the likes of Eddy Merckx.

One measure of a racer's greatness is to consult his opponents. None suffered at the legs of Merckx more than the Italian Felice Gimondi. It was Gimondi's misfortune to have the peak of his career coincide with Merckx's. Gimondi won the Tours of Italy and France and numerous classics, but he knew only too well how many more races he would have won if Merckx hadn't been born. Of course he was deeply frustrated, but after retiring he had this to say about his lifelong rival: "They say new riders will come from other parts of the world who will eclipse our generation. That may be true for some of our generation, but not for Eddy Merckx. I cannot imagine a more perfect professional. It was my misfortune to have to race against him, but at least I got to see the best racer who ever lived, or, I believe, ever will."

25

LUIS OCAÑA, 1945–1994

LUIS OCAÑA WAS one of the most talented riders to ever throw his leg over a bike. On occasion he achieved a level of fitness that was truly revolutionary, for it allowed him to upset all normal expectations of what a bike racer could be expected to do. And yet his triumphs were always associated with tragedy. His career as a top pro was relatively short, from 1970 through 1973, but in that time he appeared ready to do the impossible—beat Eddy Merckx in the Tour de France.

To appreciate Ocaña it is necessary for us to digress, for like all European road pros of the late 1960s and 1970s his record takes on meaning only when seen in context, and that context is "Le Cannibal," Eddy Merckx. Different eras present different challenges. At this time, to escape being devoured by Le Cannibal was the chief concern of most riders. In a little over a decade Eddy amassed the greatest record of all time. But more than just statistics, Eddy's style is what impressed. By gargantuan leaps he expanded on notions of what was humanly possible. He threw away energy like rice at a wedding.

Ocaña was born in Spain on June 9, 1945, just eight days before his great nemesis-to-be. Ocaña's parents moved the family across the border into France when little Luis was not yet ten. It was in his adopted country that he caught bike fever and came to recognize his exceptional possibilities.

Compared to King Eddy, Luis matured slowly. Yet even as an amateur he discovered his ability to time trial. In 1968, his first year as a professional, he used those abilities against the clock to win the Spanish pro championship (which used a rare time trial format that year).

He was also a natural climber and relied on his uphill talents to win a number of small stage races in his first years in the paid ranks. Conversely, he was a modest sprinter who generally feared the explosive accelerations certain riders could produce in one-day races.

Ocaña was also a bit fragile. He became ill easily and was, on occasion, victimized by mysterious losses of form.

By 1971 Ocaña had had some undeniable successes, most notably a second and a first in the Tour of Spain, and victories in two of France's shorter stage races, the Dauphiné Libéré and Midi Libre. To the average cycling fan, Ocaña was no more than a promising rider in the third tier of talent. (The second tier was composed of those who could actually threaten the only rider in the first tier, Eddy Merckx.) But those close to the Spaniard expected bigger things. Luis was loaded with potential just waiting for the right circumstances.

While Eddy rolled in headlines all through the spring of 1971, Ocaña made his preparations for the Tour de France in Spain, placing third at the Vuelta a España. Eddy started the Tour in his usual swashbuckling style, attacking repeatedly, forcing others onto the defensive and, naturally, making the yellow jersey a permanent fixture of his wardrobe.

Real mountains were at last encountered on stage 8, which finished by ascending the frighteningly steep Puy-de-Dôme. A *puy* is the cone of an old volcano, and there are so many in central France that they are preserved in a national park. The Puy-de-Dôme is one of the few that can be mounted on a road, and the Tour organizers, ever vigilant for ways to add interest to the race, have for years used this six kilometers of torture to bring climbing excitement to an area otherwise devoid of serious uphill obstacles.

So relentless is this grind, well over 10 percent, that the slightest weakness is revealed. July 5, 1971, was to prove no exception. What wasn't expected was to see King Eddy in trouble. In a cool fog that reduced visibility to twenty meters, Ocaña made an irresistible acceleration. It's one thing to sprint for a few hundred meters and make a gap; it's another to hold that gap. But hold it Ocaña did, in part because he was going so fast and in part because Eddy couldn't respond. In fact, two other men, the Portuguese Joachim Agostinho and the Dutchman Joop Zoetemelk, were both able to get clear of Le Cannibal. At the summit Ocaña had gained only fifteen seconds on Merckx, but the way he did it indicated exciting possibilities for the future.

Two days later those possibilities were realized when Merckx punctured in the Chartreuse mountains (an introduction to the Alps). He couldn't recover quickly enough, letting Ocaña, Zoetemelk and half a dozen others take more precious time out of Le Cannibal. Merckx lost the yellow jersey to Zoetemelk, but Ocaña was only one second behind on the new General Classification list.

Sensing that Merckx was not at his best, Ocaña decided to go for the kill. Stage 11, July 8, was only 134 kilometers long, but deceptively difficult. After only 25 kilometers the peloton encountered the decidedly abrupt Côte de Laffrey. It climbs 622 meters (over 2000 feet) in 6 kilometers, and the end result is a 10-percent grade with occasional extra-nasty pitches.

Agostinho was the first to attack, but he was soon joined by Ocaña, Zoetemelk, and the Belgian climber Lucien Van Impe. By the top of the hill the foursome already had two minutes on Merckx. For the next three hours Merckx was to lead the chase in a valiant effort to limit the damage.

Out front, liberated at last, the Spanish raptor spread his wings and simply flew. On the next big climb he dumped his three companions, who combined could not hold off being gobbled up by the chasing Cannibal.

Let's dwell on this image for a moment. A subpar Merckx, receiving no help whatsoever at the front of the chase, is still so strong he can shred the wheel suckers and catch three of the greatest riders of the time, and yet in the face of such intensity Ocaña continued to augment his lead spectacularly. Indisputably, this was one of those rare great days in cycling history. Only nine riders were able to hang on to Merckx up the final climb to the ski station of Merlette, which came at the end of what was virtually a three-hour time trial. Nevertheless, when Merckx arrived, Ocaña had been waiting for him for almost *nine minutes*. Ocaña had done the unimaginable, created a new top tier above Eddy.

To Merckx's credit, he came out swinging, declaring he would attack all the way to Paris. And he did, but with nearly ten minutes to make up Ocaña was content to lose a few seconds here and there. In a few days they'd be in the Pyrenees and Ocaña was confident he had another scintillating recital in his legs.

The stage from Revel to Luchon was intended as a Pyrenean introduction. Only the last third contained real climbs, and these were "mere" third and second category. Merckx made four attacks on the first climb and Ocaña responded easily. The second pass, the Col de Menté, was more severe, but again Ocaña appeared more than capable of handling anything Eddy could dish out. Five kilometers from the summit, a huge storm moved in. Residents of the Rockies know all about such afternoon gullywashers. They may not last very long, but often the bottom drops out of the thermometer and the intensity of the rain or hail can be quite painful.

Naturally Merckx attacked, only this time on the descent. It was a risky move. In many places the edge of the road was a precipice. Indeed, Merckx did crash, and so did Ocaña. Eddy remounted quickly, but before Ocaña could get going again he was blasted by Agostinho and then, a few seconds later, by Zoetemelk.

Merckx, unaware of the drama being played out several hairpins above, kept up his kamikaze tempo. He need not have pushed himself so hard.

Luis Ocaña, knocked out by the successive impacts, was being lifted into an ambulance, his precocious Tour terminated.

The Greeks examined in minute detail relations between men and gods and concluded that attempting to be a god was a great way to experience one's own mortality. Let us look at the rest of the career and life of Luis Ocaña. The parallel with the Greek interpretation is perhaps more than coincidental.

In 1972 Ocaña sought revenge in the Tour. Instead, he collapsed and quit. Was it bad luck? Ocaña didn't think so. He called it a "curse."

In 1973 Ocaña romped through the Tour, winning by a large margin. Just one problem. Merckx was absent. (Instead, he'd ridden the Tour of Spain and beaten Ocaña.) To a degree, Ocaña's Tour victory was tarnished by not measuring up to his own definition of success. Without that success Ocaña considered his life, in some deep way, a waste.

He was only twenty-eight in 1973, but though he competed for three more years, he never won another major race. Had he, like Icarus, attempted to fly too high, too fast? In the early 1980s he took part in a journalists' driving competition held during a Tour rest day. His car flipped and he almost died. He attempted to become a vintner but made little return on his investment.

Finally, he contracted cancer. His condition was not public knowledge and in fact he worked all through the Tour of Spain as a radio and television commentator. A week later, on May 19, 1994, Luis Ocaña died in the hospital at Mont-de-Marsan, the result of a self-inflicted bullet wound. He had ended his life, and the curse. He was buried at the Chapel of Notre Dame des Cyclistes at Labastide d'Armagnac, where his Tour de France yellow jerseys hang in memory of this tragic champion.

Tragedy has become more or less synonymous with decline and sadness. But traditional tragedy (Greek, Elizabethan) is always associated with nobility and calamity. The calamity is necessary to allow people a situation to demonstrate their noble capabilities.

Against this larger backdrop the life of Ocaña is not so sad. Great tragedies reconcile us to outward defeats for the inner victories they reveal. From the beginning Ocaña was doomed; he, only a superb mortal, a Hector if you will, who dared to openly challenge Merckx, the god, an Achilles. But what an effort, what a gesture! How many arenas are left that allow people even this possibility? In this sense tragedy is not an expression of despair, but the means by which we may save ourselves from it. Quaint notions of happiness and longevity have no place at this altitude. Even if he didn't know it, Luis Ocaña measured himself by greater standards.

26

JOSÉ MANUEL FUENTE, 1947–

THERE IS SUCH A THING as luck in cycling, and one form of it is being born at the right time. You were not lucky if you were born in the mid- to late 1940s because that put you in competition with Eddy Merckx. So complete was Merckx's dominance from around 1967 to 1975 that there wasn't much left for anyone else. You were particularly unfortunate if you were a stage race specialist, as Eddy usually took two of the three grand tours in each of those years.

A few riders came along who appeared to offer threatening possibilities. One was (yet another!) Spanish climbing specialist José Manuel Fuente. Like so many of his predecessors, he had a small body and powerful legs, which made him ideal for the mountains but little else.

His childhood was the all-too-common story in those days of a talented kid who had to scratch like mad just to get a bike that would roll and enough food to eat. One time he rode his bike to a race expecting to perhaps win it, or at least capture some primes. He was gambling on the fact that he'd make money because he didn't have enough food to make it home. But a flat early in the race lost him any chance and by the time he finished everyone had gone. He still had 100 kilometers to ride home and he was completely out of food and money. He was so weak he lay in a field for a while, and then, by now rather late at night, timidly knocked on doors and was shooed away until at last a good Samaritan fed him.

Still, he survived, did well enough to move up the ranks, and by 1971, at age twenty-four, he had become a pro for Spain's most prestigious team, Kas. They didn't waste time. That year he was entered in the Giro d'Italia and Tour de France.

The Italian race suited him well, with only modest action on the flat stages, so he was fresh enough in the mountains to take the climbers' prize. But come the Tour de France it was very much the deep end of the pool and he suffered terribly, often dragging in at the very back of the field. He had little experience in intense long, flat races, and holding the wheels in high-speed echelons was beyond his capabilities. By the time the race arrived in the Alps, he was so worn out he couldn't do a thing in terrain that was his supposed specialty.

But once he got near home, the Pyrenees, and was able to take full advantage of the second rest day, he started to show his true worth. On the first stage in those mountains he wasn't able to hang in with Merckx and Ocaña and rest of the titans, but when they all crashed on the descent of the Col de Menté, Fuente was close enough to zip away for the stage win, finishing six minutes ahead of the stars.

His life was transformed. Fuente had hurt so much for so long, but the adulation he received for winning the stage (even if the Spanish fans saw

José Manuel Fuente, the personification of the lightly built, explosive climber, won two stages of the 1971 Tour in the Pyrenees.

this as poor compensation for the hospitalized Ocaña, who seemed on the verge of the impossible, beating Merckx) so jacked him up he went out and did it on a funny little stage the next day. It was an twenty-kilometer mass start hill climb up Superbagnères. Just his kind of thing: straight up. While it is true he was so far down on G.C. no one cared about losing time to him, riders such as Joop Zoetemelk, Bernard Thévenet, and Lucien Van Impe were very concerned about gaining time on one another. They attacked relentlessly. That riders of their stature could be left behind so easily when they were trying so hard indicated that Fuente was a man who would make an impression in the future. In any event, two successive Tour stage wins in his debut Tour wasn't a bad start to his pro career!

Next year, 1972, with his talent no longer in question, especially after he won his native Tour of Spain (against admittedly modest domestic opposition), he arrived in the Tour of Italy billed as the primary opponent of Eddy Merckx. Chapter 24, on Eddy Merckx, examines this confrontation in some detail. Suffice to say that an early climb (Block Haus) gave Fuente a perfect chance to gain huge time on everyone and don the race leader's pink jersey. So far, such as in the Tour of Spain, escapades of this sort had been enough to win tours overall, but now, confronting Eddy Merckx, the master, Fuente made the mistake of thinking he was truly untouchable.

At the dope control on the Block Haus Merckx was standing outside the van waiting his turn, when he heard Fuente say to the technician that he (Merckx) would soon be packing his bags and going home. Merckx had already been considering how he might upset this Spanish upstart, but hearing such indiscreet pronouncements further inspired Merckx to annihilate Fuente on a stage when the poor young Spaniard thought he was safe.

Merckx gave his lessons the hard way. On a stage that finished with the double punch of the Sestriere and Jafferau, Fuente made the mistake of attacking on the former. Merckx was only too happy to let him go, struggle into a head wind between the climbs, and then die, as Merckx pounded by to take the stage and relieve poor Fuente of any lingering illusions he might have about who was going to win this Giro. In consolation, Fuente sealed his grip on the mountains jersey, along with second place overall, with a superb ride up the snow-walled Stelvio with its forty-eight hairpins.

In 1973 Fuente once again took the mountains prize in the Giro, but his eighth place on G.C. (behind Merckx, of course), a substantial drop from second the previous year, showed José Manuel just how difficult his self-appointed task was.

Nevertheless, 1973 was a year of considerable satisfaction. Whatever regrets he had about the Giro he rectified in the Tour of Switzerland. This weeklong race better suited his talents: almost all climbing and devoid of the sapping flat stages of the Tour de France. Fuente was only too happy to romp away to an overall win.

The 1973 Tour de France was one of those good news/bad news things. The good news was that Fuente finished on the podium in third place in Paris. However, for him as for the winner, fellow Spaniard Luis Ocaña, the victory was a bit devalued by the absence of Eddy Merckx. (Merckx had chosen that year to ride and win the Tours of Spain and Italy, and skip the Tour de France. Maybe Eddy could have won all three grand tours in one year, but his team couldn't have survived.)

It's impolite to pass over such facts as Fuente's once again winning the Tour of Spain in 1974. To win a major tour anywhere is a feat guaranteed to reconcile a rider to his ultimate fate. But this was expected of the talented but diminutive (in size) climber from Oviedo, Spain. With no Merckx around, he was supposed to win. See what I mean about the bad luck of being born into the Merckx era? Even winning could be a form of losing when everyone went away muttering, "Yeah, but if Merckx had been here ... "

Fuente started out what was to be his last great year (1974, although he didn't know it then) seeking to upset Merckx by attacking early in the Giro (much as he had in 1972) and taking the third stage, which finished just after a difficult climb. The win also brought him, once again, the pink jersey.

This time Fuente was determined to make no mistakes. Nurtured by his faithful Kas teammates, he held onto that precious jersey for the next twelve days, winning two more stages along the way. It was a formidable accomplishment, which, unfortunately, once again led to a little lapse in focus that was to have significant repercussions on G.C.

It wasn't until stage 14, a lumpy but not truly mountainous route run off in lashing rain to the famous spring classics town of San Remo, that Fuente managed to sabotage himself once again. In the midst of all the attacking Fuente suddenly fell back, losing minutes and his pink jersey by the finish. Why? He "forgot" to eat. Spanish journalist Utrillo put his face in his hands and groaned, "God in heaven! He forgot to eat! It's like a journalist coming to a race without his typewriter, notebook, and pencil!"

Fuente was to win two more stages and take a chunk of time back from Merckx, but it was not in a way that made Fuente feel good. On the second of those stages Merckx was informed that his lifetime friend and father figure, Jean Van Buggenhout, had just died. From that day Merckx rode in a trance, even not bothering to change a broken toe clip.

In the morning Fuente had a touching conversation with the great Belgian. "Eddy," José gently remonstrated, "we are all very sorry for you, but life must go on. For you and this Giro I wish you all the best for the coming days."

"Thank you, José, you are a good friend," Merckx replied.

I love little insights like this. They show what deep respect resides between even the greatest rivals in this colossal sport.

Soon enough they were back at it, this time on the famous Dolomite climb to the Tre Cime di Lavaredo. Merckx had won here in a snowstorm in 1968. Headlines of the time said, "While the others walk, Merckx climbs like a pursuiter!" But Eddy had put on body muscle since then and, although a stronger rider overall, he wasn't quite the winged climber he had once been. Fuente was the new winged climber, and his attack six kilometers from the summit was impossible to resist. Although Merckx couldn't accelerate like the flea-weight Fuente, he could certainly maintain a hot tempo guaranteed to leave most others only too happy to hold his wheel, if that.

Everyone on the mountain knew what was at stake, and most were yelling for Italians or even Fuente, anyone other than the "Cannibal" who never seemed to tire of eating his opponents. Fuente climbed superbly, gaining all the way. But Merckx never faltered either, and at the summit Merckx still owned the pink jersey of race leadership, while once again Fuente had to be content with the green jersey of best climber.

No one would have guessed it, but that was to be the effective height and end of José Manuel Fuente's promising professional career. He put in one more season, but he was nothing like his former self. At twenty-eight he was a premature has-been. Maybe beating his head against the Merckx wall had hurt him more than Merckx. Even he didn't know. He later said he could have done better, and undoubtedly he made various mistakes the astute Merckx capitalized on. But Fuente shouldn't be too harsh on himself. He kept Merckx awake at night worrying about how to defend against the Spaniard, and that's a lot higher status than almost anyone else had in this era of those unlucky enough to ride against the great Eddy Merckx.

27

THIS IS A PERSONAL story. Throughout this book I have attempted to be an invisible medium transmitting the action as directly as I understand it to you, the reader. These stories are so interesting, so dramatic, so intriguing that no editorial addition is needed. The actors and actions, properly portrayed, speak for themselves. But the first alpine stage of the 1975 Tour de France, from Nice to Pra Loup, is an exception. Perhaps if I had read about it in excavated archives, as I have many of the incidents that grace these pages, the presentation would be different, but in this case such transparency of rendition is impossible. Although I followed the Tour for many years in print (the only way to do so in the United States in those days) and saw it up close and personal as a spectator on numerous other occasions, on this date, July 13, 1975, I had the privilege to follow the action from the press caravan.

The second rest day of the Tour that year had been on the Côte d'Azur, specifically, the city of Nice. I had arrived early enough in the afternoon to see riders returning from their training sorties on their supposed days of "repose." For men so accustomed to daily racing, a day off the bike can be catastrophic. Some also indulged in social activities. In particular, I remember Felice Gimondi and his wife walking down a street, arms around each other. A sweet sight indeed, but however much their hearts may have been united, their appearances differed. She was a very voluptuous redhead dressed in a rather snug sweater and swathed in gold chains, pendants, and bangles, a sort of walking waterfall of cascading effects. In contrast, Felice was the essence of cycling minimalism. His skin was shrink-wrapped around a body of beautiful features, but there was not one hair of excess. Every vein stood out like the cables on a suspension bridge. After years of magazine photos and roadside ogling my rapture of appreciation from mere inches away can hardly be called hyperbole. I couldn't have been more enthralled.

A certain quiet before the storm pervaded the scene. Battling for two weeks around France had left the top men fairly closely grouped at the head of the General Classification list. The usual runaway dominance by Eddy Merckx hadn't materialized. Yes, he was in the yellow jersey, but only by fifty-eight seconds. The day before, a spectator had slugged him in the kidneys on the Puy-de-Dôme. I have no wish to minimize the effect such a blow might have had on a man going flat-out on such a killer climb, but the fact is that prior to that stage Eddy had done no more than win two time trials and look after himself throughout the Pyrenees. His untouchable climbing form of the late 1960s appeared to have been reduced to a proficiency that might be assailable.

Certainly twenty-seven-year-old Bernard Thévenet felt his time had arrived. Only three years Merckx's junior, his apprenticeship as a professional cyclist had been slow but inexorable. Prior to the Tour this year he called his Peugeot teammates together for a big meeting. At the time the Peugeot team was as close to a French national team as one could have wished. They were French, they were good, they were united, they were hungry for a win in their national race (which hadn't been won by a native in eight years), and they had a leader who said, "My time has come. Believe in me. With your help I can beat Eddy Merckx." This was more than a convivial slap-on-the-back agreement. It was a quasi-legal document they all agreed to and signed. In the ledger books of the Tour it states the financial rewards for stage wins, days in the yellow jersey, most aggressive rider, best sprinter, and so on, and most of all, the amount bestowed on the man who stands atop the podium in Paris. Thévenet agreed to sign away every centime of such earnings to his teammates should he be wearing the *maillot jaune* into Paris. In return they promised to have no personal ambitions but to give every drop of effort to help him win. Such agreements were by no means new in the Tour. What was new was that a team in this era of Eddy "The Cannibal" Merckx, the man who devoured all rivals, had such confidence in a leader that they were prepared to make the necessary sacrifices even when the opponent was supposedly unbeatable. Eddy had the greatest record in the history of cycling. He had won the Tour de France no less than five times, every Tour he had entered. He appeared invulnerable. To gamble everything on beating such a colossus was a gamble indeed. If the gamble failed, Thévenet's teammates would be putting a lot less bread on the family table that winter.

Nice, the elegant old holiday seaside resort, was, as already mentioned, deceptively quiet. Possibly there was a beachgoer or two from some place like Tajikistan who accepted the tranquility at face value, but for all others acquainted with the Tour de France (i.e., the entire population of the town), the quiet had an ominous tone akin to that reported by folks a half-hour prior to a tsunami.

Everyone associated with the race had examined and reexamined the challenges of the next day, which featured no less than six climbs packed into 217.5 kilometers. Two other alpine stages followed on succeeding days and then a hilly time trial, but unquestionably this stage to Pra Loup would be the single most difficult. No less than 5,266 meters (17,277 feet) would have to be ascended, and at racing speed. I throw in this last qualifier about "racing speed" because there is no end of cycling aficionados who endeavor to follow the Tour stages. Some even attempt to compare their times with those of the pros. But this stage was more than just another run-of-the-mill three- or four-pass 10,000 foot ball buster.

Any normal rider tackling this stage as a personal test would be well advised to pack a light and make arrangements to be picked up, "just in case."

The stage got off to a slow start that morning of the thirteenth. In one of those rare Tour snafus, the race had to stop because the gendarmes had not been able to remove the traffic from the road leaving Nice. Horns blasted, sirens wailed, orders screamed, helpless gestures were made, and in less than half an hour the road was clear and the race truly under way.

That Rik Van Linden, the Belgian sprinter, a man allergic to uphill gradients, should lead over the top of the first col, the St.-Martin, showed just how intimidating this stage was. Even at this initial pedestrian pace everyone knew a toll would be taken, especially since the tempo increased on every succeeding climb.

Attrition had reduced the lead group to about fifty when there was a flurry of action on the fourth climb, the Col des Champs, where Thévenet made several probing attacks, only to be immediately countered by the ever-vigilant Merckx. On the descent Thévenet punctured. But he got a quick wheel change, Raymond Delisle, his teammate, set a searing chase pace, the leaders ahead very honorably made no special effort to take advantage of Thévenet's misfortune, and by the end of the descent everyone who mattered was together again.

Now the gloves were coming off. No one can ride this far, this fast, without feeling it. But who felt what, and how much? Now was the time to find out. This next-to-last climb, the Col d'Allos, is one of those unsung cols that show up with some frequency on the Tour itinerary, but because it's between nowhere and nowhere it doesn't get much attention. The cols of the Madeleine and Glandon en route to L'Alpe d'Huez suffer the same sort of anonymity. But ask sporting cyclists who tackle these climbs, especially the ones who are ill informed about the local topography and think it'll round out their altimeter accumulation if they can bag another climb en route to the famous one farther on, and then they'll discover that anonymity in no way equates with facility.

In the story on Ottavio Bottecchia (Chapter 3) I include a firsthand description of the Allos made by Henri Péllisier in 1923. I can assure you that except for a thin veneer of pavement very little had changed by 1975. Most of the climb is little more than a one lane gravel-strewn track that slowly works its way up one side of a mountain range and down the other. It's not remarkably steep, much of it around 4–5 percent, although the incline becomes progressive, steepening to 6 percent, 7 percent, and finally 8 percent at the summit. The most daunting statistic is its length, twenty-four kilometers, and this immediately after the Col des Champs, whose seventeen-kilometer climb averaging a rude 8 percent and 9 percent is followed by a brief twelve-kilometer descent. In other words, the better part of three hours was spent on these two climbs alone!

In 1975 I was almost thirty years old. I had actively raced for fifteen straight years, including a season racing in the French Alps. I had long been fascinated by the history of the sport and immersed myself in the epics of the past. I was well prepared to see what I was seeing, but as the day wore on, as the climbs came and went, and as the speed continued to increase, I became ever more amazed, humbled, awestruck, and dumbfounded. Twenty-seven years of hindsight and many intimate contacts with the major tours have done nothing to diminish my appreciation for this stage of the Pra Loup or bring it sufficiently into focus. The old adage about "seein's believin'" did not and does not apply. I know I saw it. I have proof I was there. And I still struggle to comprehend how figures of human appearance, with arms and legs and blood in their bodies, could do what they did. I know I am not alone. This struggle to comprehend has fueled a century-long fascination with this most stupefying of sporting endeavors.

At age thirty-seven in the 1929 Tour de France, Victor Fontan made a big attack over the Col du Tourmalet and claimed the yellow jersey by nine minutes only to have tragedy strike the next day.

top Ottavio Bottecchia was the first Italian to win the Tour de France, in 1924. He repeated in 1925, when he took the lead on the 323-kilometer mountain stage from Luchon to Perpignan.

bottom Belgian Lucien Buysse took the 1926 Tour by winning both Pyrenean stages by a collective thirty-two minutes.

top Eugène Christophe was leading the 1919 Tour de France by a half-hour with one stage to go when his forks snapped and the rules decreed he had to repair them alone. He lost two hours and finished third overall in Paris.

bottom Alfredo Binda, who won the Giro d'Italia five times and the world title three times, won a record forty-one stages of the Giro between 1925 and 1933.

top Frenchman André Leducq won the Tour de France for a second time in 1932, thanks to his ability to hold his own with the best climbers.

bottom Antonin Magne gave France two wins in its national tour in the early 1930s, here showing his dexterity in leaping from his bike before shifting the chain to a smaller sprocket at the summit of a mountain pass.

opposite Solo stage wins in the Alps and Pyrenees put Jean Robic into position to win the 1947 Tour de France on the final day.

Little Vicente Trueba of Spain was the first winner of the King of the Mountains competition, which was instituted at the Tour de France in 1933.

top Ten years (and a world war) after his first win at the Tour de France, Gino Bartali returned to dominate the race in the mountains with his dogged style.

bottom Although Hugo Koblet established his supremacy at the 1951 Tour de France in a solo break on the flats, it was over the Vars and Izoard climbs in the Alps that he clinched the overall victory.

top Long, solo breakaways in the mountains were one of Fausto Coppi's hallmarks. This one earned him a seven-minute stage win at Sestriere on his way to winning the 1952 Tour de France.

bottom While using the mountain stages to win the 1953 Tour de France, Louison Bobet also showed his climbing prowess to take the hilly 70-kilometer individual time trial from Lyon to St. Etienne.

The elbow-to-elbow battle between Jacques Anquetil (left) and Raymond Poulidor on the Puy-de-Dôme mountain at the 1964 Tour de France was the highlight of Anquetil's fifth Tour victory.

opposite

top Belgian Rik Van Looy is remembered as the only man to win all the major one-day classics, but at the 1963 Tour de France he was able to rival the best climbers to finish tenth overall.

bottom Charly Gaul (left) and Federico Bahamontes (right) were perhaps the fastest pure climbers that cycling has seen. Each won the Tour de France in the late 1950s.

Eddy Merckx (center) won the Tour de France five times between 1969 and 1974, when Luis Ocaña (left) and Raymond Poulidor (right) were among his chief rivals.

above Tom Simpson is often recalled as the man who died in 1967 climbing Mont Ventoux in a heat wave, but he was also a very competitive rider in the mountains, as he demonstrated here leading eventual 1960 Tour de France winner Gastone Nencini up the Col du Tourmalet.

right Belgian Lucien Van Impe was a master of the King of the Mountains competition at the Tour de France, prior to winning the race outright in 1976.

Single-mindedness, belligerence, and brute strength made Bernard Hinault the dominant rider from the mid-1980s to mid-1990s.

Small and powerful, Irishman Stephen Roche used a smart tactical sense and fearless climbing ability to do the Giro–Tour double in 1987, which he followed up the same year by winning the world championship.

Laurent Fignon was unstoppable in the mountains of the 1984 Tour de France, but after tendon surgery he never returned to those heights in the late 1980s.

Aggression and sheer determination brought Greg LeMond his third Tour de France victory in 1990.

top American Andy Hampsten—here leading 1993 Tour podium finishers Miguel Indurain (right), Tony Rominger, and Zenon Jaskula (left)—won the 1988 Giro d'Italia with his superb climbing strength.

bottom Five-time Tour winner Miguel Indurain wasn't known as a great climber, but it was in this two-man break through the Pyrenees with Claudio Chiappucci (left) that he took the yellow jersey for the first time in 1991.

above After overcoming cancer and returning to the Tour de France in 1999, Lance Armstrong was unbeatable in the mountains.

right The fastest pure climber of the 1990s, Marco Pantani did the Giro–Tour double in 1998 with an exciting climbing style that left the opposition in the dust.

Stage wins at the Giro d'Italia in 2001 and 2002 mark Mexican Luis Perez as the climber of the future.

Like most of the journalists, we honked our way by Merckx and company in the last five kilometers of the Allos in order to get ahead on the descent. That ever charging warhorse was setting the tempo. Maybe the others were holding back for the final climb to Pra Loup, maybe, especially in light of what came later, Eddy was bluffing a bit, but the general impression all around, among observers and contestants alike, was that the tempo Eddy was setting was just about all everyone could handle, and increasing it would be tantamount to suicide. Even though the final all-out attacks had yet to begin, all teammates had been shelled out some time ago. Delisle had been the last one. Now this group was composed of nothing but team leaders: Eddy Merckx, Bernard Thévenet, Lucien Van Impe, Joop Zoetemelk, and Felice Gimondi.

I felt sorry for our driver. (I was traveling in a car from a Strasbourg newspaper.) The descent was extraordinarily narrow and serpentine. Here and there little indentations into the cliff or an extra bulge in the wall on the outside allowed cars (on normal days when the road was open to the public) to squeeze by each other. Furthermore, the road was in a wretched state of repair. Spring runoffs had torn away sections of the surface, leaving swaths of exposed rock. At each of these torn-up sections a gendarme had parked his motorcycle and stood holding a yellow warning flag.

Our driver was herding the big Citroen wagon down the mountain as fast as he dared, but between all the limiting conditions, plus the congestion of other cars in front of us, it was obvious from race radio that we would be caught. Race radio was screaming at everyone to find a place to pull off, but it was no easy matter. For most of the descent there was a wall on one side and a cliff on the other. There simply wasn't a place to pull over. Finally, a small pullout was spotted. The driver, his face streaming with the sweat of concentration and anxiety, maneuvered us in with millimeters to spare. Everyone got out the left side; there was no room on the right.

It was a good spot for viewing, as we could look back about a half-kilometer across a ravine that dropped from sight. More pertinent to our purposes, we could see the road as it wound along the big indent in the mountainside. You could see why the road was so narrow. If the cliff was 80 degrees, even whacking out a road one car (or one ox cart in the original version) wide had taken enormous work.

We didn't have long to wait. Thanks to race radio we knew Merckx had put in a big burst near the summit, enough to be ten seconds clear of Thévenet. The others, we assumed, were struggling to limit the damage. Along with most observers, either present or watching on TV or listening to the radio, I thought, "There goes the race." Eddy was a superb descender, and if he'd had the suds to get clear of Thévenet over the top there seemed to be no reason to suppose that he didn't have the suds to roar up the final climb to Pra Loup and put an end to any speculation about his continued preeminence.

And then there he was! Two gendarmes on motorcycles were trying to stay ahead of him and when he came by us, he was screaming at them to get the hell out of the way. We saw him approach one of the washed-out sections, but he never touched his brakes. He just jumped the washboard mess like a gazelle escaping a cheetah. This was bike racing! Nearly seven hours of combat had come down to this. Merckx was totally concentrated. Any little lapse, any minute mistake, and he'd be down. If he were lucky he'd be down. There was always the over-wall-option as well! The wall was low enough anyway, but in many places it had been hit by vehicles and never repaired, leaving virtually no protection from a plunge into the unfathomable abyss. It really was "unfathomable" because the cliff below the road kept curving more toward the vertical until one could see no further.

This observation became more than a matter of idle curiosity when the next rider hove into view. We had heard that Thévenet was second to the summit after Merckx, but on this vertiginous descent even the race director had to hang on for dear life and forgo his race report duties. Getting down the Allos alive was a first concern.

And that's no exaggeration. About thirty seconds later we could make out the blue jersey of . . . let's see, we have to look clear across to the other side of the canyon . . . damn, it can only be Gimondi! Ten years earlier he won this race and here he was again showing the fearless skills one would expect of a younger man. And Jesus, look at his team car! You can see the smoke from the brakes! Wow, the driver's getting sideways on a curve. He's correcting, but not much room for correcting. Ohmygawd, he's overcorrecting, he's losing it, he's launching through one of those holes in the wall with just enough rudimentary stones left to give him a good takeoff angle! He's in midair, almost hanging there. The mechanic is thrown out of the doorless rear seat, whirling musettes around his neck spinning out to a horizontal plane like some weird propeller, or a useless parachute. And my god, there it goes. There goes the car, tilting down and starting to somersault into that bottomless oblivion.

This is more than my overloaded senses can take. A car and its two occupants have disappeared into an abyss at least 500 feet deep and I'm supposed to notice which rider will be chasing Gimondi. At least the Bianchi team car's absence has been noticed and two gendarmes have stopped and are already peering over the edge. Maybe I'll burn in hell, but that's all I need. Here come Zoetemelk and Van Impe and I'm back to noting time gaps and writing comments in my notebook.

The big question, of course, is, Where's Thévenet? Race radio is still silent; anyway how could they know? Finally, here he comes, almost two minutes after Merckx! No sign of a crash. And just look at him. There's the answer, he's slow! Compared to Merckx he's a grandma. His hands are welded to his brakes. Where Merckx and Gimondi weren't even touching theirs, Thévenet is stiffly fighting his bike, and all times keeping those trigger fingers busy on the brake levers. Can there be any doubt now? Merckx has done it again! The Cannibal lives, and for good reason. He's the best! For hour after hour today I have seen him up close and personal. Maybe he isn't quite the gifted climber of 1969 anymore, but he's got so many weapons it's going to be a while yet before anyone gets the best of him. If he has thirty seconds on the next chaser at the bottom of the final five-kilometer climb to Pra Loup, it's hard to see how he's going to do anything but gain time. Eddy Merckx is not known as a man who fades at the end of a long day.

After Thévenet's tremulous passage we jump in the car, say a prayer for the poor Bianchi bastards over the cliff, and use this little window between groups to regain contact with the front. Our driver is really good and for a big station wagon full of gear, the car handles pretty well. Grab handles are conveniently placed over every window and we three passengers are locked onto them. Everyone is grimly silent. The example of the Bianchi car is something we don't want to emulate, or discuss. We have little idea how close the next rider behind us may be. The last time check at the summit had a group at about two minutes behind the Merckx group, but we've had to wait so long for Thévenet there's no telling what the gap might be now. One member of that chase group is Francesco Moser, a man famous for his kamikaze capabilities, so every time we can look back a little way we do. A theme in some philosophy classes is the "somethingness" of "nothingness." It's the sort of idea that can drive first-year students to the quick conclusion that philosophy is little more than madness playing with words. I have to smile because this is a perfect example. Looking out the back window, the "nothingness" of Francesco Moser is the "something" I most want to see!

At last we make the turn onto the final climb. It's a rudely abrupt transition. How difficult it must be on the riders. They've been flying down a mountain for fifteen minutes or more with very little chance to pedal, and now, boom, around a corner and immediately 6 percent greets stiffened legs.

We accelerate and our driver is using no less than three horns. The Citroen comes with two tones, one for town and one for country, although I never could figure the rationale for why which was which. We also have one of those multitone jobs associated with the Tour. We're using them all to keep the enormous crowds parting in front of us. It's a close thing, so close I sometimes can't look. Where possible we're up to forty or fifty miles per hour and of course the spectators fill the road looking for the next rider. They part just in time as we roar up the mountain. All it would take would be one little misjudgment, one trip or stumble, and we'd cream someone. The tolerances are so close. My elbow, for example, is definitely not out the window!

Now we see two team cars following riders and, big news, neither is a Peugeot. (The cars are Peugeots because Peugeot supplies the Tour with all the following vehicles. But these two cars are painted in the colors of the Gitane and Mercier teams so we immediately know Van Impe and Zoetemelk are just in front.) Thévenet must be up ahead. Wow, there's a surprise; this stage isn't over yet!

Our driver lays on the horn, the team cars pull to the right as far as possible, the crowds pull back just a little more, and we scoot past, getting a quick look at Van Impe and Zoetemelk. Zoetemelk, in particular, looks horrible. His eyes are so far back in his head they're practically in line with his ears. His cheeks almost touch inside his mouth. His face doesn't have streams of sweat; it's uniformly drowned in water, a pure transparent sheet of liquid covering his facial features. Both men have that hypnotic stare of pure and desperate concentration. There's enough noise to be heard on the moon, but one senses they hear nothing. All they care is to maintain their rhythm with what must be their last dregs of energy.

BERNARD THÉVENET ❧ 147

Dachau refugees on bicycles. This Tour de France stuff is really something. It's no little game where guys work up a sweat, kick each other's asses with a ball or something for an hour, and then retire to the nearest bar. This is a game of life and damn-near death.

We zoom on now, looking for the next rider to leapfrog, and this time it is Thévenet. His speed is not to be believed. We don't need a speedometer check for that. Look! He's in the big chainring, and this on the 10 percent section three kilometers from the finish! He's got a real convoy behind him, and cooperative as the other drivers try to be, it's a dodgy operation zigging around the vehicles to a spot intentionally left open for us, where we sit until the next opportunity avails itself. I can see enough of Thévenet that I'm in no real rush to get by him. Most of the time he's in the saddle just churning a huge gear. Once in a while there'll be a slight extra rise that we in the car can hardly discern, but obviously he's so close to his physical limit he must stand up to keep the gear going over these nasty bits. Our speedometer is hanging around thirty kilometers per hour. How is this possible?

Just then Radio Tour springs to life. Eddy Merckx has been caught by Felice Gimondi . . . and dropped! The whole mountain erupts with the news. In the car we think there must be a mistake. In nearly a decade such an announcement has never been made. But the announcement is repeated . . . and repeated . . . and repeated, *"Eddy Merckx est laché! Felice Gimondi est en tête!"* Talk about sensory overload!

At last we work our way by the Thévenet entourage and in no time we're up to Merckx. Oh man, no question about it, he's dying. No out-of-the-saddle for him. His head is down between his shoulders and his whole upper torso is swaying as he tries to muscle a too-big gear up the mountain. Unlike the others, he's on the left side of the road when we pass. Who has ever seen Eddy Merckx with a death mask like this? I want to lean over and pat his head. He's that close. Only willpower keeps him going. His legs are going around, of course, but there is no real force in them. The contrast with Thévenet is completely remarkable.

Once more we accelerate, this time up to Gimondi. He has always been the epitome of grace on a bike, and even now, in these extreme conditions when the dream of just possibly winning the Tour de France again is giving him extra power, he is the picture of smooth and balanced action. No wild torso bobbing. No lunging at the pedals. Everything about him is correct and efficient. But for all the poetics, is he fast enough?

We race on to the finish line and the last announcement we hear is that Gimondi was indeed not fast enough. Thévenet may not be a "pretty" rider like Gimondi. He's rather thickly built, but in the end nothing counts like forward progress. His build has hidden heretofore unknown reservoirs of power, and on this climb to Pra Loup they have been unleashed in such a devastating manner than no one has had a response.

Thévenet crosses the finish line in 7 hours, 46 minutes, 35 seconds. Everyone consults their stopwatches for the gaps. Thévenet was 58 seconds behind that morning in Nice. Gimondi arrives at 23 seconds, Zoetemelk at 1 minute, 12 seconds, Van Impe at 1 minute, 42 seconds, and finally a disconsolate and utterly whipped Eddy Merckx arrives at 1 minute, 56 seconds. What a coincidence. From being 58 seconds down on G.C. that morning, Thévenet is now exactly the same number of seconds ahead of Merckx this afternoon.

Ecstatic as France is at the heroics of its favorite son, there is also an air of exhaustion, a limpness. In their own way the fans are as wrung out as the riders. Excited words, shouts, such demonstrations almost demean what has transpired this day. People's eyes meet, they shake their heads, a *"nom de Dieu"* is muttered, and they walk on to some destination, knowing they have witnessed and participated in something indescribable. The most that can be hoped for is an attempt at appreciation, an attempt that will take a lifetime and never be successful.

The occupants of the Bianchi team car that took a swan dive off the road on the descent of the Col d'Allos were unbelievably lucky. The mechanic, Signor Lunga, was almost immediately thrown out of the cutaway rear door and landed in a tree, sparing him from the full fall of the vehicle. Unfortunately, he landed in the tree with such force that he was knocked out and broke a leg. The driver took the full 150-meter plunge, never lost consciousness, and broke no bones. With the help of a gendarme he was able to limp all the way back up to the road. Nevertheless, he was a fright to see, being literally covered in a sheet of blood from his head wounds. That driver was in no way put off by his crash. Today he is the well-known directeur sportif of the Italian Fasso Bartolo team—Giancarlo Ferretti.

Nor was Bernard Thévenet finished. The following stage included the famous Col d'Izoard. Merckx attacked early during the stage, but on the Izoard, Thévenet wanted to make a definitive statement. Monuments to Fausto Coppi and Louison Bobet grace the upper slopes and Thévenet wanted to erase any doubt that he deserved to be ranked among those greats. His progress up the mountain was a royal procession and was appreciated as such. He wasn't doing this to win the race. That had already been done. Now Bernard Thévenet was declaring his right to a seat in the halls of cycling immortality. His career did not last long at these rarified heights, although he did manage another Tour win. But time can be measured in various ways, and for three weeks in 1975 Bernard Thévenet made accomplishments so great that he is guaranteed eternity.

28

THE WORD "TOUR" has the sense of going around something, and from the very beginning the "Tour" of France has had that look, more or less a circle going around France. Unlike Italy, say, France lends itself quite nicely to this circular approach, not only because of its roughly squarish shape but because its two great mountain chains, the Pyrenees and the Alps, are on opposite sides. Since 1911, when both groups of mountains were first included on the Tour itinerary, the profile of the race, if all the days were stretched out end to end, would resemble something like that of the Golden Gate Bridge.

Not so in 2001. Now we're approaching a five-day hump in the middle. Nearly a hundred years since its inception, the Tour's directors are still experimenting. Nor is this the first time. There is one precedent, the Tour of 1976.

As in 2001, the first alpine stage in 1976 ended by climbing the twenty-one hairpins of L'Alpe d'Huez, but the approach was different, climbing part way up to Chamrousse before turning off on the Col Luitel and descending to the Romanche valley, which gradually leads up to the foot of the famous "Alpe."

The logical Tour favorite in 1976 was the Dutchman Joop Zoetemelk. Since 1970 he'd been second twice and was never out of the top five. Merckx at last wasn't in the Tour and Joop could finally emerge from that intimidating shadow. (A joke of the day asked, Why doesn't Zoetemelk have a tan after the Tour? Answer: Because he always rides in Merckx's shadow.)

Thanks to the benefits the little Belgian climber Lucien Van Impe had received from the team time trial, Joop's victories in the first two alpine stages left him eight seconds behind Van Impe.

Eight seconds, no time for a false move. Ergo, both men made them. The fourth (of six) straight days in the mountains and first in the Pyrenees saw Van Impe and Zoetemelk mark each other so closely that the very competent Peugeot rider, Raymond Delisle, in eighth on G.C. and only four minutes down, was able to get away and gain time all the way up to the ski station finish at Pyrenees 2000.

The next day was a stalemate, leaving only one, the biggest of the Pyrenean stages; like 2001, it was the fifth mountaintop finish. Without Cyrille Guimard, his directeur sportif (famous for his recruitment of Greg LeMond five years later), it's doubtful Van Impe would have had the nerve to do what he did. After all, as a six-time winner of the mountain's jersey (a record), Van Impe had never shown more ambition than to arrive in Paris in the polka-dot jersey. Not infrequently, he made the top three on General Classification as well, but that was more an unintended result of his brilliant mountain riding. Of course, in order to win all those mountain points he had to attack early on the mountain stages in order to be first over the first two or three or four climbs, leaving him ill prepared to hang with the big G.C. contenders when they caught him on the final one.

But it was a trade-off that made him happy. Van Impe took more time off in the winter to enjoy traveling and family life, used the early-season races just for training, and focused almost exclusively on the Tour de France. At the time he was criticized for ignoring his full "professional obligations," but he understood that his small build hardly fitted him for anything but the role of climber. Why beat his head against the wall finishing midpack in Milan–San Remo and run the risk of a crash? He realized his first professional obligation was to himself, just as every-one else did. (Eddy Merckx was an exception who rode many races just to bring in a gate so there would be more money for the poorer riders.) But most other riders couldn't be so narrowly focused and be success-ful. From the perspective of today, Van Impe would appear to have been ahead of his time, in the time of Lance Armstrong.

Luis Ocaña, the untouchable Tour winner in 1973, although much more human in 1976, was seriously intent on showing his Spanish fans that he wasn't dead yet. Guimard recognized the legitimacy of Ocaña's attack on the Col de Portillon and told little Lucien to chase. Already a three-time King of the Mountains winner (the other three came later), Van Impe wasn't in the habit of attacking from the bottom of a col, espe-cially so far from the finish. He hesitated. Guimard knew his man bet-ter than the man himself and shouted at Van Impe that he'd run him off the road with the car if he didn't attack! (The scene is reminiscent of one played out on the climb to L'Alpe d'Huez in 1989, when Guimard demanded that Laurent Fignon attack LeMond when he [Guimard] could see LeMond was weakening.)

Van Impe flew away and caught Ocaña and the Italian Walter Riccomi on the next climb, the Col de Peyresourde. Over the top they had two minutes on Zoetemelk and Delisle. Zoetemelk had thought to himself, "Delisle is in yellow. I'll follow him back to the front. Ocaña is prema-turely old and just showing off, and Van Impe only wants those mountain points." The theory was fine; it just didn't correspond with reality at that moment. Delisle's thirty-four years were showing, and there was noth-ing the aging Frenchman could do.

Still, there was a flattish transition after the descent of the Peyresourde, where Van Impe would be vulnerable to a concerted chase from behind. This was the very place that had made Van Impe hesitant to attack in the first place. If he went hard here, he'd be toast on the final climb to Pla d'Adet and if he cruised it he might be caught. This is where Ocaña stepped in as a saving angel. While not the imperial master of 1973, he wanted recognition for his fading glory in front of the adoring Spanish fans next to his homeland border. He showed he hadn't lost his old time trailing ability, and although blown away by the effort, he deposited a relatively fresh Van Impe at the base of Pla d'Adet.

From here it was a mere formality (given Van Impe's superb climbing capabilities) to scamper up the brutal climb and reclaim the yellow jersey. Zoetemelk made the fastest ascent of the day, but it wasn't nearly fast enough, and Van Impe had no trouble hanging on to the lead all the way to Paris.

In 1976 Van Impe achieved his only Tour victory, and he would be the first to admit that he probably wouldn't have had the nerve to attack as he did that day in the Pyrenees without the verbal knife in his back Guimard so intensely provided. (The incident, no matter how beneficial to his career, so traumatized Van Impe that he went looking for another team for the next year.) But what Guimard had seen from day one of the 1976 Tour was that those five consecutive mountain stages couldn't help put his man, Van Impe, in a unique-in-his-lifetime position to win the yellow jersey.

Lumping all the mountain stages together was a stupefying endeavor, but relatively less so for a man of Van Impe's caliber. The problem was to convince him. However good one feels, one must think about tomorrow. Zoetemelk and Van Impe showed that kind of conservatism. What broke the stalemate? An attack by "outsider" Delisle. Guimard knew that Delisle had ridden himself into the ground to grab the race lead and was vulnerable the next day. Even in his seventh Tour Van Impe couldn't see it, and even if he could have he was scared to do something about it lest it make him exposed to Zoetemelk. There are many ways to climb mountains and many ways to win a big race, but no one is predestined to win.

Imagine your own experience on a bike. How many of us have ridden four or five passes a day at any pace, never mind a race pace? Then multiply that by five days. Can we really criticize a man, even a top pro of seven years, for being concerned about overdoing it in such circumstances? Instead, let us join his native townsfolk who received him after the Tour at his newly repainted home, a home thinly painted in yellow with an undercoating of white with red spots!

29

BERNARD HINAULT, 1954–

AS THESE WORDS are written in the second year of the twenty-first century, France awaits a successor to Bernard Hinault. It's been eighteen years since the brash man from Brittany retired, and impatience around the country is palpable. The French sporting spirit is the most generous in the world—it admires excellence wherever it may come from—but it's only natural to want a home country hero. How is it that the United States produced two Tour de France winners with seven victories between them in the years since Hinault's retirement, while the host country produced none? There are no easy answers.

Rather than ponder the unfathomable, let us return to yesteryear and the glory days of "Le Blaireau" (the Badger), as Hinault was called, for his indomitable fighting spirit.

Could it have been a Napoleon complex? At 5 feet, 5 inches Hinault was definitely on the short side. Everybody's got a complex about something and no doubt Hinault had his, but what really made him stand out were his obvious attributes: superb physical talents, the fighting desire to win that all champions must possess, and the stimulation of growing up in Brittany, the hothouse of French cycling. His climb through the ranks was inexorable; by 1979 he had won two Tours de France and numerous other major stage and single-day races. At the age of twenty-five he began to look to history as a guide for his next move.

His immediate French predecessor was Jacques Anquetil. Among Anquetil's numerous claims to fame, he was the only Frenchman to ever win the Tour of Italy. It was clear to Hinault that it was time he considered becoming the second.

Between Anquetil and Hinault came Eddy Merckx. (Anquetil retired in 1969, the year Merckx won his first Tour de France, who in turn left the sport in 1978, the year of Hinault's first Tour victory.) The Tour of Italy tended to be a bit parochial compared to its sibling in France. The flat stages were often a gentle amble until the finish line came in sight, reserving the few mountain stages to determine the overall winner, almost always Italian. When a foreigner threatened to upset this formula, the home teams would drop their rivalries in favor of a united front against the intruder. Merckx, a Belgian, by ravaging the Giro (Tour of Italy) so often (five wins), had simultaneously dampened the antiforeigner reaction and dragged the race out of its insular peninsula into the modern world, where any worthy winner was supported.

In his first Giro in 1980, Hinault was content to ride a cautious race, staying near the head of affairs while not actually leading. He was only too happy to let the old warrior, Wladimiro Panizza, age thirty-five and riding his fourteenth Giro, wear the *maglia rosa* (race leader's jersey).

On the eve of the third day from the end Panizza allowed himself to dream. He knew his one-minute lead over Hinault would evaporate in the final day's fifty-kilometer time trial into Milan, but tomorrow was the biggest climbing day of the race. Panizza thought he had detected slight signs of weakness in his French adversary in earlier mountain stages. Panizza fancied himself something of a climbing specialist. Mightn't this stage tomorrow, 221 kilometers among the Alps along the Italian-Swiss border, offer a chance, especially since the mighty Stelvio pass (forty-eight hairpins mounting up to 2,757 meters, 9,045 feet) was strategically placed close to the finish? Who could blame the Italian for dreaming? After fourteen Giri Panizza knew this was the best chance he would ever get.

Hinault had his own plans. He was in complete agreement with his directeur sportif, Cyrille Guimard, that now was the time to set matters straight and leave no doubt as to who was boss. The somewhat complicated plan Guimard hatched involved a weak element. Hinault's chief lieutenant, Jean-René Bernaudeau, had been a shadow of his normal self since his younger brother was killed in an accident just before the Giro started. But Guimard's plan brought Bernaudeau back to life. Bernaudeau looked Guimard and Hinault in the eyes, and with quiet intensity he said, "You can count on me."

Not long after that stage started on June 5, 1980, Bernaudeau slipped into a breakaway. While Hinault and Panizza kept track of each other, Bernaudeau and companions gained considerable time. Over mountains and through valleys they went until they were on the final monster itself, the Stelvio. The appearance of accord among the breakaway companions soon faded on the relentless drag uphill. The Stelvio may not be the absolute highest pass in Europe, but the distance from bottom to top is arguably the greatest (arguably, because not everyone agrees on a method for making the measurements). Bernaudeau soon found himself far in front of the others. Phase 1 of the plan had been implemented perfectly.

Phase 2 looked pretty similar to phase 1, except the actors were different. From the bottom of the Stelvio, Hinault's steady tempo soon shed everyone but Panizza. Obviously Hinault was going to have to go into badger mode to rid himself of the tenacious Italian. Coming out of a hairpin between fifteen-foot walls of snow, Hinault gave a mighty lunge on a big gear. This type of acceleration is devastating to respond to when you're weak, and Panizza was weakening. But he knew how to ride with his heart as well as with his legs. He not only hung on to the Frenchmen, he even got alongside for a bit to show he was still fresh. It was a beautiful bluff, but still, it was a bluff. One more attack and Hinault was alone, each pedal stroke carrying him further away from the anguished little Italian.

Once Hinault went clear, phase 3 began. Guimard called the driver of the team car following Bernaudeau and told him to tell Bernaudeau, who was just beginning the descent, to slow down and wait. Hinault stormed over the top, dropped like a rock down the other side, and soon joined his faithful and inspired young teammate.

United, they began the fourth and final phase, in which they rode a two-man time trial at express speed over the last few kilometers into Sondrio. They never let up until they were within sight of the finish line, where Hinault allowed Bernaudeau to take the stage. Hinault could afford to be magnanimous. When the sad Wladimiro Panizza struggled in more than four minutes later, Hinault gave one of his rare smiles. The plan had worked. The Tour of Italy was as good as his.

MANY OF the stories in this book focus on the mountains of the Tour de France because those climbs produce the greatest mountain competition in the sport. So how is it that a man who won the Tour de France five times showed his best climbing talents outside of his home country?

In 1978 Hinault won his first yellow jersey by default when the stage winner to L'Alpe d'Huez, Michel Pollentier, was caught trying to cheat the dope control. Not the material for athletic epics. Hinault was incredibly strong in all departments. In the 1979 Tour he won no less than seven stages and took the green points jersey as well as the yellow. The same rider was never ahead of him at the finish of a mountain stage twice. Not only was Hinault strong, he was smart. And intimidating. He was so feared and respected that his opponents were semiparalyzed by his reputation. When he attacked they seemed to give up and say, "What's the use?" Hinault made the mountains just one part of his formula for success, and therefore a little less outstanding when viewed alone. (Hinault also put up some impressive mountain performances when he was threatened by his teammate Greg LeMond. Those performances are described in Chapter 33.) Therefore, it is outside the Tour de France that we must look to find Hinault's most heroic rides in the mountains.

In the Giro described above, Hinault wanted to make a definitive statement to show he was a big winner of the Giro and not some mouse who somehow slithered by for the win. Later in his career he began producing exploits for a different reason: weakness. Occasionally he would lose time in places, particularly big climbs, where he never would have before. He found himself having to wait for a day when he was his old self in order to rectify matters. What part did psychology play? Was he really weak on those occasions when he shouldn't have lost time, or had racing become so boring that he spiced it up by giving himself a handicap? These questions can never be resolved, least of all by Hinault himself, who was such a master at disinformation that it is hard to know which statements from him are to be believed. But there's no denying the results were spectacular.

Bernard Hinault's 1983 spring program showed uncharacteristically spotty performances. When he announced that he intended to ride the Vuelta a España (Tour of Spain), many observers thought he might use it as a training ride for the Tour de France. Hinault protested otherwise, but one day late in the race he lost minutes in the mountains, and even two minutes in the time trial the next day. Observers could hardly be criticized for thinking that regardless of what Hinault's original intentions may have been, he might have to consider the race a training ride.

Hinault's fans were worried. He'd always been so reliable. When he wanted to win something big he did it, and usually with panache, a sort of bravado style that showed he had energy to burn. Whenever he indulged in badger talk ("I intend to win race X") and followed it up with badger riding (winning the race), everything appeared to be in inevitable alignment. What were the fans to think when their hero was talking tough but not riding that way?

Time was running out. Only two stages remained until the finish in Madrid. The first was fairly flat with one modest pass to climb 100 kilometers from the stage finish. The following and final day had two major climbs. The Spaniards, who were not above transcending team loyalties for national honor, couldn't help but feel confident. Where could the French invader get the upper hand?

As so often before, Guimard and Hinault put their heads together and hatched a plan. They agreed the Spaniards needed to be surprised. They picked a spot in plain view, the modest climb of Serranillos, the "modest pass" referred to above. Of course no climb is "modest" if you go fast enough. A simple idea: Drop everyone on the climb and time-trial 100 kilometers. Simple, and apparently ludicrous. Let's see, drop these born Iberian climbers on their strongest terrain when the Frenchman has been able to do nothing like this for the previous two and a half weeks, and then hold off a chasing peloton alone on terrain where an organized group has all the natural advantage? To these objections Hinault blandly stated, "I was convinced I could do it because I didn't have any other choice."

Come the Col de Serranillos, Hinault put the hammer down so decisively that the race leader, Julian Gorospe, overreacted and blew himself up. Nor was he the only one.

Another miracle was that Hinault was not alone. On this day was born a great star of the future, Laurent Fignon. Hinault's young teammate not only held the leader's wheel but gave invaluable help all the way to the finish in Avila. The leading Spaniards desperately tried to organize themselves but to no avail. It was a triumph of the first order.

Just to make sure no one missed the message that the Badger was back, Hinault led over the two big climbs on the next and last stage at such a commanding tempo that no one could attack. Avila, a city known for saints and miracles, had done it again!

Bernard Hinault had three years of his illustrious career yet to complete. By the end of it he had won five Tours de France, two Tours of Italy, and two Tours of Spain. Jacques Anquetil had an identical record except for only one victory in the Tour of Spain. The "miracle of Avila" (as this Vuelta has come to be known) was even more miraculous than anyone had originally dreamed.

30

STEPHEN ROCHE, 1959 –

ON THE SCALE of great climbers it's difficult to classify a man like Stephen Roche, one of the two recent outstanding pros from Ireland (along with Sean Kelly). Yet classifying can be a step to understanding. Certain short riders have an obvious power-to-weight advantage. Others are so loaded with all-around talent that they can't help but be good climbers too, and so on. From the beginning of his career Stephen Roche displayed all the characteristics of a truly great rider. Yet year after year passed when it just didn't come together in the biggest races: a misjudged sprint, illness, crashes, an off-day. By 1987 Stephen Roche was a frustrated man who was on fire to prove himself.

In the spring of that year he either won or did very well in a number of big races. He entered the Tour of Italy intent on final victory. But there were problems. He was one of only three foreigners on the Italian Carrera team. The other two were men he'd brought with him, Belgian teammate Eddy Schepers and mechanic Patrick Valcke. Another teammate was Roberto Visentini, the previous year's winner. It's not unnatural to suppose that all Italy, not to mention all the Italians on the Carrera team, anticipated another Visentini victory. As indicated, problems.

The Irishman's defense was to go on the offensive early. For ten days he wore the leader's jersey, the famous pink *maglia rosa*. And everywhere Roche went Visentini was sure to follow. Roche felt that he had to control the race himself, that given the chance, his team would stab him in the back, and that Visentini was laughing to himself all the way. At the end of those ten days Roche was physically and emotionally drained, and on the eleventh day he rode a very poor time trial, losing over two and a half minutes to Visentini.

The Italian fans, the press, and the Carrera team all felt the Tour of Italy was now a done deal. Visentini had the legs and backing to carry him safely through to the finish in Milan, where he would once again be crowned the winner. Where does loyalty to the group (in this case the team) end and loyalty to oneself begin? All sorts of general rules can be applied, but in the end the individual must weigh all sides and come up with an answer he can live with. When that individual is a supremely talented athlete who has been attempting to do something for years and may never have the chance again, it is at least understandable if he opts for himself. Stephen Roche decided to give himself, as he said, a "second chance."

The next stage was flat and offered little opportunity, the day after was severely lumpy, and the third the most mountainous of the Giro (Tour of Italy). Stephen reasoned that Visentini would be expecting a major assault on that third day and therefore might be more vulnerable the day before. The reasoning is worth investigating. (1) Visentini had made a huge effort in the time trial and would need time to recover, especially because (or so Stephen reasoned) Visentini hadn't prepared for the Giro as fully as he should have. You had to be more than a one-day wonder to win a big three-week stage race. (2) Roche knew himself. He had prepared properly. Yes, he'd overextended himself and had had a bad day, but he was pretty sure he would recover quickly and be ready to mount a major attack soon. (3) Roche knew Visentini would be expecting something on the big climbs of the third day. Between the recovery time and the mental preparedness Visentini would have, as well as some doubts about his own abilities in the high mountains, Roche could see it had to be all or nothing in two days' time.

The first 100 kilometers of that 224-kilometer stage to Sappada were relatively flat. Three climbs followed. Roche followed an attack over the top of the first one but found Visentini right on his wheel. Getting desperate, Roche attacked again, on the descent, literally risking his life on every bend. Looking back, he could see riders on the hairpins above flying off the road and hanging in trees, as well as Roberto Visentini trying to stay upright on a gravel bank.

Roche was a free man. He quickly caught a previous solo breakaway and the two settled down to cruising quickly. Team director Davide Boifava arrived soon enough and, leaning out the car window, inquired what the hell Roche thought he was doing. An increasingly heated exchange ensued. Roche's defense was that surely other teams would chase, giving Visentini a free ride. Stephen was not prepared to hear that the Carrera boys were leading the chase. "In that case," Roche replied, more incensed than ever, "you better go back and tell the boys that if they're going to ride after me they better be prepared to ride for a long time!" And with that Roche moved up to the fourteen-tooth sprocket, a substantial gear on the gradually rising road. This was war.

In places Roche could look back and see the chase a kilometer or so behind. He got this view often enough to see the peloton wasn't catching up. The thought only made him go faster.

In time, another team car came screeching up, driven by Stephen's friend and mechanic, Patrick Valcke. Boifava hoped that Valcke could get Roche to slow down, but Valcke did no more than relay Boifava's cease-and-desist order. Valcke was trying to be neutral, but when asked his own opinion, he gave a wry smile and said, "Steve, if you have balls, now is the time to show them." As the philosopher Friedrich Nietzsche said, "I may speak crudely, but I don't wish to be understood crudely." For Roche, these words were all the poetic justification he needed.

He'd been out front for more than fifty kilometers, and as the road began to lift in anticipation of the final climb the bunch was truly breathing down his neck. Roche was determined to make them suffer to get him and the result was mayhem. Riders were dropping off the bunch in whole groups, many of them Carrera men. Visentini was hurting as well and went to Moreno Argentin's team for help. They just laughed. Visentini, this peacock of the peloton (he was a famous playboy, fast car, girls, the usual, including a big head), had said some pretty nasty things about Argentin and company recently, and now they were only too happy to let him hang out in the wind to die.

As the leaders began to engulf Roche, he was pleased to find Eddy Schepers at his side. Boifava noticed and ordered Schepers to drop back to help Visentini. Schepers refused. Even when threatened with dismissal that night, Schepers refused. Rarely have battle lines within a team been so clearly drawn.

Midway up the climb was a particularly steep section and Roche was in trouble. Schepers nursed him as best he could, but as the gradient eased Schepers blew. His last words were, "Stephen, you have got to get up to that group. This is the day you win the Giro."

At moments like this great men show what great means. Any physiologist checking Roche's lactate levels at this time would have said Roche was ready for a wheelchair. Instead, he rode with his will. He clawed back to that front group. His world was reduced to focusing on the wheel just before him. Where Visentini or anyone else was he had no idea. All he wanted was to stay with that wheel and for the pain to end. Eight kilometers remained, an anguished eternity. An eternity he survived.

Roche had started the day 2 minutes, 42 seconds down on Visentini. By the time he crossed the finish line and had begun to collect himself, three minutes had passed. Then four. He was called to the podium. Finally, as he was donning the *maglia rosa* again, Visentini crawled by directly beneath him, nearly six minutes down.

With that jersey on his back Roche had no fear of being sent home. He struggled at times in the last week of the race, but no one knew it. He had had the will to get the jersey and he was going to have the will to keep it to the end in Milan.

Winning the 1987 Giro d'Italia was just the beginning of a fabulous year for Roche. In three weeks he was lining up for the Tour de France. It presented its own share of problems, but after the infighting of the Giro he felt he could handle anything.

Stephen Roche knew he had good form, that he could be a contender, but there was plenty of competition. He didn't feel he could rely on his Carrera team, even without Visentini's presence. He needed to lay low, remain near the top but not at the top, and ideally not go into yellow until the final time trial the day before the finish in Paris. Most riders would have told you Stephen Roche was a damn fine climber, and he was. But Roche himself knew he climbed well because he was an overall superb rider. In a Tour with seven mountain stages, all of which finished at or near a summit, Roche was justified in fearing the climbing specialists, the men who could drastically alter their tempo on a climb. With that caveat in the mix of considerations, Roche saw himself as hoping to survive the climbs. Understandably, he kept his fears to himself.

The first two weeks of the Tour had all sorts of little surprises for Roche, but he arrived at the foot of Mont Ventoux for the beginning of the final week in third place, only 1 minute, 25 seconds down on the leader, Frenchman Charly Mottet.

Mont Ventoux, the "Giant of Provence," the scene of the Simpson tragedy twenty years earlier, was always an intimidating prospect, and never more so than when it was the scene of a time trial, as it was this year. In the end, Roche was both pleased and displeased with how things turned out. He finished in fifth, only forty seconds behind the super-climber from Colombia, Luis Herrera, and twenty-eight seconds behind the man he feared the most, Spaniard Pedro Delgado. Shockingly, Jean-François Bernard, a young French pro, vaulted over everyone with a brilliant victory to lead the race with no less than 2 minutes, 34 seconds overall lead on Roche.

Immediately Roche put his mind to work. Bernard was a lot better than anyone had thought, but he had put out an enormous effort on the Ventoux. He must not be allowed to take it easy. Roche wasn't the only one with such thoughts. The following morning the former *maillot jaune*, Charly Mottet, had a quiet word with Roche. No one had to explain "situation ethics" to Stephen. "Listen," Mottet said, "today we climb into my home region, the Vercors. The feed station is in a tiny town, Leoncel. The road down into town squeezes across a narrow bridge in the village and starts climbing immediately. We all [i.e., his System U team] are taking extra food from the start so we can skip the feed and attack climbing out of town. If Jeff (as Jean-François Bernard was popularly known) is just a little way back, he'll be held up by the riders slowing for the bridge and then the feed." Roche smiled and filled his pockets with more food.

The plan was a good one, so good the bike gods decided to help. Two hundred meters from the summit of the Tourniol (the col before Leonçel), Bernard flatted. That meant he had to let everyone go by before he could get a new wheel. He was quickly back in action and taking risks to pass others on the descent to get back to his place in front. But just as Mottet predicted, the narrow bridge and following feed zone forced the peloton to compress like a two-wheeled accordion. The road was so clogged Bernard even had to put his foot on the ground. It was a full minute before the mob cleared and word of the big attack filtered back. (Earphones had yet to be introduced to cycling.)

Bernard looked around; not a teammate in sight. Some were ahead and some were behind and it took a little time to collect everyone around the *maillot jaune* and begin a proper chase. Although it contained no big climbs, the road didn't have a flat bit in it for the next fifty kilometers. Thirteen men, including Roche, flew away at the front, while Bernard's team (led by Canadian Steve Bauer) fought to limit the damage.

On the final climb the string snapped. Roche and Delgado leaped ahead (without Mottet) while Bernard, his team now a wreck, was forced to chase with no help. In the end Bernard lost 4 minutes, 13 seconds to the new *maillot jaune,* Stephen Roche. So much for waiting until the last time trial to take the jersey!

After years of domination by Bernard Hinault, the race, now wide open, ignited the public. The top riders were well balanced, and each was probing for any weakness in the others. More changes were soon to come.

The next day, one of numerous difficult climbs, the leaders arrived together at the foot of the last one, the dreaded Alpe d'Huez. Herrera and Delgado attacked from the bottom, and Roche was content to let them go. He'd worked all this out already. Delgado was a little over a minute down on G.C., so Roche could afford to lose about 1 minute,

45 seconds and still be in striking distance. Keeping the jersey was immaterial at this point.

Roche admitted he probably could have stayed with Delgado, but at what price? He had to keep something in reserve because there were still two mountain stages to go. His plans worked out perfectly. Delgado went into yellow and he was at twenty-five seconds. If Roche didn't lose any more time it was an amount he could anticipate regaining in the final time trial. Meanwhile, Mottet lost more time and Bernard finished just ahead of Roche at the Alpe. Both were therefore crossed off Roche's danger list. The list was now one man long: Pedro Delgado.

The next day, the fourth straight mountain day, included the classic climbs of the Galibier and Madeleine, and once again there had been energy-draining tussles along the way only to find all the top men together at the base of the ascent to La Plagne. As expected, Delgado attacked early. An eighteen-kilometer uphill pursuit was on.

Was this the end? Was Roche so cooked he couldn't respond? Stephen remembered later, "I knew I could never hold Delgado when he went. I told myself, 'Be calm. Stay steady. Wait for the five-kilometer sign, then give it everything.'" Although Roche was hardly crawling, the gap continued to widen. With ten kilometers to go, it had reached 2 minutes, 20 seconds. If he continued like that, Delgado had the race.

Of course Roche was getting time checks the whole way. He had to weigh that information against what his body was telling him and his estimation of Delgado's condition. This is cycling sophistication of the first order. Through the pain and suffering one has to keep room for an even greater level of pain and suffering while not panicking about the size of the time gap.

Delgado started to cooperate. He'd made too big an effort too early and now he was paying the price. Between ten and five kilometers to go, the gap was reduced to fifty-five seconds. Over the next four kilometers

Roche whittled back another twenty seconds. Everyone who could was riveted to their radios and TVs.

Up around the last corner Delgado came, weaving across the road, his body bouncing to every labored pedal stroke. Painful to see, painful to be. Suddenly a roar from around the corner. Roche is in the big chainring, out of the saddle and sprinting. He just missed catching the Spaniard by four seconds. His chance at the yellow jersey was saved.

Roche crossed the line and collapsed. Patrick Valcke laid him on the ground, covered him with his own jacket, and yelled for the medics. Roche was lifted onto a stretcher, given oxygen, and whisked off down the mountain to a hospital.

At home in Dublin, Stephen's mother stared at the TV in disbelief. A rising tide of impotent hysteria gripped her. She feared her son was dying. The next scene in the ambulance would have reassured her.

Doctor: "I see color coming back into your face. Your heartbeat is dropping. You're going to be okay."

Roche, with an Irish twinkle in his eye, removing the oxygen mask: "Good, but no women right away, okay?"

Roche was back at the hotel and in the tub when his faithful friend and teammate, Eddy Schepers, arrived in the room. He had finished way back today. When he heard what Stephen had been through, he almost cried. "What I saw before me was an innocent boy who needed my protection. I thought how poor I was to be so far behind today when he needed me. I told myself, 'If he can suffer like this, so can I.' I swore to him, then and there, 'Stephen, tomorrow I will be with you on the Joux-Plane.'"

And he was. The Joux-Plane, the last of six (!) climbs on this last day in the Alps, was the obvious showdown spot. From bottom to top Schepers kept the pressure on, Roche glued to his wheel and Delgado unable to go faster. Eddy had fulfilled his promise.

Schepers's parting gift was to leave a little gap on the descent that Delgado just couldn't close for the simple reason that Roche rode flat out the whole way down. The eight-second gap at the bottom grew to eighteen seconds by the finish line five kilometers later. Now Delgado's lead was only twenty-one seconds overall, not enough to hold off the insistent Irishman in the final time trial.

After taking the Giro and the Tour in the same year, Roche could be forgiven for leaning on his laurels, but a month after the Tour he won the world road championship. It was a year when it all came together for Stephen Roche; it never would again at this level. But while it did, he gave a perfect demonstration of how to race with your head, and your heart.

31

LUIS HERRERA, 1961–

THE UNIVERSAL APPEAL of cycling has never been better illustrated than in the case of Colombia. The sad condition of that country is all too well-known. A large sector of the population is impoverished, and the country is torn by civil wars and rampant kidnappings and murders. Cycling may not need a material base like that of, say, Formula One Grand Prix racing, but given the fact that good bikes cost three times as much in Colombia as they do in the United States and the roads are often quite poor, it is a miracle that the sport exists at all. And it not only exists but flourishes.

In the 1970s the true worth of the Colombians remained difficult to judge. Aside from the odd encounter with American teams on intermediate territory in Mexico and Venezuela, they remained happily at home in their mountain seclusion, content to pump out a mythology of incomparable mountain-climbing prowess.

It remained for an American promotional genius, Michael Aisner, to invite the Colombians to his Colorado stage race, the Red Zinger, and later the Coors Classic. They had first come in 1980 and showed they indeed had wings on the climbs but could do little else. Patro Jimenez changed all that by winning the American stage race outright in 1982. The following year he was duking it out with Lucien Van Impe for the climbing jersey of the Tour de France!

But the Colombian talent pool was hardly depleted. The next year, in 1983, another young climbing star arrived in Colorado. His name was Luis "Lucho" Herrera and he was only twenty-two years old. He was already famous at home, but no one had heard of him anywhere else. That changed as soon as the Coors Classic started when he tied Ron Kiefel in the opening hill climb time trial up Flagstaff Mountain outside Boulder, Colorado.

More was soon to come. One of the hardest stages of the Coors came the following day on the famous Peak-to-Peak Highway, which entailed no less than 6,800 feet of climbing. Herrera and his teammate, Israel Corredor, quickly disposed of the field. That they should be ahead on the climbs wasn't a total surprise, but that they were able to survive a howling hailstorm on the descent (so deep was the hail on the roads they had to ride in the ruts created by the lead vehicles) and then thirty miles of relative flat back to Boulder, where they arrived no less than 3 minutes, 57 seconds ahead of the group containing their supposed opposition.

The rest of the field looked helpless. Herrera obviously had the legs to pick up more time on the climbs, and he could easily afford to lose a little here and there in the criteriums. And that's exactly the pattern the race followed until the last day from Cheyenne, Wyoming, down to Denver, Colorado. The flat 115 miles with a following wind made for a style of racing not found in Colombia.

As soon as the race started, the East Germans went to the front and set a tempo few could follow. Among those who could were four 7-Eleven team riders, as well as Doug Shapiro and Dale Stetina. There was only so much room in that front echelon. Those dribbling off the back had no protection. Even Canadian star Steve Bauer couldn't cross a gap created by someone else in front of him, and if "Bauerpower" couldn't do it, then it was no shock the waif-like form of Luis Herrera couldn't do it either.

In Denver the lead group arrived in under three hours for an average speed of over thirty miles per hour! Herrera's loss of seven minutes dropped him to third overall. However tragic for the Colombian in the moment, he had nevertheless made it quite clear that he had world-beating talents. Like Jimenez before him, Lucho was off to the Tour de France in 1984.

There have been a lot of rags-to-riches stories in cycling, but Herrera's was one of the most exotic. He was born in a rundown farm-house surrounded by banana and palm trees. The nearby town of Fusagasuga, about thirty miles west of the capitol, Bogota, is the center of the country's flower industry. By the time he reached high school age, little Lucho dreamed of racing bicycles, but his father could hardly afford the luxury of buying his ambitious boy a bike. So Herrera dropped out of school, worked in the fields, and saved his money until he could invest in a proper machine. His faith in his capabilities was quickly realized and he was soon doing amazing things in the big races in his home country.

Herrera was made for Colombian racing. Endless thirty-mile climbs, almost no flat, and altitudes ranging from 7,000 feet to 14,000 feet suited the prodigy perfectly. The Coors showed his weaknesses, but they weren't enough to prevent him from joining the first amateur team to ride the Tour de France. The Tour organizers, always interested in "mondi-alizing" their race, took a look around at the Colombians already doing big things in Europe and figured it wasn't much of a risk to invite the Colombian national team.

As expected, the team was nowhere on the flat, but once in the mountains they more than looked after themselves. The first big alpine stage to L'Alpe d'Huez looked to be a showdown between a subpar Bernard Hinault struggling to return to his former glory after a knee injury and his former understudy who had won the 1983 Tour, Laurent Fignon. To the stunned amazement of all Europe, who should emerge from this clash but Lucho Herrera, twiddling his pedals as though there were no resistance in them. His victory on this famous stage made him an instant national hero. It was the first in Tour history by an amateur and a Colombian. That evening he received a call from his country's president congratulating him on his historic win and the honor he had brought to his entire nation.

Colombia even made the sacrifice of allowing Herrera to skip the midwinter races in Colombia so he could better prepare for his next European campaign. At the 1985 Tour, he did not disappoint. He won two mountain stages and could have won another to Lans-en-Vercors but graciously handed it to his fellow Colombian, Fabio Parra. He could afford to be so generous; he already had the King of the Mountains jersey glued to his back.

His second "mountain" win that year was particularly interesting because it revealed the progress so necessary to become a more complete rider. On the stage to St. Etienne it was no surprise to see him dance off the front on the upside of the Col de la République, but unlike his other wins that came at summits, this one entailed twenty miles of descending from the top into the town below. Nor was this a gift stage in which the race leaders didn't care because of Herrera's lowly place on G.C. Attacks to get rid of Hinault meant the peloton was descending furiously. Herrera knew he had to take risks, and on one corner he took one too many and went flying off into the bushes. Fortunately, he was able to remount and ride so effectively that he hung on for the stage win. In Paris he was in seventh overall, an incredible accomplishment.

Overall, 1986 was something of an off year for Herrera, although twenty-second in the Tour de France would more than please most riders. But he came back in 1987 to new heights. In the spring he climbed so well he won the Tour of Spain outright. He was a little lucky in that Sean Kelly had appeared set to win but had to retire because of a saddle boil, but this was no hollow victory. Behind Herrera were such riders as Fignon, Vicente Belda, and Pedro Delgado. When Herrera returned to Bogota, more than a million Colombians were waiting for him at the airport.

That year Herrera returned to the Tour and terrified the eventual winner, Stephen Roche. Roche was absolutely blunt about it. "When Herrera wants to go, there's nothing any of the rest of us can do about it. On the climbs he's in a class of his own. Unfortunately for him, his team isn't very strong and he's missed out on some of the key moves which have put me ahead of him. But otherwise ..." "Otherwise" wasn't so bad, even if it did fall short of Colombians' dreams. In 1987 Herrera again took the mountains jersey and finished the Tour in fifth overall.

Herrera peaked in 1987, although finishing sixth in the 1988 Tour hardly indicated a precipitous drop. He carried on until 1992, when he retired from racing and returned to Colombia. Eventually he married a beauty queen and settled down to a quiet life in a new house he built in the countryside.

Alas, this is Colombia, where notoriety is a curse. In January 2000, a more recent Colombian star, Oliverio Rincon, was kidnapped by narco-terrorists, and six weeks later it was Herrera's turn. He was marched for seven hours through the jungle and released thirteen hours later after an undisclosed amount was forfeited to the kidnappers. It is rumored that he is still paying in order not to be kidnapped again—a tragedy for a man who showed all his countrymen they can play by world rules and still win.

32

HOWEVER YOU MIGHT describe the appearance of a professional bike racer, it probably wouldn't apply to Laurent Fignon. He had a certain intellectual look, mostly due to the wire-rimmed glasses he wore, and a body type that seemed too smooth for a top pro, whose skin is so thin that every underlying morphological nuance is revealed. But, as often remarked, "appearances can be deceiving."

His performances in the amateur ranks caught the attention of Cyrille Guimard (directeur sportif of the all-conquering Renault team led by Bernard Hinault), who snapped him up in 1982, when Fignon was still a relatively tender twenty-two. Earlier, Guimard had made another prescient acquisition when he signed Greg LeMond. Although LeMond had been a year younger, his and Fignon's careers were to be intertwined in many fascinating ways. Fignon soon proved his worth by becoming Hinault's strongest lieutenant, most notably by helping his leader snatch a last-minute win in the 1983 Tour of Spain.

That would have been plenty of responsibility and heroics for most young riders, and certainly Fignon had no grandiose plans for the upcoming Tour de France. There was even some argument in the team as to whether Fignon should be included. After all, he wouldn't turn twenty-three until August, and this would be his second grand tour of the season. Nor was Guimard the kind of director to bleed his young men of their talent by racing them too much and then discarding them. But it had been a near thing in Spain; Hinault's former mastery seemed to have declined a bit, and Guimard determined that Hinault just needed the best help the team could give him. Conversely, Guimard promised Fignon he'd keep a close eye on him. If he started to show signs of exhaustion, Guimard wouldn't hesitate to have him retire from the race.

Shockingly, on the eve of the Tour de France, Hinault announced he had a tendinitis problem so grave that he couldn't participate. Suddenly the "all-conquering Renault team" looked anything but. A poll was taken of eight of France's leading cycling commentators canvassing their prognostics for the 1983 Tour. Not one of them listed Fignon in the top ten. Without the "patron," Hinault, in control, the Tour appeared to be wide open, and the decapitated Renault team would have to be satisfied with whatever it could scrounge in the way of stage placings.

The first half of the race confirmed the anticipated Wild West shootout, with the yellow jersey passing across several backs. France forgot about Renault as it turned to cheer on another Frenchman, Pascal Simon, who emerged from the Pyrenees wrapped in the *maillot jaune*. He seemed to have the legs and the team to hold his lead all the way to Paris—until he crashed and sustained a hairline fracture of his shoulder blade. For five stages Simon refused to quit. His determination and ability to withstand the obvious pain are the kinds of qualities that so endear this race to fans.

But on entering the Alps, he succumbed to his broken body, and who should be there, ready to inherit the abdicated *maillot jaune,* but Laurent Fignon. He had ridden a superbly judged race, avoiding the ferocious duels that had immolated some pretenders while never losing critical amounts of time. Fignon had floated to the top of the heap by showing the best combination of head and legs, riding with ice-cold self-restraint, and the yellow jersey did nothing to change these qualities in him.

Only within sight of Paris did he discard his tempered prudence and go all-out to crown his race leadership with a win in the final time trial, thereby confirming to any remaining skeptics that he was no accidental winner.

This book is devoted to climbers, and thus far Fignon had not shown himself to be anything other than a very good all-around rider who just naturally did well enough in the mountains. As such, this description of Fignon's 1983 season doesn't justify inclusion in this book, but it provides a perfect backlight for 1984.

In 1984 Laurent Fignon became his supreme self. In some religious circles it's called a "state of grace." In that year, Fignon became the new "patron." He should have won the Tour of Italy. There was only one true mountain stage, which he won by two minutes, enough to wear the pink leader's jersey. He had every reason to expect an extension on his already apparently comfortable lead when the only other true mountain stage had its main challenge, the Stelvio, removed from the itinerary at the last moment, supposedly because of too much snow. That brought the race down to the final time trial, and Francesco Moser (not unfairly) took advantage of every new aerodynamic advantage then available, while Fignon did not. It was a lesson the tradition-minded Frenchman had a hard time adopting. He just couldn't appreciate the difference between disc wheels versus spoked, plunging bars versus normal, and as a result he lost the stage and the race. Five years later he made the same mistake in his famous eight-second loss to LeMond at the 1989 Tour.

But come the Tour de France in 1984, Fignon rode with deliberate and debilitating ease. In all, he took five stages. He quietly admitted that it was his traditionalist respect for his fellow riders that kept him from winning more stages, which he was sure he could have done with only one leg. Last to give in to this new imperial dominance, because he himself had had that role for so long, was Bernard Hinault. Now on a new team after a year's absence due to tendinitis in his knee, he had attacked all the early-season races with a raging desire to regain his earlier form. The results had been less than glorious, but when he won the opening prologue time trial in the Tour it seemed that maybe Hinault had timed it just right and that the "Badger" was back.

Race fans in general, and all France in particular, sat back to watch this intriguing match between former guru and disciple. But once through the Pyrenees there could be no more doubt: Hinault was not his old self. Yet his attitude remained almost suicidally aggressive. On the stage to the famous Alpe d'Huez, Fignon and Luis Herrera, the Colombian climbing prodigy, detached themselves from the front on an earlier climb, the Côte de Laffrey. I purposely say "detached themselves" because they hadn't really meant to create a break. It's just that the cruising tempo of these two wonder boys was so superior to everyone else's desperate best that they created a break without meaning to.

A descent and a long, gentle climb led to the grim finale up the twenty-one numbered hairpins of L'Alpe d'Huez. Over these transitional kilometers Hinault chased like a man possessed. He hated the idea of being dropped, hated it so much that when he got back to Fignon and Herrera, he did something only an unthinking, obsessed, and possessed man would do: He immediately attacked. Fignon was injudicious enough to later say that Hinault's attack "made me laugh." Fignon didn't mean the remark to be as derisive as it sounded. It was just the honest recognition of their relative merits in that time and place. Fignon knew that as soon and he and Herrara got to the "Alpe" they'd swallow up the Badger who was surely expending his last bit of energy on this semiflat approach.

Both men soon sucked up Hinault, and after dropping him Herrera attacked to go on to become the first Colombian stage winner in Tour history. Fignon, second at a comfortable minute, was only too happy to extend his lead over everyone else. Hinault finished the stage well behind, his face a scowling mask of defiance and despair.

Two more mountain stages remained, and on the final climb to Crans-Montana, Fignon demonstrated the type of mastery every winner in the grand tradition is expected to display. He followed earlier attacks with deceptive ease and then, with no apparent extra effort, surged ahead, never deigning to get out of the saddle or look back. He *knew* no one could follow.

Still only twenty-three, Laurent Fignon could hardly be blamed for thinking that he was set for one of the greatest careers in cycling. He had every right to expect that he would only get better. "But" (you could almost hear that "but" coming) Fignon began to suffer from a malady similar to Hinault's and had to withdraw from competition for an even longer time than the famous Breton. The comeback road took longer too.

The comeback roads for Greg LeMond and Laurent Fignon wandered their separate ways through the mid- and late 1980s until the two men met again in the 1989 Tour. Both men had competed in that year's Tour of Italy, but at opposite ends of the peloton. While Fignon won the race he felt he'd been cheated out of back in 1984, LeMond struggled the whole way, only his iron willpower and his wife's support getting him to the finish. It wasn't until the time trial on the final day of the three weeks that LeMond showed signs of his old self.

In the Tour neither man was quite as good as he had formerly been, but each was still superb. Both were often at their limit but did all they could to bluff each other. The first to crack was LeMond in the Pyrenees. Fortunately, it was just before a final summit and there was little overt damage. Covertly, since LeMond had been decisively dropped when he did not wish to be, everyone had to wonder just how deep his fitness truly went.

We found out once again on that killer climb to L'Alpe d'Huez. At the bottom LeMond attacked in his big ring! Not once, but several times — hardly the appearance of someone with a thin layer of fitness. And yet

Cyrille Guimard, the man who had brought both into the professional ranks, soon noticed a subtle change in LeMond's style that indicated fatigue. He quickly drove up to Fignon and demanded that he attack. With a third of the climb yet to go, Fignon was understandably hesitant. But this is what good coaches get paid for. Guimard knew these guys better than they knew themselves. When Fignon attacked, LeMond had no reply, and struggle as he might, he lost so much time that he had to surrender the yellow jersey to Fignon.

Once again the dominator, Fignon attacked on the climb to St. Nizier, the next stage into the mountainous Vercors region. LeMond and Delgado did all the chasing and couldn't make a dent in Fignon's brave and paying move. It was a true bravura performance that left him with an apparently insuperable fifty-second lead over LeMond.

We all know how that final time trial played out in perhaps the most thrilling comeback in Tour history, but one last time Fignon had showed what he could in the mountains. Comparing him to the famous ruler of Renaissance Florence, Lorenzo the Magnificent, French papers called Laurent Fignon "Laurent le Magnifique"! A fitting comparison indeed.

33

GREG LEMOND, 1961–

IN SCIENCE THERE is an idea that progress has come in considerable measure as the result of coincidences, the random juxtaposition of events that managed to add up to something looking suspiciously like momentum or direction or even intentionality. One need look no further than the life of Greg LeMond to find support for this idea. Born near Los Angeles, California, and raised near Carson City, Nevada, he had no business discovering competitive cycling, let alone becoming one of the world's greatest practitioners of the art. Yet Nevada and top-level cycling in Europe anchored the ends of his bike racing demi-orbit.

It's in our democratic blood to believe that anyone can do anything, but cycling is so difficult that no one can make it to the top level without genetically loaded dice. Thurlow Rogers tells the story of how he and Greg and a number of other elite juniors were being tested in the newly created Olympic Training Center in Colorado Springs, Colorado. "We were each being tested for our VO_2 max," Rogers recalled. "As each guy vented all the air possible the guy monitoring the test would say, 'That's good. Next!' But when Greg blew it out the guy yelled, 'Jesus, guys, look at this!'"

But there is a big difference between being physically appropriate for an activity and being a champion in it. LeMond had bridges. Parental help didn't hurt. Loving the activity helped. Being recognized by a small circle as particularly talented was a boost. All things considered, being in the right place at the right time with that kind of potential put Greg right where he needed to be to break out of the American bubble and onto the stage of world cycling.

By the time he was twenty-one, he was a pro in Europe devastating the opposition. It was at this tender age that he was first given the opportunity to unleash his full firepower. The Tour de l'Avenir (Tour of the Future) for amateurs and young pros was (and is) a mini Tour de France, with a bucket of big-time climbs thrown in to let riders know what the big Tour is all about. In that year, 1982, the Avenir featured a severe climbing day in the Chartreuse, a subdivision of the western Alps.

LeMond treated it as a playground to destroy the opposition. On that day alone he left French climbing specialist Raymond Martin behind by 5 minutes, 25 seconds. Even further behind were riders destined to play great roles in the professional ranks, and their lagging behind LeMond enhances the stature of his ride. On the final G.C. he was 10 minutes, 18 seconds up on Robert Millar, 12 minutes, 3 seconds on Colombian Luis Herrera, and no less than 18 minutes, 48 seconds on the 1980 Olympic champion from Russia, Sergei Soukoroutchenkov.

LeMond was a complete champion, performing every dimension of cycling very well or superbly. And that, oddly, was the source of his principal obstacles to success. He signed on with the Renault team, which initially did a great job of giving him the Goldilocks treatment—not too much too soon (not too hot), not too little too late (not too cold). By 1985 the essentials of the team were riding under the banner of La Vie Claire, and LeMond had the maturity to rule the world of cycling. On the same team, however, was one Bernard Hinault. Having won four Tours de France before 1985, he can hardly be blamed for desiring to win the Tour de France that year and equal the record of Jacques Anquetil.

Throughout 1983 and 1984 LeMond learned about his new profession from its acknowledged master. But by 1985 Hinault was no longer at his apogee and was having to resort to psychology to get the desired results. He started that year's Tour in such an intimidating manner that all his opponents were soon just looking for a way to survive. Hinault had them where he wanted them. After the first week he could relax. But a nasty crash broke his nose, which, coupled with fatigue from his big efforts in the Alps, left him vulnerable in the Pyrenees.

There Stephen Roche went for a stage win at Luz–Ardiden. Hinault wasn't worried, since Roche was no danger on General Classification. But when LeMond jumped on board the Roche train, everything changed because Greg could get towed into the lead. The team car came up and in no uncertain terms Greg was told he had to drop back.

LeMond was devastated. He understood that Hinault was the designated winner in Paris, but not being allowed to win a stage? He was dutiful and followed orders, but the tears and anger at the finish line were obvious expressions of the depth of his deception.

At the finish of that Tour Hinault publicly promised to help a promising young man win the next Tour. Not without justification, the cycling world assumed he was referring to Greg LeMond.

When 1986 arrived, LeMond was going better than ever. By Tour time he had every right to believe this would finally be his turn. He had the form, the momentum, the team, the experience, and Hinault's promise. At the foot of the Pyrenees Hinault led the race by less than a minute from LeMond. (Hinault gained that little lead in the first time trial, a stage in which Greg punctured.)

On the first day in the Pyrenees, Hinault, with no warning, attacked. Greg was paralyzed. What should he do? He could hardly chase his own teammate and drag rivals along with him, but to sit still would be to lose the Tour. It would take an enormous mental effort, because who of us is endowed like Greg LeMond? But imagine, try to extrapolate from whatever level of cycling you've achieved to the one of a potential Tour de France winner. You've got the most important ingredient, the legs. Stir in the rest of the recipe, how to use the legs, the motivation to use them, the justification to use them, the years of waiting to use them, and then get stuck in a bad morality play. What would you do?

Hard to believe (but easier if you've been in the European pro ranks for long), LeMond played the dutiful teammate and followed the chasers who were losing time, eventually five minutes. He said it aloud, "I've lost the Tour."

Many of the stories in this book fall into one of two categories. There are numerous examples of genius expressed; riders who had the legs and used them. Other stories describe climbers of less than superman status who still managed to do very well in the mountains, usually thanks to a massive dose of wits. Greg LeMond represents a third category. He may not have been a climbing specialist, but then neither was Fausto Coppi nor Eddy Merckx. They all were so endowed that they excelled in every domain. Because climbing is so disproportionately important in the grand tours, that attribute gets disproportionate attention. There is tragedy in LeMond's life. We all know that. But it extends far past the gunshot incident. In riding with and against Hinault, Greg could not give full expression to his capabilities. That's the third category: genius stymied. For a long time LeMond was prevented from showing his real worth.

The next day in the Pyrenees appeared to be a repeat of the previous one. Again Hinault took off unexpectedly. He once told me he liked to "play" with cycling, and doing something this outrageous two days in a row may have been his idea of play. No one will ever know because even when he explained himself, Hinault played with words. And when credibility disappears so does reliability. Was this a gamble to win the Tour in a super-dominant manner? Was he trying to tire out the opposition so LeMond could go easily into the lead? Was this a bold gesture for the hell of it, a "playful" gesture? Who can tell because Hinault's actions could be interpreted in myriad ways, and his words, intentionally deceptive, meant nothing. On such a "solid" basis, LeMond had to make decisions. Kafka wrote whole books about situations such as the one LeMond found himself in.

Greg bit his lip and sat in. The only thing worse than a morality play in which he was cast as the loser hero was a repeat of that play. But three mountains remained, and going over the second (Col de Peyresourde, second of those remaining, third on the stage) it became obvious that Hinault was starting to fade. In the town of Luchon at the foot of the last climb, Superbagnères, the nine leaders were all together.

Attacks came in staccato succession and Greg had the legs to follow. Hinault didn't. The pressure was on, but still LeMond was undecided and continued to follow. In a peculiar irony, it remained for his teammate and countryman Andy Hampsten to make the decisive attack seven kilometers from the summit. Hampsten pulled as long as he could, and then breaking through the cloud of indecision and misgivings plaguing LeMond, he yelled for Greg to go for it and win the stage.

It was the decisive moment LeMond had been waiting for. He soared away as only the most superb can. French papers called it a "day of destiny." They recognized that LeMond was finally realizing his proper destiny. Once unchained, he did nothing but gain time on everyone. At the line he was over a minute up on the climbing specialists such as Herrera and Millar, but, more importantly, he'd pulled back no less than 4 minutes, 39 seconds on Hinault. Hinault was still in yellow, but by only forty seconds, a difference a liberated LeMond could easily obliterate.

Except for this one stage LeMond was back on restriction for the rest of the race. If he went into yellow over the Izoard and up the Col du Granon, it was because chief outside rival Urs Zimmerman (Switzerland) dragged LeMond away from Hinault and into the overall lead.

The last mountain day that year ended atop L'Alpe d'Huez. Hinault asked LeMond to go slow for him, and LeMond not only backed off but gave him the stage. LeMond was able to defend his lead all the way to Paris, as much with his psychological and political skills as his athletic prowess.

In 1987 Greg was shot.

In 1988 Greg recovered.

In 1989 Greg began racing in the early season and did little but suffer and get dropped. By late May he was riding the Tour of Italy but still suffering at the back.

Day after day he dragged along, trying to beat the time limit and praying for some sign of form to appear. His predicament was not appreciated by everyone. Some felt he wasn't training hard enough. Others thought his fitness was now a thing of the past, that he could no longer reach competitive form. It was very discouraging. Finally he called his wife, Kathy, in Belgium and confessed his physical weakness and inability to carry on slogging like this. She said something to the effect of, "Hang in there, I'm coming down." And off she flew to Italy.

Once on the scene she gave him a major dose of tough love. This race was pivotal. It was too soon to conclude he'd been permanently damaged by his hunting accident. Carrying on, no matter how painful, was the only way he could ever make a proper determination of his new potential and his future possibilities in the sport. And if he didn't do that now, he'd hate himself forever.

History has shown that her intuition was right. She really did know her man, even better than he did, and her faith was justified. But go back to those agonizing stages before the final time trial in which he suddenly came out of nowhere to finish second. Couldn't Kathy LeMond be seen as some sort of misguided domineering vicariously unfulfilled presence? What if she had been urging her man to protracted, endless torture? Wouldn't the average wife have seen her husband in all his anguish, been understandably moved to infinite pity, and implored him to quit, to come home to an easier life where he was loved?

Certain mysteries can never be solved. LeMond himself sees it as a sort of miracle. But Kathy's faith was justified, form did return, and Greg went on to ride a superb Tour de France. Given his form of 1986, he could have won that Tour with one leg. As it was, he only did very well in the mountains, not superbly, and therefore had to win in the last stupefying time trial. Greg LeMond was back, all right, but slightly diminished from before the accident. His future was going to depend on his utilizing those diminished powers ever so wisely.

This "diminished" Greg LeMond rose to the challenge in what I believe was his greatest Tour victory, that of 1990. This is another example of the "genius stymied" category alluded to earlier. This time the genius wasn't denied by intrateam intrigue, but permanently diminished capabilities. For a man of LeMond's natural capabilities this meant that he was reduced athletically to being on a par with a number of others. To win, he would have to make the difference with his mind.

It was hard to see where that "mind" fit in when a break of four gained 10 minutes, 35 seconds on the first stage. True, it contained his own teammate, Ronan Pensec, and three others, but still it was a lot to give away. None of the four had any reputation as climbers, which contributed to the slothful inertia of the peloton.

As they emerged a week and a half later from the Alps, it was obvious that there was a ringer in the front four, Claudio Chiappucci of Italy. No longer a lowly *gregario,* he fought well to hold on to no less than 2 minutes, 54 seconds over LeMond as they began the key day in the Pyrenees. Not only did the American have to keep an eye on the precocious Italian, but in second place overall between them was Dutchman Erik Breukink, 1 minute, 52 seconds down on Chiappucci and 1 minute, 2 seconds over LeMond.

Three severe cols dominated the 215-kilometer stage. The Aspin, Tourmalet, and Luz-Ardiden were all packed into the final eighty-seven kilometers. The Tour was to be played out here and everyone knew it. The question was how?

Chiappucci had a startling answer. He attacked from the foot of the Aspin. Neither LeMond nor Breukink made any special effort to haul him back. The difference was only thirty-four seconds at the Aspin summit, but that translated for Greg into an overall deficit of 3 minutes, 38 seconds. In moments like these, images conjured by phrases characterizing professional cyclists as "beasts of the bicycle" fall flat. While working plenty hard, even if not flat-out, LeMond had to calculate the growing gap against what he estimated his opponents' strengths to be and what his own strengths were, and then distribute them over the remaining terrain in such a way as to arrive at a satisfactory conclusion. Even today in the era of so technical Lance Armstrong, the computer has yet to be invented that can make such calculations more precisely than the human mind, particularly Greg LeMond's superhuman mind.

On the descent of the Aspin and first half of the Tourmalet, Chiappucci pushed his lead to 3 minutes, 20 seconds, or more than five minutes overall. Crunch time was approaching, as LeMond was only too well aware. With five kilometers of the Tourmalet remaining, LeMond made two attacks of such severity that he soon had only Pedro Delgado and Miguel Indurain (at this point, still just a teammate for Delgado) for company. By the summit he had halved Chiappucci's lead. And Breukink had been definitively dropped.

Twenty-one kilometers later at the bottom of the descent, LeMond was with Chiappucci. (So easy to say, so hard to do. Greg has always been a great bike handler, but this descent was the kind that can give nightmares. Still, for the Tour de France, one risks all, and if one can go fast enough the descents can be as important in one's calculations as the ascents.) Thirteen and one-half kilometers to go and 2 minutes, 54 seconds by which to jettison courageous Claudio.

The Italian tried to ride strongly at the front, but Greg knew it was a bluff. Yet the bluff lasted over ten kilometers. Finally, Colombian Fabio Parra attacked. LeMond responded immediately, and the two were joined by Indurain and another Spaniard, Marino Lejarreta. Parra soon dropped off, so Greg remained the driving force all the way to the finish line. The tempo was enough to drop Lejarreta near the finish, but Indurain's surge so close to his homeland's border could not be denied.

LeMond, of course, was interested in the damage done, which was considerable, not the stage win. For the moment, Chiappucci was still in yellow, but only by five seconds, which would be easily eliminated in the final time trial en route to Paris. LeMond had won his third Tour de France in the mountains, all right, not just by brawn but by brains as well.

34

ANDY HAMPSTEN, 1962 –

ONE SIGN OF the growth of serious cycling in the United States is that the talent pool is no longer clustered around a few hotbeds of the sport. In the 1950s there weren't many racers from outside the greater New York, Chicago, San Francisco, and Los Angeles areas. Two decades later a kid from North Dakota could turn into a top European professional! That "kid" was, of course, Andy Hampsten.

He was a bit overshadowed in the amateur ranks because races weren't long enough and steep enough to let him show his full capability. (Levi Leipheimer is a similar example.) But a surprise invitation to ride for the 7-Eleven team at the 1985 Giro got him into the spotlight: Hampsten won a stage finishing on a mountaintop late in the race. His climbing talent was confirmed by a trip to Colombia in October 1985, where he won the Caracol de la Montaña stage race, beating all the famous Colombian mountain goats on their home turf. This was during a time when a steady stream of Europe's elite had gone to Colombia, including Bernard Hinault and Laurent Fignon, and come back with nothing but lowly placings to show for their efforts.

Colombia billed the Caracol de la Montaña as a sort of unofficial world mountain climbing championship, and so when Hampsten won that after his stage win at the Giro people took notice, including Greg LeMond's La Vie Claire team. They quickly signed him up and the following season the precocious twenty-four-year-old was en route to his dream, the Tour de France.

Although cast in a supporting role for LeMond and Hinault, he rode superbly and finished fourth overall. It was a stupendous performance that vaulted him into the rarified group of riders who had the potential to win the Tour.

Later that summer he returned to the United States to compete in what was then our national tour, the Coors Classic. In the perverse way of professionalism (no matter what the sport), Andy entered that race at the head of his old Levi's–Raleigh team, making him the instant adversary of his recent teammates in the Tour de France. In this and the previous year LeMond had won the stages into his then hometown of Reno, and Hampsten strongly wanted to repeat that feat when the race arrived in Boulder, Colorado, where he had taken residence.

Unfortunately, Boulder was at the lower end of the eighty-eight-mile Boulder Mountain stage, so Hampsten was compelled to attack on the first climb just eighteen miles after the start. He continued to open a gap over the next thirty miles of ups and down, but the five minutes he eventually acquired wasn't much in light of the final thirty miles on flat and rolling roads into a head wind.

Greg may have won the Tour de France that year, but the team still belonged to Hinault. When the Frenchman decided to teach the young Hampsten a lesson, no one argued. Hinault was "le patron," the boss, and he controlled his own team. When he said, "No one attacks," no one from any team attacked. The whole field knew he had the power to nullify any unsanctioned aggression. Hinault could just as easily have taken a sympathetic point of view and controlled things in a way that ensured Hampsten's success, but Hinault's combative nature was piqued by the implication of Hampsten's breakaway. Hinault didn't want anyone to think that this young upstart could hold off the world's best. He saw it as a stupid attempt at glory and intended to give Hampsten a lesson in the merciless ways of cycling.

The field rolled up to a minute behind Hampsten, Hinault raised his hand, the chase was tempered, and there the bunch sat, with Andy often in sight a bump or two of the rolling road ahead. While Hampsten flogged himself in desperation, knowing smirks spread around the peloton. For the better part of an hour the slow torture continued, and only with the Boulder city limits in sight was Hampsten gobbled up. Then he exchanged one sort of anguish for another.

In a revealing moment after the race, LeMond said to Hinault, "I knew we'd catch him." "Oh no," Hinault chuckled, "we didn't have to catch him. He came back to us." And they both laughed. This too is high-level cycling.

La Vie Claire fell on hard times that winter of 1986–1987, leaving this extraordinary collection of riders to jump the sinking ship and search for new sponsors. Hampsten went to the American-sponsored 7-Eleven team, which had been amazing Europe since 1985. The only thing missing from their lineup was a big Tour contender, and in Andy Hampsten they were pretty sure they had one. Just how right they were was to be revealed in the 1988 Giro d'Italia (Tour of Italy).

Americans had been penetrating the European road scene since the 1950s, and 7-Eleven was the next logical development. For example, in 1960 Mike Hiltner (today, Victor Vincente) was the first American in the twentieth century to win a race in Italy (an American had won in the nineteenth century), in 1976 Mike Neel was the first American to become a professional in Italy, around 1980 George Mount rode the Giro d'Italia several times, and in 1985, 7-Eleven became the first American team to compete in the Giro.

European competition is a major step beyond anything in the United States. Attempting to bridge that gap has been a daunting athletic challenge for Americans. Problems such as language difficulties, food, lifestyle, loneliness, finances, and so on, contributed substantially to the sketchy record of success by our solo American cycling warriors. 7-Eleven, in creating an American cocoon of sorts, immeasurably reduced the distracting distresses of competing abroad. Now they could focus exclusively on that original project, the athletic challenge.

Not only did 7-Eleven have the deep pockets of a major corporate sponsor and an Italian cosponsor in Hoonved, it had raced in Europe for two years, had a seasoned and highly professional support crew, including Shelley Verses, Europe's first female professional soigneur, and most of all the former American pro in Italy, Mike Neel, as directeur sportif. He knew the American psyche and the European reality and how to be the perfect buffer/translator between the two worlds. His deep knowledge and calm assurance imbued the 7-Eleven men with a level of self-confidence they'd been hard-pressed to find on their own. Signing Andy Hampsten was the capstone to this entire edifice.

From the first day of that 1988 Giro, Hampsten rode like a potential winner. His thirteenth place in the opening nine-kilometer time trial showed just how strong the supposed mountain specialist was. (In contrast, Greg LeMond, still convalescing from his hunting accident, could manage only 155th!) On stage 6, the first truly hilly stage, Hampsten moved up to eighth overall. Six stages later there was a major climb to the finish in Selvino, and Hampsten made the most of it by winning. His third attack had finally gotten him clear, with only Dutchman Erik Breukink able to hold on. Andy tried to get Breukink to share the work, but Breukink could only gasp in explanation just after the finish, "I couldn't come through. Hampsten is the strongest climber here." Now Andy was fifth on General Classification, just 1 minute, 18 seconds out of first, with the really big climbs, his terrain of predilection, still to come.

Thus far Andy had shown a logical progression toward the *maglia rosa* (pink jersey the race leader wears), but the final step called for attributes far beyond those of inertia. Stage 14, a mere 120 kilometers from Chiesa Valmalenco to Bormio, had its profile dominated by the mighty Gavia Pass, an 8,600-foot brute with gravel-strewn percentages on the order of 16 percent in places. Challenge enough, one would think, but nature decided to transform this severe but normal task for grand tour riders into one of those epic stages that are told and retold in annals such as this for generations to come.

The riders had some intimation of things to come from the start. A chill rain should have warned them of possible conditions at higher altitudes. The nasty weather kept the peloton together until the start of the Gavia, where Johan Van der Velde made the first attacks. He expected the climb to be hot work, even in the steady downpour, so he jettisoned his rain cape. Andy led the chase, comfortably spinning his 39x25, a gear Neel had wisely insisted on mounting, while all around other riders had to struggle on 23s.

Neel also made sure the team cars were spread up the mountain to be on hand to supply the riders with warm clothing and hot drinks. Practically no one else had envisioned what conditions would be like at the summit and they paid dearly for their lack of forethought. The freezing rain turned to snow six kilometers from the top, and still the semi-naked Van der Velde led the way. In those conditions, however, the uphill was the easy part. After only one kilometer of descent he dove into a team car where his clothes were cut from his frozen torso. He finished the stage more than three-quarters of an hour behind the stage winner.

Similar stories abounded as these normally hard men were pushed beyond their extraordinary limits in these diabolical arctic conditions. Roberto Visentini, the Giro winner in 1986, had to stop three times, once to plunge his hands in warm water offered by a bystander, once to change clothes, and once to run a bit to warm his feet. He lost only fifteen minutes. Bob Roll, Hampsten's 7-Eleven teammate, finished well in terms of placings, but not in terms of body temperature. Even with extra clothes he was hypothermic and had to be rushed to the hospital; he was on the start line the next day. Eyes frozen shut from tearing were common. This was no longer a race but a test of survival.

When Van der Velde abandoned the lead, the next two, Breukink and Hampsten, led the stage. Andy's boyish appearance had made some observers fear he didn't have the fortitude for this sort of severity, but in fact he had endured such conditions back in Colorado and knew exactly what to expect and how to cope with it. Breukink attacked at the end to win the stage, but Hampsten went into pink.

It had been a sensational ride, one that put minutes on most of his opponents (except Breukink, who was at fifteen seconds on G.C.), but in the minds of those opponents there were doubts that the Giro was finished. They weren't prepared to accept the American upstart's ascendancy. They thought of him as having profited from a lucky day. There was still a week to go and they had every intention of testing not only his but his team's ability to hold on to the coveted race leader's jersey.

During that week, over and over, day after day, the team was forced to dig deep, and deeper, to answer the endless attacks. But answer them they did, sheltering their leader in the chases and leaving him with enough strength to win the final mountain time trial that opened up the gap on the chief antagonist, Breukink, to some two minutes. Today, fifteen years later, Andy Hampsten remains the only American to have won the Giro d'Italia, a marvelous accomplishment under any circumstances, but for those who love the sport the fact alone is not as exciting as appreciating how the victory was achieved.

Italy fell in love with the cute boy from Colorado who spoke their language with an attractive accent and showered him with adulation. The cute boy was seduced and, after retiring from competition nearly a decade later, went to live in the land that had adopted him.

Hampsten never found the right combination again to win a major tour, although two victories in the Tour of Switzerland and other prestigious events attest to his continued presence at the highest levels of cycling, but in 1992 he put in a ride that ranks with his Gavia triumph.

Of all the famous mountains in the Tour de France, L'Alpe d'Huez has achieved the most notoriety in the public mind even though it wasn't introduced to the Tour until 1952 and then not again until 1976. However, in the last quarter century it has become an almost annual staple of the Tour. It's probably those fantastic TV shots from the helicopters revealing the enormous crevasse of the valley of the Romanche River and the serpentine road that stretches up the north wall around twenty-one numbered hairpins to reach the ski town of L'Alpe d'Huez that has stuck in the memory of viewers and participants alike. The spectacle and its implications for bike riders are hard to forget.

Difficult as the climb to L'Alpe d'Huez may be, coming as it always does after numerous other leg-breaking passes, its influence on race results is often greater than its own statistics (1,000 meters, 3,280 feet, of ascent in 13.4 kilometers) might imply. The result is a unique measure of prestige that comes with winning this stage.

Therefore it's no surprise to find a man of Hampsten's talents playing with the idea of "doing something." The questions of where and when would be determined by the roads en route to the Alpe and the behavior of the other actors on the tortuous stage the roads provided.

It was on the third of four climbs that day, the Croix de Fer (Cross of Iron), one even longer and steeper than the Alpe, that Hampsten joined three others in the search for glory. It's all too facile to characterize a major move in such a mundane manner. Hampsten may indeed have been riding within himself in order to save something for the last obstacle, but the pace had already been intense enough to drop the likes of Gianni Bugno, Laurent Fignon, Erik Breukink, Stephen Roche, Jean-François

Bernard, and Greg LeMond (who, so sadly, retired from the Tour for the first time that day)! It was no casual matter to commit to this attack twenty kilometers from the summit of the Croix de Fer and seventy-five kilometers from the finish atop L'Alpe d'Huez.

Hampsten could probably have ridden away from the other three in those twenty kilometers of ascent, but he'd been around too long to waste precious energy on foolish bravado. After the summit of the Croix there were more than forty kilometers of downhill and flat where he would need their help. And help they did, no one shirking his turn at the front, so that by the time they arrived at the bottom of the Alpe they had a four-minute margin on the chasing Indurain-Chiappucci group.

Andy began the climb spinning his 39x23 and then increased his tempo all the way up progressively using the 21 and 18. He was on his own from the first hairpin, free to fly away through the screaming multitudes who had waited hours to vociferously salute the man who could dominate this most celebrated of stages.

Immortality can be measured in many ways, but conquering the Gavia and Alpe d'Huez are two of the most endearing for a cyclist.

35

MIGUEL INDURAIN, 1964 –

A CENTURY HAS passed since the Tour de France was invented. In that time it has spawned enough statistics and comparisons to delight any baseball fan. Normally, more information leads to greater understanding. But sometimes assembling the facts leads to a struggle to find an explanation that makes sense of the facts. This phenomenon is a mystery in broad daylight.

Take the issue of multiple Tour winners. Philippe Thys (Belgium) was the first to win three: 1913, 1914, and 1920. World War I eliminated the Tours of 1915–1918, so there is a high probability that Thys could have won more. But it wasn't until Louison Bobet's three-peat of 1953–1955 that Thys's accomplishment was recapitulated. So it took a half century to get a second three-time winner.

How, then, has it happened that in the succeeding half century there have been not only two more three-peaters, but no less than four men who have won the Tour five times? Many explanations have been offered, none perfectly convincing.

The most recent of these five timers only deepens the mystery. Miguel Indurain, after five years in the pro ranks, gave little hint of what was to come. He didn't appear to have the right mentality, physicality, or nationality. Oh, he had given hints. He dropped our own 1984 Olympic champion Alexi Grewal over the famous Izoard to win the Tour de l'Avenir. As a young pro, Indurain won some prestigious second-tier races such as Paris-Nice. But he was big and heavy and seemed to excel in a support role as a teammate. Being Spanish wasn't necessarily a plus either. Iberian stars were often brilliant but erratic.

It wasn't until 1991 that it all started to come together for him. He became the designated team leader and lost enough weight to climb well.

He was reminiscent of Jacques Anquetil in basing his Tour victories on accomplishments in the time trials. He got the nickname of "extraterrestrial" in the "races of truth" and then rode just hard enough in the mountains to defend the lead he'd gained against the clock. Anquetil had used a similar formula for success very effectively. Perhaps Indurain could have climbed even better than he did, but there was no good reason to do so. His stupefying power allowed him to be a momentum climber. Climbing specialists might pop off the front from time to time, but "Big Mig's" "big mo" would just roll them back in the succeeding kilometers. It wasn't a crowd-pleasing style in the manner of Merckx or Coppi, but for five years no one could find a card to trump Indurain's basic game plan.

As the early-1994 season unfolded, a wave of climbing stars seemed prepared to engulf the Tour de France. Tony Rominger, Piotr Ugrumov, Armand de las Cuevas, Luc Leblanc, Richard Virenque, Pavel Tonkov, Gianni Bugno, Claudio Chiappucci, and Marco Pantani all believed Indurain was vulnerable on the big climbs. Indurain knew the Tour route profile as well as anyone, but if he had any qualms he didn't reveal them. Known as a great example of the strong, silent type, he was then even more so.

The first ten stages across northern France deposited the Tour at the foot of the Pyrenees with Indurain adorned in his customary yellow, thanks to a strong showing in the first time trial, and everyone peering into the mountain mists trying to discern just how much of a challenge the new (to the Tour) climb to Hautacam would be. The stats, 1,000 meters (3,280 feet) of vertical gain in 13.6 kilometers of road ascent, looked pretty fearsome. But this is exactly what the pure climbers wanted: the steeper the better. Less "big mo" for "Big Mig."

With so many men wanting to be in on the climbing action, there was an intense race to get to the race up Hautacam. Teammates massacred themselves to pull their leaders into proper position up front at the bottom of the mountain proper. The results of this mad scramble became obvious when the true ascent began. It was as if a bomb had exploded in the field with most going backward (relatively speaking; Lance Armstrong, for example, was to lose over seven minutes, and many would lose more than double that) and just a few going forward.

Marco Pantani, second in the 1993 Giro, was anxious to show how he had done so well. In a style that was to become famous, the waif-like Italian stood up, leaned out over the handlebars, and pounded away into the swirling clouds where he was soon lost to view. Being more than fifteen minutes behind on G.C., Indurain wasn't much concerned by the attack of the precocious Italian. Indurain still had a teammate, Jean-François Bernard, who continued to ride flat-out up the 10 percent gradient. One by one the front dozen were reduced as the unrelenting pace left no room for recuperation.

Halfway up and Bernard pulled off the front, his job done. Indurain looked around at all the suffering behind him and maintained the killing tempo. His opponents' gasping breath, desperation in the eyes, lunging style, and search for the right gear that didn't exist were all signs that Indurain had nothing to fear.

Now a new Indurain emerged. Winning time trials may be effective, but it doesn't have that *mano a mano* or wheel-to-wheel intensity that both participants and spectators consider a definitive statement of relative worth. Miguel Indurain, age thirty, had reached full maturity. He was at the peak of over a decade's preparation, and he was finally in a position, as much psychologically as physically, to declare that he was indeed the premier cyclist of the professional peloton. He wanted there to be no doubts about who was *le patron,* the boss. He remembered the previous five-time Tour winner, Bernard Hinault, and the intimidation that was the hallmark of the Badger's (Hinault's nickname) performances. Into that tradition the big Spaniard swept.

Indurain never looked back. In two kilometers he reduced the wheel suckers to two, Frenchmen Richard Virenque and Luc Leblanc. One kilometer later and only Leblanc could hold the pace, with four kilometers remaining. From time to time the air of magisterial progress was shown to come at a price; Indurain's teeth were showing. At two kilometers Pantani was caught and quickly discarded. That fact alone gives some measure of the climbing performance Indurain was putting on.

Leblanc now had the temerity to attack, but Miguel was not flustered. The gap grew to 100 meters and then melted. Hats off to Leblanc for even trying; he was obviously doing the ride of a lifetime, but only birds were going to get away from Indurain this day.

At the line Leblanc found enough energy for another pop, enough to win the stage, but Indurain knew he had made his point. "Scrap among your-selves for the lower placings," he seemed to say, "but this Tour is mine."

It's easy to pick out the Hautacam climb as an example of Indurain's mountain brilliance because it stands out so much from his normal pat-tern of "just" defending. There is another example, however, that is even more audacious. Apparently he liked the move on Hautacam so much that he decided to incorporate it into his bag of tricks for the 1995 Tour de France. Only this time he didn't wait for the real mountains. Why wait a week and a half when you can get everyone to whine in sub-mission even earlier?

This time Miguel picked a stage in the decidedly lumpy region of southern Belgium. And they weren't just any lumps. Each had a name and each had a history as they marked the final five challenges in the oldest of all classics, Liège–Bastogne–Liège. None climbed more than a few hun-dred meters, but their combined viciousness was to spread out the field as though it had just traversed the Alps.

The prestige attached to winning this stage was lost on no one, and once on the Liège–Bastogne–Liège course attacks followed in rapid suc-cession. Lance Armstrong was one of those out front putting on the pres-sure. In those days he was a pure power man and this was his preferred playground. On Mont Theux, the next to last hill, Armstrong and six oth-ers (one of whom was Johan Bruyneel, direteur sportif of U.S. Postal Service these days) had a little lead of fifteen seconds.

And then, twenty-six kilometers from the finish in Liège, it happened. Miguel Indurain burst from the bunch at a speed that immediately put him on his own. In seconds he was on the break and blasted by it at a superhuman rate. Armstrong tried to react but admitted, "When Mig took off, he rode me off his wheel." A statement of honesty, incredulity, and admiration. (Two days earlier Armstrong had crashed heavily, which more than likely took a little off his ability to react. Obviously torn up as he was, Armstrong never used the crash as any sort of excuse.) The one man who did hang with the sensational Spaniard was Bruyneel, and over the top of Theux they disappeared.

Down the other side and up the two-kilometer Côte des Forges Indurain pounded. Under orders (he was defending for his team leader Laurent Jalabert), Bruyneel could only sit on. He would have been the first to admit, though, that it was all he could do to stay glued to Indurain's rear wheel. On the descent of the Forges they touched eighty kilometers per hour. Indurain had planned this attack, all right; he'd mounted extra big gears for the downhills.

He needed them. The pack, led by the *maillot jaune,* Bjarne Riis, was desperate to keep Indurain from gaining time and to prevent the humiliation of being beaten by one man on roads where a group (now down to 50) had a huge advantage. At the summit of the Forges, Indurain learned he had forty seconds and set about gaining more over the final twelve kilometers. On broad avenues, all downhill and flat, he gained another ten seconds in conditions that would have seen any other rider eaten up. In the end, Bruyneel and Indurain arrived fifty seconds ahead of the bunch.

The implications were obvious. This man really was extraterrestrial—invulnerable—and it was useless to attack him. If that's the lesson the others drew, it was fine with Indurain. But just in case there were any lingering doubts, he rubbed everyone's nose in his superiority in the next day's time trial.

36

MARCO PANTANI IS one of the more enigmatic members of the modern peloton. At a mere 125 pounds, he has the build of a classic climbing specialist, and yet he has managed, sometimes, to transform himself into a more all-around rider, putting up surprising performances in flat time trials and being where he needs to be throughout long stage races. As his notoriety has increased, so has his flamboyance. An earring, a nose stud, bandanna, goatee, and several nicknames have helped bring him fame, but his performances underlie everything else. Flamboyance without substance means nothing. His persona has been tarnished with allegations of drug use, a subject I won't touch here because he has never been convicted of these offenses. If he does seek to artificially enhance his natural abilities, he is not unique. Although drugs may supplement inherent potential, none has been invented that can create potential at the level Pantani has displayed it. Despite the cloud that hangs over his name, Marco Pantani must be recognized as one of the finest riders of the last decade.

He first attracted attention with a third-place finish in the 1990 amateur Tour of Italy. Two years later he won the same event, thanks to his dominating performances in the mountains, and, needless to say, the offers to turn professional came flooding in.

His apprenticeship didn't last long. The 1994 Tour of Italy was one of the most savage in recent years. The heretofore invincible Miguel Indurain was repeatedly attacked by Eugeni Berzin, a Russian riding for the Italian Gewiss team, as well as Gianni Bugno, Claudio Chiappucci, and Pavel Tonkov. Indurain, having won the Giro twice and the Tour de France three times, was in no mood to be humiliated, even if he wasn't in top form. That Pantani could hang in with such fierce company and arrive at the foot of the Dolomites in tenth position overall was a wakeup call for those who had thought of him as a midget novice climbing specialist.

That wakeup call grew louder when Pantani rode away to win that first monster mountain stage. He leaped to sixth overall. Whatever benefits he had derived from not being taken too seriously, you could be sure there weren't going to be anymore. He was now on every leader's "marked man" list.

The next and biggest mountain stage of the Giro was going to see all-out "war," Indurain predicted, "and so much the better." The gauntlet had been thrown down, and all Italy held its breath to see who would attempt to pick it up. The 188-kilometer stage would include the forty-eight hairpins of the Stelvio, the ultra-steep Mortirolo, and finally the often 15-percent grind up to Valico di San Cristina. That the winner's time for the stage was expected to be almost seven hours indicates its incredible severity.

It wasn't until the Mortirolo that Pantani decided to show he wasn't just a one-day man. As soon as the lower slopes steepened, he danced away on an enormous gear. As much as the others wanted to keep him in check, no one could do it. Also, of course, there were the sophisticated calculations top pros constantly make about when to respond without helping another rival.

Indurain held his fire until three kilometers from the summit. At that point he rode up alongside the race leader, Berzin, looked him in the eye, and turned up the tempo. In just a few pedal strokes he was alone. Once over the top he flew down the descent and caught Pantani. The four rivals who could hold his wheel left Berzin to do all the chasing. He dug deep and gave an honest self-appraisal. "I knew what I had to do, and in the end I think I did it well. One should be dignified when racing with the pink jersey."

Obviously, the whole race was coming down to this stage-ending climb of the Valico di San Cristina. Utterly unawed by the presence of Indurain, Pantani left the famous Spaniard in his wake as he set off for the summit. Was Pantani too audacious? Was Indurain simply being cautious? Was he suffering from the bonk? Was this not his kind of climb? Even Indurain was unclear, but his power left him and he struggled all the way up the mountain. Two of those who had sat on Berzin, Chiappucci and Wladimir Belli, used that free ride to slingshot past the man in pink and then, a little later, even the mighty Indurain.

It was a sensational stage, the kind that fans talk about for years to come. Pantani did so well that he leaped up to second on general classification. Although Indurain gained a few seconds on Berzin, the Russian remained in the race leader's jersey. Meanwhile, Indurain was stuck in third just over three minutes down on G.C., and that's the way the leadership *tiercé* held to the finish in Milan.

To heck with Berzin, Pantani had arrived, and as the first and most unexpected Italian!

That year (1994) Marco Pantani went on to ride the Tour de France. "Only for familiarity," he said. But of course when the Tour got to the mountains it was difficult for a rider of Pantani's means to restrain himself. Imagine yourself in his position. You're supposed to be tired, but you don't feel tired. Chumps you have little respect for have been taking minutes out of you every day. The desire to show everyone you're not just some young wheel sucker is overwhelming. You're only twenty-four and "restraint" is hardly a word in your vocabulary. So of course when the race finally started to climb, you wanted everyone to understand you were no couch potato on wheels.

Come Hautacam, the first big climb in the Pyrenees, you're ready to throw caution to the wayside and attack. There's a sorting-out attack at the bottom so you're prepared to sit on the wheels and wait, but three kilometers into the climb (leaving more than ten) there's an ebb in the surge, and now you know it's your time to go.

And go Pantani did, intent on winning the stage and boosting his G.C. position. In Italy, the month before, this type of effort had been enough. Now Pantani found a different Indurain, a big man at last truly fit. Indurain and French rider Luc Leblanc had combined their considerable talents to drop everyone and eventually pull in Pantani. Leblanc went on to win the stage, Indurain the Tour, and Pantani, who finished third on the stage, a new respect for the Tour de France. This was a transformed Indurain from the man he'd assaulted so often in the Giro.

Unlike so many others who were cautious after beating their poor bodies against the impenetrable Indurain wall, Pantani, in his infinite youth, saw lots of opportunities to unseat the master. The very next day he was back on the attack, finishing second on the big Pyrenean stage and taking over three minutes out of Indurain. A few days later in the Alps, Pantani did the by now expected—jumping away on the final climb of the day to L'Alpe d'Huez and pulling back 1 minute, 15 seconds on Indurain. That still left Pantani almost ten minutes in arrears of the race leader, but now he was fifth on G.C. While Indurain still felt his margin of security was sufficient, those in second, third, and fourth were definitely looking over their shoulders at the Italian upstart.

Those who hoped that a crash the next day would reduce Pantani's effectiveness severely misjudged his resiliency. With the aid of faithful teammates, he not only got back to the front but had enough suds left to pull one and a half minutes out of Indurain on the last climb to Val Thorens. That ride put Pantani in third on G.C., a position he beautifully defended in the mountain time trial two days before Paris, thus guaranteeing him a place on the podium on the Champs-Elysées.

I have lavished detail on Pantani's first big year in the pro ranks to remind us of the excitement this man generated. If he could get on the podium in both the Giro and the Tour in his first year, who knew what lay ahead? No one could say for sure, of course, but it was fascinating to contemplate.

However, Pantani fans were doomed to frustration for the next two years. Terrible crashes almost ended not only his cycling career but his life. It wasn't until the 1997 Tour de France that Pantani was able to return to the front line of competition. So demanding are the top levels of professional cycling that lengthy time off the bike means a lengthy time getting back to true competitiveness. And in 1997 it appeared that a new Indurain had been born. His name was Jan Ullrich. Not only did the German win all the time trials with "extraterrestrial" type margins (the term "extraterrestrial" being first applied to Indurain to describe the mammoth margin of his time-trial victories), but on the Pyrenean stage to Andorra he accelerated away from Virenque and Pantani on the final climb without even getting out of the saddle.

Pantani made a superlative demonstration on L'Alpe d'Huez, climbing most of it in the big chainring and setting a record that stands to this day. But he still wasn't the Pantani of old, and the next day he lost over three minutes. His final third place in Paris was a triumph of fortitude, and deep down Marco knew he was a long way from fully fit.

The following year, 1998, marked his triumphal return and the creation of the Pantani cult. Bandannas and goatees sprouted on amateur imitators around the world. He handily took the Tour of Italy in his swashbuckling style of old, dominating in the mountains and doing superbly against the watch. All but diehard Italians know that the Tour de France is generally more difficult than the Giro. To be number one in Italy is no modest achievement, but to be acknowledged as the best in cycling requires winning the Tour de France.

Pantani almost didn't go to the Tour in 1998. If Ullrich was in anything like the form of the previous year the only possible place to challenge him would be on the climbs, preferably ones that ended at mountain tops. In 1998 there weren't many stages fitting that description on the Tour itinerary. On the other hand, Pantani knew he was back to his old self, and being a stage race specialist he was not likely to throw away this opportunity.

It proved a wise decision. Ullrich had been unable to resist the blandishments of fame and had put on a lot of weight over the winter. He spent all spring struggling to lose that girth and find form. However, the way he started the Tour implied he had it all back together just in time. All day long, day after day, he was at the front controlling the race, just as you'd expect the defending winner to do. And then, in the first time trial, he rode with total dominance, taking no less than 4 minutes, 21 seconds out of Pantani. (Incidentally, second and third in that time trial were Americans Tyler Hamilton and Bobby Julich.)

Pantani came back in the Pyrenees to reclaim a couple of minutes, but this was a game Ullrich appeared quite capable of playing to his own advantage all the way to Paris.

Pantani bided his time until the alpine stage over the Galibier and ending at Les Deux-Alpes ski resort. He had marked this one as one of the few stages that suited his specialty, climbing. Then the gods threw in a violent freezing storm to set the stage for one of those truly epic days.

Aside from a few brave escapees, the rather large front group of twenty-five was hanging together on the Galibier in a collective desire to get over this frozen misery together. Six kilometers from the summit,

Pantani attacked. In his favorite style, out of the saddle holding onto the hooks, stomping a huge gear, he just flew away from everyone. No one attempted to go with him. Not only was Pantani in a league of his own athletically, but with forty-eight kilometers to go, including a lengthy descent before the final climb, there was every chance of rolling him back with only modest effort.

The Anquetils and the Indurains are respected for the iron mastery of their eras. Who can blame them for winning in a manner that favored their particular talents? But cycling enthusiasm thrives on the audacious, the spectacular, the risk-taking, and who since Bernard Hinault and, before him, Charly Gaul had dared win with bravado? The repressed starvation for the heroic inspired not only thousands of fans shivering at the roadside but millions of viewers ensconced before their TV sets.

And it inspired Pantani himself. He said later, "I was at the limit of being overcome [by cold] on the descent [of the Galibier]. Then, on the last climb [to Deux-Alpes], I had incredible determination. It was the day when I had the will to put everything together."

He was remarkably cool, given the circumstances. He stopped at the summit of the Galibier to put on a rain jacket and warm gloves, this when he knew every second counted. He then descended like a madman and managed to catch the riders from an early break, who were of great help along the gradually descending valley to the base of Deux-Alpes. They worked so well together that they continued to gain on the theoretically stronger Ullrich group.

The leaders had 2 minutes, 47 seconds in hand commencing the last climb of 8.5 kilometers. Of course the Italian attacked right from the bottom and was immediately alone, free to pursue his wonderfully mad fling. He never faltered, frequently staying out of the saddle for long stretches in order to keep the biggest possible gear turning, but was always smooth, always powerful.

Ullrich was in exactly the opposite condition. The deep fitness he needed now deserted him. The sins of the wasted winter had come back to haunt him. His strength was gone, the final ascent was one long semihallucinatory agony. Pedaling on residual willpower and pride, he plodded along, a frigid pedaling metronome set on a very slow beat. He arrived at the finish just three seconds shy of nine minutes after his Italian nemesis.

To his credit, Ullrich would go on to attack on other mountain stages, but Pantani easily followed his every move. Although Ullrich of course won the final time trial, he took only two and a half minutes out of an amazing Pantani, who, inspired by the yellow jersey, finished the stage in third place.

The ancient Greeks believed that the luckiest of men died at their greatest moment because the rest of life was a declining afterthought. Such sentiments seem harsh to our modern sensitivities, but they recognize that in the total scheme of things a living death can be worse than an actual one.

The following year Pantani was yanked from his bed two days from the finish of the Giro, had his blood tested, and was found to have a hematocrit in excess of 50 percent. The implication was that he was using the blood booster, EPO, at the time undetectable, but his ejection from the race was based on his health. He claims he has been unfairly demeaned, and perhaps so. Either way, the accusations have shattered his self-confidence and ever since he has either failed to finish a major race or done poorly—excluding the two mountaintop finishes he won at the 2000 Tour de France. For a man of Pantani's stature, this is a form of twisting slowly in the wind. As of 2003, he is a master of his own team and claims he is preparing for a proper comeback. He's in an awkward box. If he does well, some will say he is able to do so thanks to a new form of enhancement. If he does poorly, the same critics will claim the new controls have forced Pantani to ride without boosters, and without them he's not so hot.

I wish he had bowed out quietly some time ago. Watching this former giant of the sport struggle in the peloton and in the courtroom is not a pretty sight. I want to remember Marco Pantani for the glorious excess he brought to the sport, for those days when his performances made everyone who saw them pinch themselves and say, "Thank God I am alive to see this." At age thirty-three in the year of the one-hundredth anniversary of the Tour, he is possibly a little over the hump. But, bless him, he doesn't believe so. The pelotons are intoxicating and he has nothing to replace that elixir. He has enacted so many self-resurrection miracles before; who can blame him for trying the supposedly impossible one more time? If he loses on this last throw of his cycling dice, he will have died to the sport, in some ways a worse than normal death. But whatever happens we can never forget what he gave us, over and over and over. Grazie Marco!

37

ROBERTO LAISEKA, 1969–

IT'S FUNNY (funny peculiar, not funny ha-ha) that a race of the magnitude of the Tour de France in the second half-century of its existence has seen a trend toward domination by individuals for up to five races, when only one rider, the Belgian Philippe Thys, was able to approach that sort of control (winner in 1913, 1914, and 1920) in the first half-century. Something similar has happened with the world hour record, in which in late 1990s records by Tony Rominger and Chris Boardman saw them add up to a kilometer over the previous records, whereas giants such as Coppi, Anquetil, and Rivière were more than content to add a handful of meters to what had been already established. No doubt the ability to identify men of extraordinary talent and train them to a peak unimaginable in earlier decades has something to do with these trends, and of course better roads and tracks and equipment raise the overall speed. But there's still a mystery about it.

One result has been to relegate men who might have been more successful in other times to the role of sparrows picking up crumbs off the ground next to picnic tables where the supermen dine at their leisure. A good case study is Roberto Laiseka. He was born in Guernica, a Spanish city made infamous by Pablo Picasso, who painted its horrors during the Spanish Civil War of the 1930s. The complexities of the situation were (and are) compounded by the existence of the Basque people in northeastern Spain. Although their origins are unclear, their identity and language are far from Spanish, and they have long felt oppressed by their more powerful Spanish neighbors on the Iberian Peninsula. When Roberto was three years old (1972), the Spanish dictator, Generalissimo Francisco Franco, executed two Basques by twisting a pointed screw through their neck vertebrae. These repressive tactics may instill fear, but hardly loyalty. Spain has undergone a fantastic transformation in the subsequent thirty years and is very much a modern nation today. Life for the Basques has improved immeasurably, but under the surface there is still tension.

No matter how bleak the landscape, people can hang on if there is one ray of hope. The Thirty Years War (1618–1648) in the German–speaking principalities scraped a raped and plundered landscape clean of every vestige of civilized life—no houses, no food, and certainly no inspiring architecture and poetry. Then the people turned to music and transformed it from a pleasant and entertaining diversion into a new lifeblood. The heart had to be fed before the stomach.

While the Basque situation never descended to the levels of early seventeenth-century Germany, it's been desperate enough to transform every individual Basque success into a statement of hope and worth for the community. Nowhere has this been more obvious than with their bike riders. In John Wilcockson's book on the 2001 Tour de France, *Lance x 3*, he gives a poignant example of the elevated devotion that Basque bike riders inspire. He noted a scene in which the Euskaltel-Euskadi (an all-Basque bike team until recently supported primarily by donations from the Basque people, and after a decade of existence riding its first Tour de France in 2001) team bus stopped in front of an outdoor café in the stage start town of Tarbes. Three Basques sat at a table. "If they'd been French fans," Wilcockson writes, "they would probably have politely applauded; Germans would have blown air horns or chanted their heroes' names. But these were Basques. They put down their beers and went down on their knees, as if to worship the ground on which the Basque bus was standing."

Roberto Laiseka grew up in of one those cycling-mad Basque families. He was more than inspired by annual bus trips to the nearby Pyrenees to see the Tours of France and Spain. He became a decent local amateur and at age twenty-four turned pro for (who else?) Euskaltel-Euskadi. For five years he devoted his life to the cycling religion without one victory. As the better riders on Euskaltel were snapped up by better-paying teams, Laiseka was grateful to at least be able to continue improving himself in this difficult milieu. It wasn't until his sixth year (1999) that he finally won a mountain stage in the Vuelta (Tour of Spain), and in 2000 he repeated the feat and finished the race in sixth overall.

In 2001, at age thirty-two, when many pros consider retiring, Laiseka got a crack at riding the Tour de France. Only now had his modest team been sufficiently recognized to deserve an invitation. Stories of the stars are always exciting and inspiring because their achievements shine so brightly. But for every star there are hundreds of Laisekas who deep down believe that if only they can hang in long enough they too can improve to

The Basque climber Roberto Laiseka embodies the traditional Spanish cyclist's gifts of leanness and climbing speed.

a point where they can have at least a moment of glory. Such unrewarded devotion, even more than the success of the stars, demonstrates the kind of attraction that cycling has.

From the beginning of the 2001 Tour the Euskaltel team struggled. The opening flat stages hardly played to their strengths. By the time the Tour arrived at the Alps, the Basque team was last and Laiseka languished in eighty-sixth place, fifty-seven minutes down. But once the roads began to climb, Laiseka and the rest of the orange-clad team began to justify their wild-card selection to the Tour. Laiseka arrived in ninth place on the memorable stage to L'Alpe d'Huez, took a fabulous fourth in the Chamrousse time trial, and placed second on the first Pyrenean stage to Plateau de Bonascre.

Laiseka, whose diary appeared in *El Mundo,* had no illusions about that second place. He wrote:

> Yesterday, Lance Armstrong could have won another time. But he just did not want to. When Ullrich launched his attack, Lance followed him. He looked like he was whistling, like he wasn't making any effort. I caught him later and I stayed beside him for a few minutes, watching his extremely serene face and observing his impressive cadence. After resting for a while, I attacked and Lance made a little gesture to me. He didn't say anything at all, it was just like a little grin. He meant I was free to go chasing after Cardenas (Felix Cardenas, a Colombian riding for the Kelme team). His behavior was fair to me. If he had wished he could have dropped me easily.

But even with the help of his teammate David Etxebarria, Laiseka couldn't close that last thirteen-second gap on Cardenas and had to settle for second on the stage. It was a performance to be proud of, of course, but it was so close that it gave Laiseka the desire for more. Yet Laiseka wasn't too carried away. He readily admitted that

> in the final kilometer, once more Lance's behavior was fair. He almost caught me, but he chose to stay behind me and let me take second place. He could have beaten me even riding with one leg. In the final part of the ascent I saw many (Basque) flags and listened to many people cheering me. But at the end I wasn't able to listen and see anybody. I was just asking for the finish to arrive as soon as possible and not to be eaten by the Tour's "Lion King," Lance Armstrong. Right now he rules, and we have to abide by what he decides.

And then disaster. On the second Pyrenean stage, to Pla d'Adet, Laiseka experienced a sudden and inexplicable off-day that reduced him to seventy-eighth on the stage, thirty minutes behind the winner, Armstrong. The probable explanation is that Laiseka is only human. Even for a natural mountain man, five successive mountain stages can be wearing. Laiseka could only pray that it was just an off-day, one he could bounce back from. He knew that he had one hope of leaving his mark on this race and crowning his career with something immortal to point to forever as justification for all the sacrifices he had endured for so many year: the last Pyrenean stage leading up to Luz–Ardiden, where eleven years earlier he had cheered on Miguel Indurain to a stage victory over Greg LeMond.

One chance left, one more roll of the unknown-fitness dice. At the bottom of the final climb there were only ten men left in the lead group (including Laiseka), survivors of the severity of the previous mountains that day, the Aspin and Tourmalet. Four men were strung out up the road in front of the ten. Roberto Laiseka knew his moment of truth had arrived.

Looking at a 1 minute, 18 second-gap up to the leader on the road, Wladimir Belli, Laiseka violently attacked the last thirteen-kilometer haul up to the summit at Luz-Ardiden. Once again, he was pretty sure Armstrong would be content to follow Ullrich, so there might be an opportunity for an ambitious sparrow to pick up a major crumb after all.

To some degree Laiseka resembles a sparrow. He has carried his dedication to the climber's art to the absolute edge. One more lost pound and he'd be in a hospital. Bones, taut muscles, and just enough skin to cover it all. His deep-set eyes suggest knowledge of profound suffering. He would be the first to admit that he doesn't have the natural talent of Lance Armstrong or many others, but on this climb he brought to bear absolutely everything that a decade of devotion to his profession allowed him to develop. Beyond morphology and the supposed peak watts such a human design should be able to produce, there is another, more mystical, dimension—the will.

Not just the ample will of Laiseka, but also the will of the Basque fans lining the mountain who pooled their collective energy to lift their new idol to the summit. It's an intoxicating mixture, which, if realized, can justify any sacrifice. The mixture worked. Halfway to the top and Laiseka had caught and dropped Belli. There could be no faltering now. And there wasn't. There couldn't be. Focused, determined, and inspired, Laiseka never let up for a second and with every pedal thrust gained time on Belli. At the line the Basque sparrow had, on that day, become a giant; if not in his painfully realistic assessment of the conditions that permitted him to win, then certainly in the eyes and hearts of the thousands of Basques who had practically blown him up the mountain and then dropped to their knees in gratitude and appreciation for this heroic performance by one of their own.

38

WHAT IS IT with our two American superstars who have to handi-cap themselves in order to make a real impression on the rest of us? Greg LeMond probably could have won at least five straight Tours de France if it hadn't been for that frightful hunting accident in the spring of 1987. Yet to nearly die and then come back for two more Tour victories—the qual-ity of the empathy his last two victories aroused more than made up for the missing Tours.

Lance Armstrong has done something similar. Everyone knows about his terrible struggle with cancer and how he resurrected himself. His original career was plenty spectacular: world champion shortly after arriving in Europe, winner of the San Sebastian Classic (1995), Flèche Wallonne (1996), Tour stage winner, and oodles of high placement in top races. Most pros would be ecstatic with such *palmarès.* If not for can-cer, perhaps Lance would have continued on this path. It's hard to say exactly what happened (from what I read, even Lance can't quite per-fectly articulate the transformation), but in a sense his cancer time (mostly 1997) was a sort of pupa stage, and when he emerged from the chrysalis he began to show signs that he was a new man.

Even more than his Tour of Luxembourg win earlier in 1998, his fourth place in the Tour of Spain immediately followed by a fourth in the world road championship showed that Lance was back, and better than ever. He had lost weight and could climb better, much better. He was instrumen-tal in obtaining a new directeur sportif, Belgian Johan Bruyneel. He sought scientific training advice from real experts such as Chris Carmichael. And he decided to eschew tradition in order to focus on one race and one race only, the only race Americans had ever heard of—the Tour de France.

At the 1999 Tour he completely blindsided the European racing establishment. Far from being an invalid on the comeback trail, he won the prologue, wisely relinquished the yellow jersey to the sprinters for a few days, and then grabbed it definitively in the first long time trial.

Various rationalizations about how a good classics rider might be able to make the adaptations necessary to become a fine time trialist on a flatish course justified the amazement of the dumbfounded, but there were no handy rationalizations available on the next stage when Armstrong defied a chill rain and top opposition from Alex Zülle, Fernando Escartin, and Ivan Gotti to win the first mountain stage to Sestriere.

Gotti, winner of the Tour of Italy earlier that year, and Escartin, a Spanish climbing specialist, both got away at the bottom of the final climb. When their lead mounted to thirty seconds, Armstrong picked up the tempo. He quickly noted that he was alone and then really turned on the juice. He crossed the gap to the two leaders in a very short time, passed them, and roared on to not only a stage victory but an announcement that the *new* Lance Armstrong had indeed arrived.

With a lead of over six minutes on Abraham Olano, number two on G.C., the new Armstrong was now in a position to follow events. Even so, at the top of the famous hairpinned road to the L'Alpe d'Huez, Armstrong's G.C. lead had grown by almost two minutes to 7 minutes, 42 seconds.

It wasn't until the Tour reached the Pyrenees, six stages after Sestriere, that Armstrong got a chance to prove he was more than a one-day wonder. On a stage to Piau-Engaly Armstrong became progressively more isolated as his lieutenants gave their all and succumbed to the tempo. His principal opponents had teammates in breakaways, so over the last two climbs Lance had to ensure the tempo. His sophistication showed in his ability to go fast enough to keep the break within a safe distance while simultaneously keeping enough in reserve to answer the inevitable attacks. It sounds simple, but to make these kinds of judgments in the midst of intense physical exertion is a skill few can master.

A day later he emerged from the Pyrenees with 6 minutes, 15 seconds on Fernando Escartin, and two days after that he added almost four minutes to the gap in the final time trial. Poor Escartin even lost his second place on G.C. to a hard-charging Zülle. But what did Lance care? While the others scrapped over the placings, he rode in triumph up and down the Champs-Elysées before thousands, friends and skeptics alike, who still couldn't believe their eyes.

Besides revolutionizing himself, Lance Armstrong revolutionized race preparation. The standard dictum had always been that riders needed to race in order to race. No amount of nonrace training could ever substitute for the exigencies of competition. Lance and his cohorts showed that for them, at least, another approach was possible. The new training hangs on precise scientific preparation and, of course, Armstrong's physical qualities. In addition, Armstrong is uniquely dedicated to the Tour de France. His diet in November is structured with the Tour for the following July in mind. He races through the spring to verify his training, although even that racing is pretty impressive, as two second places in the Amstel Gold Race testify. In June 2001 he won the Tour of Switzerland, but even here he was controlled, choosing to go all-out in the hill climb time trial. Of course that one effort won him the race! Throughout the spring the team visits key stages of the upcoming Tour de France and rides them, sometimes many times.

One critique of Armstrong's first Tour win was that his opposition was second class. Zülle was too old. Escartin couldn't time trial. And Marco

Pantani and Jan Ullrich hadn't made it to the 1999 Tour. In 2000 that was to change.

Unlike Jan Ullrich, who gave up restraint at the table after his first Tour win in 1997, Lance Armstrong never lost focus. Even when he relaxes he does so in a way compatible with reaching the next Tour in the best possible condition. Furthermore, his whole team is on the same page. A few weeks before the Tour, Armstrong played the role of perfect teammate for Tyler Hamilton in the weeklong Dauphiné Libéré. A gesture like that guaranteed Hamilton would do everything to reciprocate. And it showed in the Tour's team time trial, as the U.S. Postal team took a superb second place, putting Ullrich and Pantani, who both lost time, on the defensive.

A few days later, when the Tour met the Pyrenees, it was indeed Marco Pantani who attacked on the final climb to Hautacam. He didn't get far before Armstrong was on his wheel. There was a marked difference in style. While Pantani tends to spend lengthy periods out of the saddle turning a large gear at a moderate cadence, extensive testing (once again, that incredible attention to detail) had shown that Armstrong was at his optimum turning a low gear at a high rate. We hadn't seen this approach to climbing since Charly Gaul in the 1950s. It must have taken a lot of work to adapt to this style because Lance's enormous strength lends itself to pounding the big gears. But once convinced this approach would lead to better results, he did what it took to make the change. The benefits for such incredible application were soon obvious when seeing the ease with which Armstrong got across to Pantani.

But Armstrong wasn't satisfied with just containing Pantani. The American soon slipped by the pink-clad Italian and picked up the tempo. At times Lance was out of the saddle, but in or out his style belies the effort because he's so smooth and his legs are turning so quickly. While others are pushing on pedals that have a fair amount of resistance, Lance spins away with no great sign of work. Only when the likes of a Pantani are getting dropped does Armstrong's speed become obvious.

And what about that German guy, Herr Ullrich? Once again Jan had to struggle to recover from a chubby winter and he paid the price by being under his best form. From the moment Pantani attacked, Ullrich was dropped.

Perhaps Armstrong would have liked to hold off turning on the gas until higher up the climb, but once Pantani had kicked open the door and the two were away, what could Lance do but continue the effort? And what an effort! Pantani soon disappeared backward while Lance flew up the remaining ten kilometers to Hautacam. He reeled in a breakaway left over from a previous climb, most of whom struggled to hold his wheel for a moment, but only Banesto's José Maria Jimenez was able to hang on for any appreciable time.

The stage was actually won by Kelme's Javier Otxoa, who at one time had a seventeen-minute lead. On the line he preserved a bare forty-two seconds on the hard-charging Armstrong. Of course Lance was more concerned with those behind than those ahead. His first-round punch had been pretty impressive: Zülle at 3 minutes, 5 seconds, Ullrich at 3 minutes, 19 seconds, and Pantani, paying a big price for his early aggression, at 5 minutes, 10 seconds. Overall, Ullrich was at 4 minutes, 14 seconds and Joseba Beloki at 5 minutes, 23 seconds. Pantani was so far out of the picture his only hope could be stage wins.

This was "Badger racing." Bernard Hinault, five-time Tour winner in the late 1970s and early 1980s, nicknamed "the Badger" for his constant aggression, loved to knock the opposition back on its heels at the first major confrontation, be it in the time trials or mountains, and then control the racing from then on, defying his adversaries to find a weak spot for a counterattack.

Three days later the Tour finished at the summit of the dreaded Mont Ventoux, the "Giant of Provence." In the Pyrenees Lance's Postal Service teammates had been shredded before the last climb. Fortunately, Lance was strong enough to handle matters on his own, but on the approach to the Ventoux there was no shredding. First, Tyler Hamilton set a hot tempo from the bottom (having won a stage on the Ventoux a month earlier in the Dauphiné Libéré stage race), which reduced the front group to a handful. Then Kevin Livingston took over, further reducing the party to Armstrong and himself, Ullrich, Roberto Heras, Beloki, and Pantani, and Pantani was yo-yoing off the back. Once out of the trees and onto the bare face of the mountain, there was no protection from the howling wind. The group slowed, and Pantani and Richard Virenque were able to catch back on.

Virenque made one of those suicidal for-the-cameras attacks. He was easily countered and then dropped. More seriously, with five kilometers to go, Pantani went away and was quickly joined by the Colombian, Santiago Botero. When their advantage reached eleven seconds, Pantani surged again and was quickly on his own. But not for long. Armstrong made his expected move and was irresistible. He makes it look so easy. There are no wild gyrations. His legs wind up that small gear and he's gone. In no time he was past Botero and on to Pantani. Three kilometers remained, and over this distance they shared the work, the shrieking wind visibly buffeting them. With a kilometer to go they had thirty seconds on Ullrich and Beloki, and that gap held to the finish line, where Armstrong slowed enough to allow Pantani the stage win. Lance thought he was making a nice gesture to a famous rider, but Pantani took it as a demeaning gesture and said so to journalists who were only too happy to report his comments.

The next two alpine mountain stages, huge and testing as they were, saw no change in the overall picture as Armstrong and his team controlled matters from beginning to end. But the third alpine stage to Morzine in Haute-Savoie had an unexpected climax. Pantani attacked on the first of the day's four climbs. The jagged profile for the stage put the brash Italian in an all-or-nothing mood. It was a magnificent ride, but nevertheless deficient. In the transition between the third and fourth cols he was caught, and starting the final col, that of the Joux-Plane, was summarily dropped, not only from the peloton but, that night, from the race as well.

The Joux-Plane is not one of the famous cols, like the Galibier, L'Alpe d'Huez, or Tourmalet, always associated with the Tour de France. But its statistics are sufficiently formidable after three other grand cols and 170 kilometers of hard racing. It averages 8.5 percent for eleven and a half kilometers. Such an average for such a distance is intimidating enough, but the Joux-Plane is actually much more difficult. The average is tilted by the first two kilometers that are only 5 percent and 7 percent, but the rest is never under 9 percent, and three of the last four kilometers are no less than 10 percent. Such an incline allows for little momentum and the slightest weakness is punished immediately.

Halfway up, spectators were disbelieving when the heretofore invulnerable Armstrong started to drift back from Ullrich. Obviously Lance was feeling terrible. He later claimed he'd run out of food, but given his meticulous attention to such matters, that claim might have been a bit of disinformation to cover a sudden and inexplicable malaise. In any event, he fought heroically to limit his deficits and succeeded in losing only a little over one and a half minutes on Ullrich. Armstrong's depths were never so obvious. When he couldn't pedal on fuel he pedaled on willpower.

It was only a temporary glitch. Three days later he won the final time trial and made sure he would be leading the Tour into Paris for the second consecutive time.

According to various pundits Armstrong had no real opposition in 1999, and when that opposition showed up in 2000 they weren't properly prepared. Ullrich felt he could take on the American if he could regain the form of 1997. To his credit, he spent the winter of 2000–2001 preparing properly, staying fit, and not gaining weight. Then he capped his spring preparation by riding a quiet Tour of Italy. He arrived at the Tour de France claiming to be in the best form of his life. Since he was already billed as the most talented rider in the modern peloton, this attentive approach should have turned the trick. Meanwhile, Pantani allowed himself to lose all form and his pathetic Giro guaranteed he wouldn't be invited to the Tour.

Armstrong and his U.S. Postal team had spent the same time improving everything possible. In particular, they picked up two top Spanish climbers, Roberto Heras and José Luis Rubiera. Too often Armstrong had been left isolated late in mountain stages, and one teammate, Livingston, had changed teams to help Ullrich! Meanwhile, Armstrong got on with his training program in the spring in his usual applied manner. He arrived at the Tour start, if anything, fitter than ever and had researched every key stage of the Tour.

The 2001 Tour had an unusual configuration: All the mountains were lumped together in the middle of the race. This had been tried once before, in 1976. Furthermore, each of the five stages ended in a summit finish. It was a beastly sequence with no margin for weakness. Great climbers of the past, such as Federico Bahamontes, the "Eagle of Toledo," must have been wondering, "Where was a Tour like that in my day?" Back in the 1950s and 1960s the mountain stage finishes were normally at a town in a valley far from the summit of the last climb, a configuration that allowed less talented climbers to come back on the descent.

The opening week went off at a searing tempo, but Ullrich and Armstrong were content to hide in the peloton and let others collect the glory. They knew well enough that their time would come beginning on the first mountain stage, stage 10, from Aix-les-Bains to L'Alpe d'Huez. The 209 kilometers encompassed three *hors categorie* climbs that are so long and steep they're beyond categorization. The first two cols, the Madeleine and the Glandon, are longer, and in places steeper, than the more famous final climb, L'Alpe d'Huez. But the Alpe gets the notoriety because, the concluding ascent looking like a tortured snake struggling up the cliff side of the Romanche valley, the decisive moments of the stage are usually played out around its famous twenty-one numbered hairpin turns.

Ensconced by his pink guard (which included the turncoat, Livingston), Ullrich and his Telecom henchmen set a hard pace from the first change in angle beginning the Madeleine. Uncharacteristically, Armstrong dangled at the back of the ever-diminishing lead group, and at times he appeared to struggle. Was he having a bad day? Was the renewed Ullrich finally going to get his chance to emerge from Armstrong's shadow? So the game went, up the Madeleine and down the other side, up the Glandon and down the other side, all the while the screws getting ever tighter with the lead group being reduced on every steep turn.

With the Alpe in sight, the tempo leaped. Ullrich was led up the first steep ramp by his teammates until the supposedly hurting Armstrong flew by on the wheel of a sprinting Rubiera. Ullrich gave it everything to get up to Lance. Obviously, the American wasn't so dead after all.

What happened next was one of the most memorable moments in cycling. Thanks to video distribution it will be played over and over in homes around the world as long as people love cycling. Rubiera pulled over, his job done. Ullrich was right on Lance's wheel. Armstrong was out of the saddle, turned his head around to look Ullrich directly in the eyes for a long moment, then turned on the gas in a glorious burst of acceleration. Ullrich, already at full stretch, had no reply. The next time Armstrong looked back there was nothing to see.

The German didn't die. He rode magnificently and, absent Armstrong, would have appeared to be a superman because he ended up second on the stage, having dropped everyone else. But his second place was two minutes after Armstrong! While Armstrong is not a climbing specialist, he is nevertheless the greatest living climber. Everyone knows that when Lance turns it on, no one, absolutely no one, in the modern peloton can stay with him.

Armstrong has managed to pare his weight down to the minimum, nearly twenty pounds less than his precancer days (when he hardly looked fat), while increasing his strength. Power-to-weight ratio is the single greatest factor in creating a climber, and Armstrong's compares more than favorably with any emaciated mountain man one could point to. In addition, however, his tremendous strength, beyond that in relation to his weight, makes him unbeatable in the time trials as well. It's a winning formula and sounds simple to express, but only a handful of pros in the history of the sport have been able to put it together at this level. Hinault, Merckx, Koblet (two years only), Coppi, Bartali—this is the league Armstrong has placed himself in. Rarified company indeed.

The Tour is remorseless. Immediately after this first mountain stage, when huge efforts had been made by all, there was no chance to recover. On the next day was the Chamrousse mountain time trial out of Grenoble, a stage calling for maximum effort.

Poor Ullrich. He rode superbly, even beating Armstrong on the second timed section of the time trial, but a look of despondence was on his face when he crossed the line. At that moment Armstrong was less than two kilometers behind, and all too soon (to be precise, one minute too soon for Ullrich), Armstrong sprinted across the line. Ullrich was in despair. Quite honestly he lamented, "If, as some people say, I'm the most talented man in cycling, what can you call Armstrong?!"

It wasn't difficult to feel some pity for the once mighty German. In 1996 he had finished the Tour in second behind his teammate, Bjarne Riis. The next year he won in such a dominating manner that cycledom thought it was looking at the birth of another era dominated by one man. But Ullrich lost focus, and now when he'd finally got everything together to fulfill the destiny long prophesied for him, an even greater rider had arrived on the scene and deprived him of his expected glory. It looked like Ullrich would have to settle for another second place, the fourth in six years; for a true champion, this is really hard to take. Without him, Armstrong's victories might have appeared somewhat hollow, but a supporting role was hardly what Ullrich had in mind after his Tour win in 1997. It is to his credit that he handled the demotion with dignity.

There was, at last, a rest day after the Chamrousse time trial, but it was spent shuttling across France to the Pyrenees, where three successive killer mountain stages awaited the Tour entourage. Aside from the Ullrich–Armstrong battle, there was the little matter that neither of them was yet in yellow. A break had gained over thirty minutes earlier in the race, and the main benefactor had been François Simon. As often happens in these situations, the man was inspired by the privilege of wearing the coveted *maillot jaune* and fought with everything he had to hold on to the precious jersey. Ullrich and Armstrong couldn't just mark each other. They had to keep up the pressure to gain time on Simon.

Consequently there was no "piano" time with the bunch relaxing over the first climbs of each Pyrenean stage. Telekom and U.S. Postal put the pressure on from start to finish to make sure Simon lost a substantial hunk of that huge lead every stage. Inevitably, this meant there was a pretty exclusive group headed by Ullrich and Armstrong beginning the last climb of each day. On this first day in the Pyrenees to Plateau de Bonascre, Felix Cardenas and Roberto Laiseka were allowed to go for the stage win.

Armstrong just sat on Ullrich until the Telekom captain began to falter, at which point Armstrong flew away to gain another twenty-three seconds.

The next day, to Pla d'Adet, Armstrong was more intent on victory. The stage passed by the memorial to Fabio Casartelli, Lance's teammate who died in a crash on this route in 1995. Lance was very fond of his young Olympic champion teammate and has attempted to honor his memory at every opportunity since. On the stage following Casartelli's death Lance had made a point to win, crossing the finish line pointing to the sky and saying, "Today, I had the strength of two."

But first there was unexpected drama on the descent of the Col de Peyresourde, the fourth of the stage's six passes. Ullrich misjudged a sharp left hairpin, went into it with way too much speed, and wisely avoided the guard rail by going off the road before the rail began. He slid down through bushes, and then, when he reached the drop-off into a creek, he went over the bars into the water. While the fantastically dramatic scene was captured on film, Ullrich soon reappeared, bike in hand. Aside from scrapes and bruises, he was ready to roll. In a gesture indicative of the respect and honor between these two ostensible enemies, Armstrong, who saw the whole thing, immediately slowed and waited for Ullrich to return.

On the final climb Postal's winter acquisitions, Heras and Rubiera, earned their pay. By the time they pulled off, Ullrich and Armstrong had only each other to watch. Ullrich made an effort to attack, which Armstrong matched with debilitating (for Ullrich) ease. And when the American decided to go there was, once again, no chance for a response. The moment of weakness Armstrong had shown on the Joux-Plane the previous year was not evident in 2001. He did what he wanted when he wanted, and this time his wants for the stage win were double. First, he wanted to win to honor Casartelli. He crossed the line once again pointing to the sky. Also, he finally wrested the yellow jersey from the weary shoulders of François Simon.

The last mountain stage, this one to Luz-Ardiden, and once again run off in brilliant sunshine, saw the all-day winnowing process leave lesser lights to win the stage, Ullrich make one last desperate attack, and Armstrong make one more easy defense. At the finish line Armstrong slowed a bit to let Ullrich take third on the stage. As Ullrich rolled by, he extended his right hand to shake Armstrong's as a sign of defeat, but a battle well fought. The time bonus for third place was just enough to boost Ullrich into second on G.C., his rightful place after two weeks of intense racing.

The hierarchy of Armstrong, Ullrich, Beloki that had finished 1-2-3 in 2000 repeated again in 2001; and with Ullrich not starting in 2002, the Tour podium was comprised of Armstrong, Beloki and Raimondas Rumsas. As of this writing, there doesn't appear to be any possible challenger in this race to Armstrong. Gilberto Simoni, winner of the 2001 Tour of Italy, claims, "I can beat Armstrong in the mountains." He bases his prophecy on finishing ahead of Armstrong on two mountain stages of the 2001 Tour of Switzerland. But there Armstrong was riding according to a preparation program for the Tour de France. In the hill climb time trial, the only stage of the Swiss Tour where Armstrong went all-out, Simoni lost over two minutes. It would be wise for such men to speak less and pedal more, lest they appear foolish later. Pantani is promising another comeback, but that's a yawn. There's a phalanx of promising Spaniards, but it's hard to see how any of them can aspire to the levels where Armstrong routinely flies. No doubt the depredations of age will eventually take their toll even on Armstrong's extraordinary physique, but that time doesn't appear imminent!

39

LIKE EVERY OTHER American bike nut in the summer of 2001, I signed up for the Outdoor Life Network daily live transmission of the Giro d'Italia (Tour of Italy). Just because Mount Everest is the highest peak in the world doesn't mean other peaks aren't interesting, and so it is with today's climbers. Lance Armstrong is indisputably Mount Everest, but there are lots of other interesting climbers. And besides, Armstrong wasn't riding the Giro.

Rather early in the race, on stage 4 no less, came the first mountaintop finish at Montevergine di Mercogliano. The eleven-and-a-half-kilometer climb averaged 4.68 percent to top out at 1,263 meters (4,143 feet). The Dolomites might be forgiven for sneezing in contempt, but one could be pretty sure that sprint specialist Mario Cipollini wouldn't be first to the line. Go fast enough and any hill gets tough, and this one was sufficiently difficult to guarantee that only those with good uphill form would be in touch at the summit. You didn't have to win this stage to win the Giro, but you certainly couldn't be dropped if you wanted to win.

Imagine our surprise when we saw a small, dark figure riding in the colors of the almost unknown Panaria team explode from the peloton no less than seventeen kilometers from the finish. This was the climb before the climb, one of those places where the tempo is squeezed just enough to drop any weak racers, but too far out for any serious moves to be made. Or so went the conventional wisdom.

It took a moment for the commentators to identify this guy; we at home weren't the only ones who had never heard of Julio Perez (his mother's name, Cuapio, being dropped). As we were scratching our heads wondering how any European, even a Spaniard, would come up with the Mexican name Julio, out from the TV came the explanation that this guy was truly Mexican. Stop a second. Unknown rider from an almost unknown cycling country, and here he was gaining time in a difficult place over some of the best riders in the world. Very impressive.

But we had to keep the compliments on reserve because we were going to run out of adjectives if he kept up this superb pace that was taking time out of everyone else with every pedal stroke. This was no fluke. There can be no faking effort of this sort. Kilometer after kilometer slipped by and his lead climbed to thirty seconds; but as things heated up behind, the lead started to shrink.

With four kilometers to go, after thirteen kilometers of intense riding, he appeared to have the juice to go all the way. If he were to be caught, those behind would have to increase their pace markedly. And then catastrophe. He was rounding a sharp left turn; as he started to exit the curve and stood up to regain his former tempo he suddenly pitched forward, his legs spinning madly. His chain had broken. He clicked out of his pedals, looked down again to make sure that was indeed the problem, and then threw the bike onto the grass verge at the side of the road where he stood helplessly as the chasing group roared by.

All the while the announcers began dribbling out information about this fascinating young man. "He comes from the small town of Txcala, Mexico, about 100 kilometers south of Mexico City. He has six brothers and sisters." Later I discovered that he took up bike riding for something to do in his spare time. He immediately experienced success in any local race with a hill and was noticed by fellow Txcalan Miguel Arroya, who arranged for his first trip to Italy in 1997. But he returned the following year, again with Arroyo's help, and this time things started to click. He won two races, and then seven in 1999. By the time he'd won five, Panaria was waving a contract under his nose. He was only too happy to sign and begin his entry into the big time. At age twenty-two not a whole lot was expected, so his two victories that first year as a pro were more than satisfactory for Panaria.

The stage was set for 2001. No doubt his Panaria bosses hoped for a promising ride in his first Giro, but his mad dash up to Montevergine blew their minds. However disappointed by his bad luck, he told himself he wasn't going to let it get him down.

He was going to need all the optimism he could muster because the very next day he was involved in a brutal crash that sheered off his front forks and sent him flying to the pavement directly on his face. Perez lost two upper teeth and a lot of blood but bounced up, grabbed a spare bike, and took after the disappearing peloton. More than ever he was determined to show his capabilities.

There would be plenty more opportunities. Three days later on stage 8, he attacked on a rolling 185-kilometer stage and stayed in front, alone or with others all the way, eventually taking ninth. This had been a ride to convince himself that he was set for real action again. Perez said, "I really did this ride just to show I'd recovered from the bad luck on that climb ending stage 4 and the crash the next day."

Perez was getting set for stage 13, with its four major climbs—the Rolle, the Pordoi, the Marmolada, and then the Pordoi again with a summit finish. At 128 pounds Perez knew this was his promised land. He also knew this would be the day Gilberto Simoni would make his big attacks to take the pink jersey from Dario Frigo. All day long (eventually almost seven and a half hours) Perez shadowed the two race leaders, and when Simoni made his first big attack near the summit of the Marmolada, Perez was one of only four who could hold his wheel.

Once onto the Pordoi for the second time, Simoni made one searing acceleration after another. Frigo and the others gave way, except for the gap-toothed Mexican, Julio Perez. Perez took his turn at the front, but near the top he began to show signs of weakness. Simoni eased a bit to keep them together, and at the line motioned the twenty-three-year-old Giro debutant to go past him. Simoni was overjoyed to take the pink jersey, but his joy was no greater than Perez's. "I'd trade two teeth a day for a day like today! I have to thank Simoni for letting me win. That was very gracious of him. Mexico will be very happy!"

Only one other mountain stage remained and whatever ambitions Perez had for that disappeared with an overnight drug raid and the cancellation of that final climber's showdown. Perez proved his climbing skills again in the 2002 Giro, by winning the major Dolomites stage that crested the Marmolada and Pordoi, scene of his victory a year before.

Perez is more than a promising exotic rider. His abilities throughout the Giro imply that at age twenty-five Perez has an exciting future ahead of him. He's exotic because he's the first Mexican to win a stage in the Giro. Augustin Alcantara won a stage of the Tour de l'Avenir (Tour de France for amateurs) in 1969. Raul Alcala won two stages of the Tour de France in the late 1980s. The list of successful Mexican riders in Europe is not long. But in the interests of continuing to open the sport to the world and in seeing what this young star can do, we can hope he will continue to show his amazing abilities. No, he's not Mount Everest, but he's certainly a very interesting emerging volcano.

OWEN MULHOLLAND has been a lifetime cyclist. He has raced on track, road, and dirt for forty-three consecutive years, and toured extensively in the United States (including a cross-country trip at age 16 with his twin in 1962) and Europe. Most of his riding these days is with his partner, Kathy, on their mountain tandem. He lives in Marin County, California.

Mulholland's first article on cycling was published in International Cycle Sport in 1972. Since then his writing has appeared in many American and foreign magazines and books. He was the first American in recent times to follow the Tour de France in the press caravan (1975), something he continued to do regularly for the next decade. Although his journalistic efforts cover all of cycling, from race reportage, to bios, and even technical articles, he is particularly well known for his historical pieces.